"**The Everyday Genius** is a wonderful journey into the world of childhood, learning, and creativity. Not only does Peter Kline provide hundreds of practical ideas for encouraging learning at home and at school, he also makes us all think a little bit harder about what learning really means in our lives. I recommend it to anyone who cares about our most precious natural resource — the children of the world."

*— Thomas Armstrong, author of **In Their Own Way:***
Discovering and Encouraging Your Child's Personal Learning Style

★ ★ ★ ★

"Peter Kline opens the door and gives us a view of tomorrow's education, a vision of empowering growth and human enhancement. The learning process is intrinsic to a fulfilling life, and, as Peter Kline makes clear, is a joyful one. The activities he describes provide easy steps to the synergy of integrative learning."

— Paul Messier, Senior U.S. Government Educational Research Analyst

★ ★ ★ ★

"In **The Everyday Genius** Peter Kline provides parents with specific approaches to expanding the joy of learning for themselves and their children. He shows how, through the use of family ritual, games, and the specialized use of music and art, parents can build a lasting foundation for learning for every family member, a foundation which integrates the imagination, the emotions, the body and the intellect; a foundation which makes possible extraordinary performance."

— James Quina, Wayne State University,
*author of **Effective Secondary Teaching, Going Beyond the Bell Curve***

★ ★ ★ ★

"At precisely the right time in the uneven and currently depressing history of education, Peter Kline has written a comprehensive review of leading-edge cognitive research and successful educational strategies.

"Though written primarily as a handbook for parents, it should be required reading for every educator and students in every school of education. There is no time to waste in putting this powerful information in the hands of every teacher. And isn't that every one of us?"

, Director
Learning

THE EVERYDAY GENIUS

Restoring Children's Natural Joy of Learning

— And Yours Too

Peter Kline

GREAT OCEAN PUBLISHERS
ARLINGTON, VIRGINIA

For Susan Kesslen
who has helped make this book possible
by living the principles of Integrative Learning.

Book and cover design by M. Esterman.
Cover art and text illustrations by Paige Billin-Frye.

For information contact
      Great Ocean Publishers, Inc.
      1823 North Lincoln Street
      Arlington, VA 22207

First Printing

Library of Congress Cataloging in Publication Data

Kline, Peter, 1936-
    The everyday genius : restoring children's natural joy of learning,
and yours too / Peter Kline.
        p.   cm.
      ISBN 0-915556-17-0.   ISBN 0-915556-18-9 (pbk.)

      1. Home and school — United States.   2. Education — United States —
Parent participation.   I. Title.
LC 225.3.K58   1988
372'.21 — dc 19   88-18068
                                                     CIP

Printed in the United States of America

Contents

PART ONE: The Promise of Integrative Learning   **1**

We now know a great deal about how we learn — and how well we are capable of learning. This knowledge will enable us to fill the urgent need for a better education than our schools now offer.

Your children have much greater talent than can be developed by our current educational system. You are going to have to help.

And how traditional methods of teaching fail to match the way we naturally learn.

An explanation of the three components of the learning process: input, synthesis, and output. How Georgi Lozanov's innovative approach speeds learning, and makes it more enjoyable.

The development of Integrative Learning by Lozanov and his followers, and my experience adapting it to a wider range of applications.

Recent research on the brain is yielding a better understanding of paths — and obstacles — to learning.

A first-hand look at a public school where Integrative Learning is changing the lives of students and teachers.

PART TWO: Setting the Stage for Integrative Learning 94

How to create an environment in which learners and learning will thrive. For parents, teachers, and other adults this may require some changes in attitude. But your children can help, and the benefits are immediate.

PART THREE: Falling in Love with Learning 142

A collection of activities which have helped many people to discover the deep reserves of intelligence most of us never realize we possess. They can inspire you and your children to collaborate in the search for your everyday genius.

Games & Exercises

A partial list of activities to stimulate learning. It is not necessary to read the whole book before trying out these activities.

Acknowledgements

It should be obvious that no book with objectives such as this can be the product of one person's thinking, and the significant influences to which I am indebted are legion.

First, the subject, form and style of this book were suggested by Jonathan and Wendy Lazear, who provided valuable editorial advice during the early stages of its composition.

At a later stage that role was transferred to the publishers, Mark and Margaret Esterman, whose interest in the manuscript transcends professional concern. It was a wonderful experience to be able to meet with them frequently to discuss changes and to explore its effect on their children, who indirectly left their mark on what is here. In a case like this, editorial work plays such an important role in the outcome of the book that the result is essentially a collaboration.

Other help with the manuscript was provided by my close associate, Bernard Saunders, who helped shape the thinking in the early stages, and who is the source of some of the most useful exercises and ideas contained herein. Bernie and I are currently collaborating on a similar book for the business community, and have also led many workshops together.

Susan Kesslen provided excellent editorial suggestions and, partly thanks to her recent tutelage from Lozanov, understands the Integrative Learning process as well as anyone I know.

My current close associates in the business of spreading Integrative Learning, with whom the subject has been explored exhaustively, include Laurence Martel, Jerry Perez de Tagle, Charles Bubar, Kay Farrar and Robin Smith.

The list of those who were of indirect help is impossibly long. I must first mention my colleagues at the Thornton Friends School, which I helped to found as a means of exploring the implications of Integrative Learning when applied to the classroom. These include Edie Crane, Evelyn Knowlton, Lynn and Bill Godwin, Don Cassidy, Amy Christianson, Dennis Jelalian, Bob Coleman, Marion Scodari, Doug and Jane Price, and of course my co-founder Nancy Kline. I would also mention many of the students from whom I learned perhaps more than I taught, but doing so would risk essential omissions. I am sure they know who they are.

Earlier influences of importance came from Barry and Ann Morley, Thorny Brown, Brooke Moore, Rebecca Cooprider, Sally Oesterling, Amiel Francke, Ev Cooper, Edwin Burr Pettet, Jose Silva, Ron Williams, A.E. Claeyssens, Hunter Mulford, Harvey Jackins, Georgi Lozanov, Hazel Parcells, Merl and Lovell Glasscock and Harold Isen.

My three daughters, Stephanie, Maureen and Wendy, and their mother, Barbara Gardner, have contributed extensively to this book for obvious reasons, as well as my brothers, Mike and Jeff. Of course the book carries throughout the profound influence of my parents.

Next I must thank hundreds of public and private school teachers and corporate trainers and managers with whom I have worked and from whom I have learned. Special among these are the excellent staff of the Guggenheim Elementary School, surely one of the most inspiring teams one could ever wish to work with.

Particularly to be singled out are the following: Maxine A'hearn, Michael Alexander, Ivan Barzakov, Carl Biehl, Joan Bokaer, David Borchard, Anne Brady, Jenny Bricen, Bobbie Brooks, Lewis Buchsbaum, Don Campbell, Ed Cap, Linda Carlson, Sharon Carlson, Phillip and Libyan Cassone, Dolly Colzetto, Gary Crawford, Ron Ennis, Nancy Ellis, Susan Fagrelius, David Finsterle, Car Foster, Ann Friend, Paul Froiland, Betty Gebbia (and her son Jason), John Grassi, Sharon Grant, Jane Hale, Lawrence Hall, Ray Harris, Cliff Havener, Larry Hearn, Dean Held, Marilyn Herr, Ron Herring, Sandra Hopper, Gary Hovda, Sigrid Grassner-Roberts, Norie Huddle, Wayne Jennings, Becky Johnson, Jay Kesslen, Ruth Kiah, Merrill Leffler, Ann Lewin, Vi Levett, Elena Levy, Karen Locke, Michael Luft, Kanya McGhee, David Meier, Paul Messier, Philip Miele, Allison Miller, Jack Mitchell, Louis R. Mobley, Ginny Monteith, Taylor Munroe, Brian Nelson, Patrick O'Brien, Roger Olsen, Leonard Orr, Chris Owens, Lyelle Palmer, Don Petrie, Joan Pilot, James Quina, Pamela Rand, Mary Regnier, Charles Reinert, Mark Rew, Larry and A.B. Reynolds, Patrick Rohan, Sara Rossman, Susan Rosenthal-Krauss, June Sasson, Charles Schmid, Bev Schroeder, Donald Schuster, Robert Schwenger, Margaret Seagears, Paul Scheele, Rita Schulnicht, Jacqueline Simmons, Lilly Sprintz, Susan Stacey, Tony Stockwell, Kaia Svien, Carl Vogt, Arthur Waldstein, Lynn and Todd Waymon, Julian Weissglass, Win Wenger, Ocie Woodyear, and Sidney Zagri.

Finally, I am indebted to Carl Schleicher for many favors, the most relevant of which is that he made it possible for me to pursue and develop Lozanov's work, which he played a crucial role in introducing into the United States.

Of course, none of these people is in any way responsible for the many flaws a book of this kind must necessarily contain.

Preface

by Michael Alexander
Principal, Simon Guggenheim Elementary School

What happens to a dream deferred?

Does it dry up
Like a raisin in the sun?
Or fester like a sore —
And then run?
Does it stink like rotten meat?
Or crust and sugar over —
Like a syrupy sweet?

Maybe it just sags
Like a heavy load

Or does it explode?
— *Langston Hughes*

Every year millions of parents, teachers and wide eyed students entrust their dreams of learning and its accompanying success and happiness to schools of every sort nationwide. In spite of the billions spent on schooling and millions of hours expended participating in schooling, the dream, for many students, is deferred and allowed to sag. This is a tragedy of enormous proportions, with terrible implications for all of us. But it does not have to continue.

Students dropping out of schools from Maine to California in urban, suburban and rural areas attest the obvious — that traditional teaching methods fail to meet the needs of too many potential learners. For the past three centuries we educators, assured that what we did was correct, always blamed students when they failed to learn. So assured in our rightness, we developed labels and many new specializations for teaching "defective learners," and guess what? Many students continue to fail and drop out of school!

Recently, rather than blaming non-learners for not learning, educational researchers have begun exploring the learning process to figure out the who, what, why, when and where of learning. The most insightful of these directed their investigations toward the study of successful learners, for example, pre-school age children, people with photographic memories, and "geniuses."

The essence of these discoveries and their application to successful learning and teaching in any environment is lucidly described in *The Everyday Genius*. This book will intrigue, and entertain many readers. I would like these readers to know that Peter Kline's ideas are not only exciting — they work.

The Simon Guggenheim Elementary School, of which I am the principal, is in an economically depressed area in the southside of Chicago. It has about 400 students and 21 teachers in kindergarten through eighth grade. Soon after I became principal three years ago I had the opportunity to use some State Title I funds to improve the school. Realizing that the school's dedicated teaching staff was its greatest asset, I decided to find the best way to upgrade their skills and morale. I hoped to provide them with something dynamic, which would give them a common experience and point of view to draw on in their teaching. Having had some interest in accelerated/Integrative Learning, I sought out someone who could train our staff. The expert recommended to me was Peter Kline, the genial dynamo of Integrative Learning.

The teachers, whose average tenure was twenty years, were skeptical at first. But it was agreed that there would be no pressure on them to use the principles and techniques of Integrative Learning. It was up to them to apply what they found valuable. As principal, I would support their efforts by introducing an orderly and disciplined environment into the school so the students could focus more effectively on this new way of learning, and back up the Integrative Learning workshop with other training. They would receive thirty hours of training, away from the school, while substitutes paid for by the school replaced first one half, then the other of the entire staff.

The teachers loved Peter and embraced Integrative Learning with great enthusiasm, and the rest is history — or at least the beginning of a new era of achievement and hope for our students and our school. The impact on the school even in the first year was dramatic. Our student attendance rate rose to 94%, a very impressive rate for an inner city school. And our growth rate in reading and math rose spectacularly.

By the end of the first year after the introduction of Integrative Learning, the percentage of our students advancing a whole academic year in reading increased 103% over the previous year, and for reading and math combined the overall gain was 83% over the previous year. Projecting this gain through nine years of elementary schooling, our students would exceed the national norms at graduation by a full two grade levels, graduating from the eighth grade with an average ability in both areas of nearly eleventh grade. And we feel the program is far from reaching its ultimate potential.

Other results have been more subjective. Some of them are dramatically and movingly recounted in this book. I remember when the teachers returned to school after first receiving the training, some of their students asked, "What happened to our teachers? They're so much nicer now!" I am told this response is typical when teachers return to class after this kind of training.

During a Guggenheim summer program where only Integrative Learning was used, a typical parental response came when one mother exclaimed, "What did you do to my child? He wants to come! He likes it!"

Now at Guggenheim teachers no longer blame the students for not learning. Meanwhile, visitors (including professors from universities and teachers from other public schools) have noticed something here that is distinctively different — a sense of accomplishment and caring. "It's hard to believe school really can be like that!" one visitor reported.

Teacher Nancy Ellis told me, "Before Integrative Learning I was frustrated enough to quit teaching." Now she runs a class for students who are unsuccessful in regular classes — she calls it the "Superlearning Lab." Although she's taught for twenty years, she says she's more excited about teaching than she's ever been, more than in her first year in the classroom. And her students are ecstatic about the experience.

"When we first started going to the class they thought we were dumb," seventh grader Steve said of his higher achieving classmates. "But they see us coming back smiling and telling them all we've learned."

"They want to get in bad," adds his classmate Alton.

The teachers at Guggenheim are now aware that the total environment must be orchestrated to support the learning process, and that the teacher's every move supports or detracts from that process. And so I predict the number of success stories will continue to grow, the achievement data will improve, and students graduating from Guggenheim will perceive themselves as able learners and school a desirable place to be.

Recently our success has begun to be recognized beyond our own school — most significantly in the form of generous grants from the Joyce Foundation and the Chicago school system. These grants will enable us to effectively train all our teachers in the methodology of Integrative Learning. We will then be able to study such questions as: what happens when the children are taught all day long (not just in one or two classes) using Integrative Learning? How do teachers adapt? What are the optimal uses of the methodology?

I believe that by implementing Integrative Learning throughout our school's staff and programs, we will be able to improve our students' rate of learning and retention by two to five times over what it would otherwise be — and to do it in a stress-free atmosphere. We intend to document and validate the effectiveness of Integrative Learning and we hope to become a pilot program for our city and the nation, and a resource for teaching other teachers.

If what is happening here today can be maintained and replicated in school systems throughout our country, there may be no need for drying up, festering, crusting, sagging or exploding. Instead, we may be able to eradicate students' learning problems altogether. Maybe then dreams of learning will be deferred no longer.

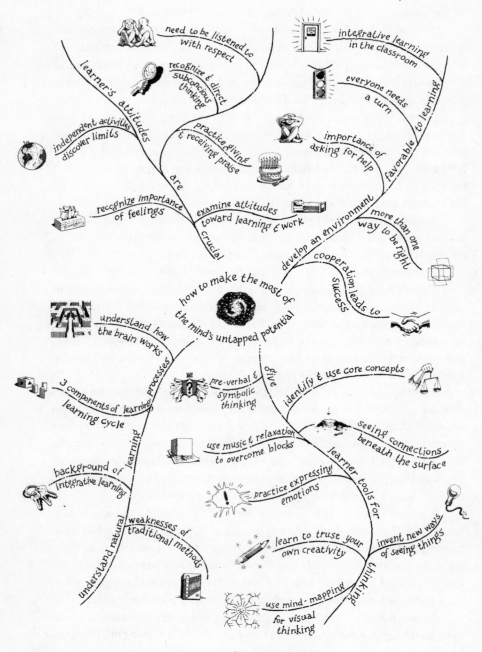

need to be listened to with respect

learner's attitudes

recognize & direct subconcious thinking

independent activities discover limits

practice giving & receiving praise

recognize importance of feelings

examine attitudes toward learning & work

are

crucial

integrative learning in the classroom

everyone needs a turn

favorable to learning

importance of asking for help

develop an environment

more than one way to be right

cooperation leads to success

how to make the most of the mind's untapped potential

understand how the brain works

3 components of learning

learning cycle

learning processes

background of integrative learning

understand natural weaknesses of traditional methods

pre-verbal & symbolic thinking

give

identify & use core concepts

seeing connections beneath the surface

use music & relaxation to overcome blocks

learner tools for

practice expressing emotions

learn to trust your own creativity

invent new ways of seeing things

thinking

use mind-mapping for visual thinking

a mind-map of "The Everyday Genius"

INTRODUCTION

HOW TO USE THIS BOOK

Remember the feeling you had as a child when you unwrapped a brightly colored package, wondering what was inside? Remember when a parent's supporting hand let go and you knew you were riding your bicycle on your own? That excitement, whether it's the mounting thrill of a nuclear physicist on the trail of a previously unknown subatomic particle, the creative ferment of an author plotting a new book, or the exhilaration of a star hitter as ball and bat connect for a home run — that excitement is the powerhouse of learning.

I've sat and watched an artist in front of a canvas lose all track of time teaching himself how light and shadow dance together in the inner darkness of the woods. I've seen the biochemist's keen gaze probing through the microscope the chemistry that shuffles and reshuffles life. I've walked with a child wondering at the mystery of the stars, exploring realms of possibility with growing enchantment.

In all these events I've witnessed the elusive, joyous and deeply satisfying adventure of learning — an adventure that should be as commonplace as breathing, but that too many of us have lost sight of or forgotten.

For every one of us has a profound capacity and drive to learn, and to enjoy learning. The more we can satisfy this desire, the more likely we are to realize the enormous potential each of us has. This in turn is a measure of our happiness and success, and of the contribution we can make to the lives of others.

This book is dedicated to making this excitement and satisfaction more generally accessible — to you, your children, and the classrooms and workplaces of the world.

WHY THIS BOOK IS FOR PARENTS . . .

Because so much of learning begins in the home, I've addressed the book primarily to parents, who are, of course, their children's first teachers and models. Reading it you'll be reminded of your parents' experiments in raising you and, appreciating their successes, perhaps become better able to build on them yourself.

If you're a parent, you might wonder why I spend so much time discussing classroom activities. That's partly because all these activities suggest what you could do or be preparing for at home, and partly because it makes sense to see your work as interactive with that of the classroom teacher.

It's easy to do things at home that will set the stage for success in school. You can start enriching your child's life the moment you take a breather from reading this book. It should be equally helpful whether the young people in your life are new-born or nearly ready to set out on their own.

Parents should keep in mind at all times, though, that the most effective nurturing of the average person's everyday genius does not require special technologies or high pressure education. Indeed, these could actually impair the process. And it's certainly not wise to force-feed knowledge at an early age. Some parents, albeit with the best intentions, push their children into forms of early learning that can actually cripple later development.

Love and understanding remain far more central in the process of education than any sort of technique, theory or technology can ever be. But love must be informed, and understanding sensitively expressed. That's why it's important to widen the circulation of information about the optimum conditions for learning and how they can best be implemented.

If you're dealing with a significant learning problem, the book shouldn't be a substitute for professional diagnosis and treatment, and therefore should be used only after consultation with your doctor or learning specialist.

...AND TEACHERS

I hope that the teachers among my readers will benefit from the exercises and examples taken from the classroom, just as I have learned from observing and working side by side with many of the inspiring and resourceful teachers mentioned in this book. There are many suggestions and activities here, particularly in Part Three, that can be used in a classroom immediately.

In addition, I believe teachers will find useful the material aimed specifically at parents. By thinking about the problems parents face, teachers may be better able to encourage and support their students. Knowing the relevance of students' home environment to their achievement and happiness in school, teachers should have much to offer parents who want advice on how to cooperate in their children's education.

YOU CAN DECIDE HOW TO USE THIS BOOK

The first part of the book deals with the theory of Integrative Learning. The principles of this theory, while differing substantially from those observed in most traditional classrooms, are in themselves simple. People who feel they already understand them, or want to get started immediately, should go directly to Part Three, which offers specific games and other activities to stimulate learning.

Others, who would prefer to take the time to explore the theory and its implications, will want to read Parts One and Two first. Part Two offers some practical self-help philosophy for the reader (because you may have to change yourself before attempting to change anyone else).

IT WORKS AT EVERY LEVEL OF DEVELOPMENT

While a few of the activities require some degree of intellectual maturity, new parents or primary teachers should consider using these themselves, to help prepare a thoughtful environment for children to grow into. Although some of the activities might seem "childish" to a junior high student, all have been used with adults, so their value at the most advanced stages of intellectual development has been tested. When they're used, results can be dramatic.

Indeed, I have repeatedly been amazed at the extent to which we can use the same activities with both pre-schoolers and corporate executives (as well as everyone in between). Often the most basic exercises can help Ph.D.'s straighten out confusions they've lived with for years. That's because what's elicited by most of these exercises is so basic in human experience it has meaning at every level of one's growth process.

ADAPT IT TO YOUR OWN NEEDS

I assume that when you've tried some of the exercises in this book, you'll want to invent others of your own. In designing them I have not been concerned with specific subject matter, which is really the job of curriculum developers, and which I'll be reporting on in subsequent books, but rather with the process by which that material may be brought to life and made most useful to the learner.

AN IDEA WHOSE TIME HAS COME

There is virtually unanimous agreement that our society and the world as a whole are facing many challenges and crises which are bound to intensify soon. The information explosion accompanying all this ferment requires that we learn to deal on a daily basis with situations more complex than ever before in history. This problem gains immediacy if we remind ourselves that the world's information doubled between 1900 and 1950, but is expected to increase sevenfold between 1980 and 1990. Improving our educational system and practices may not solve all our problems. but it is indispensable to meeting these challenges.

I believe the resources now available enable us to substantially improve educational practices throughout our society, and beyond. Integrative Learning, the delightful and effective process I've described in this book, is already working in many school systems and being readied for early adoption in many others. The results from pilot projects have been so remarkably effective that responsible educational leaders are increasingly eager to replicate them. And they should be, of course, for to do less would be to default on their responsibility. As one top administrator put it to me, "The time has come that if they think the old way is better, they ought to have to prove it."

I hope you'll enjoy your adventure with Integrative Learning. Dip in now and see what captures your imagination. Then have the courage to begin what you may have always wanted to try but perhaps never before dared.

1

THE INFINITE POSSIBILITIES OF
YOUR CHILD'S MIND

Your children have much greater potential than can be
developed by our current educational system.
You are going to have to help.

"Just talking about it gives me goose bumps," Bev Schroeder was saying. "They learned the material so quickly and retained it for weeks. What's more, now they know how to succeed in school. This kind of thing has got to transform the whole educational system."

Bev was one of a group of teachers who had recently learned the principles of Integrative Learning — a philosophy of learning that is revolutionizing classrooms all over the world — and had just applied them for the first time in her own classroom. Other teachers at the meeting were equally eager to report on their remarkable successes. There was a growing feeling in the room that history was being made, the history of a new kind of possibility — the unlimited development of the human mind in that seemingly unlikely place, the public school classroom.

A spirited, exciting teacher, Bev has an elementary special ed classroom in Columbia, Maryland and now takes time from her busy schedule to share the highlights of what she has learned with other teachers. The big change in her students began with one simple exercise you'll find in Chapter Twenty-Four. It's called mind-mapping, and it's one of a variety of techniques for parents and teachers presented in Part Three of this book. These techniques are based on the assumption that the whole person is involved in every phase of the learning process. Most of the difficulties children develop in school, as I'll show you, stem from ignoring this fundamental principle.

ON BOOSTING STUDENTS' GRADES IN A HURRY

The philosophy of Integrative Learning, together with some techniques, games and exercises designed to help bring that philosophy to life in the home and classroom, will help give you a taste of what is now possible for teachers, students and parents. You'll see why Bev, and many others like her, have found it surprisingly easy to help students raise their grades from D or F to A or B in a relatively short time — without the unpleasantness so often associated with remedial work. And you'll see why students who achieve excellent results in traditional classrooms also have quite a lot to gain from Integrative Learning.

The techniques you'll find in this book are remarkably simple. Why? Because they are based on a growing understanding of how the brain processes the information that will become the knowledge and skill of a lifetime. Many of these processes have been understood only recently. The principles of teaching and learning which can be derived from this understanding have yet to be applied in most schools. Not surprisingly, however, in schools where Integrative Learning has been tried, it is being rapidly accepted.

IS THERE A GENIUS GROWING IN YOUR HOME?

This book is a guide, an outline of principles, to help you tap a hidden treasure: the mind's profound capacity and drive to learn, and the joy of learning when the proper environment for it has been created. I call this treasure "everyday genius."

I believe it is possible for nearly all human beings to perform at a level of excellence that only top performers could achieve in the past. That's because the brain is an instrument that can be used either well or poorly. It's not hard to use it well, but many of the influences now entrenched in our educational system condemn us to use our brains less effectively than we could. I'm not talking about basic intelligence (which is a good deal higher in most people than currently available tests can measure); I'm talking about quality of performance, which is likely to be far below what it could be.

What it comes down to is that all of us — you, your children, your neighbors and their children — are everyday geniuses, even though the fact is unnoticed and unremarked by nearly everyone. That's probably because school hasn't encouraged us to notice what's hidden inside us, waiting for the right environment to express itself. But if you adopt the philosophy described in this book, you should be able to influence the developing mind of a young person whose mental and emotional resourcefulness will delight the world. Not the nervous, demonic scientist with horn-rimmed glasses — all too often the stereotype of the genius — but an everyday genius, a normal person who is sensitive, alive, fully capable and can help make the world a better place.

ON THE REVOLUTIONARY CONCEPT OF HAVING FUN

Lots of fine teachers intuitively understand the same thing that children do: learning flourishes naturally when it's fun. How sad, then, that we've turned the tables on nature and fostered a system of education that reinforces the opposite notion that learning only occurs when one isn't having any fun.

Later I'll point out some things about the structure of the brain that will help you understand a little better why learning should just naturally be the most entertaining activity you can engage in — even if you're a law student studying for the bar exam. For now, emblazon these words on your mind as the most important ones in this book: **Learning is most effective when it's fun.**

LISTENING FOR GENIUS IN YOUR CHILD

As you work with the book you'll become better able to listen to and inspire the young people in your life. In the process, you'll discover a depth and range of intelligence that should excite, amaze and sometimes baffle you. And you'll become acquainted with an approach to education that should make it possible for you to influence young people to develop their abilities fully, so they're not wasted, stifled or misled into destructive channels.

It is simply **no longer necessary** to settle for many of the learning problems, low grades, poor motivation and terrible test scores that plague so many classrooms. The knowledge to make school a joyful experience for everyone is available right now, and the resources should not be long in coming. You don't need a Ph.D. in psychology or education to do something about the problem. You do need to be sensitive enough to respond to the rich treasure of ideas and experiences children usually keep to themselves. A loving parent or concerned teacher can use any of these techniques. All that's really necessary is . . . to get started.

THE BOY WHO SEEKS THE SECRETS OF THE UNIVERSE

I know an eleven year old boy who, when he was six, said to his father, "Dad, when I grow up I want to find out where the universe makes itself." Unfortunately, his school didn't have any teachers like Bev Schroeder, and the ones who were lucky enough to have him in their classes believed they had to stick to their lesson plans, which didn't have anything to say about where the universe makes itself. Convinced that his classroom experiences had nothing to do with his dreams, he decided school was not worth bothering about. So he disowned school, and each year retreated further inward. Now, five years later, he is diagnosed as "learning disabled." It's what they call in the medical profession an iatrogenic problem — in this case a learning problem caused by educators.

Perhaps along the way someone could have listened to him and, with the creative insight that makes a great teacher, helped him structure his studies around his remarkable interests. He would have loved that, and his teachers might have learned a lot too.

WHAT WERE YOUR CHILDHOOD FANTASIES LIKE?

Can you remember any of your own childhood dreams or fantasies? Surely there was a time when you hoped someone would listen and help you bring one of them to life. Didn't you run gleaming-eyed to a parent to report a thought that seemed magical, only to be told that when you were older you would understand reality better? I've watched many adults cry about how hurtful it was to them not to be listened to as a child. And watching a child being really listened to is sometimes enough in itself to bring tears to their eyes.

Most people can remember how they speculated whether our universe is a tiny atom in some giant's universe, or how they tried to make up a new language or invent some magic machine. Young people love to dig to China, to be the Last Starfighter, the first person in outer space, a film star, or a discoverer of miracle cures. Parents and teachers calmly inform them that their dreams are unrealistic, and insist they bring their attention back to important things like multiplication tables. And thus we unthinkingly squander our most precious natural resource: the enormous potential of the human mind.

Pay attention to young people and you can sense this potential in the often picturesque language they speak: sometimes humorous, sometimes eloquent, sometimes cryptic. While they speak from their hearts we often listen with half an ear, or none at all. Perhaps we're too busy worrying about what's "good" for them.

No, I'm not forgetting there's an important difference between the creative process in children and adults. Picasso said that when he was a child he could paint like an adult, and when he was an adult he had to learn to paint like a child. The child follows an inner light, while the adult needs to have been schooled in the discipline required for true and meaningful innovation. A gulf of experience separates the two. But the experience of childhood creativity, and the response it evokes in adults who are important in the child's life, sets the stage for what will happen later. Unimaginative responses may cause children to grow up to be unimaginative adults.

We need to help children intermix their creative responses with the acquisition of knowledge and discipline, so they can keep alive the magic of their vision while acquiring the tools for mastering the adult world. The basics — learning the alphabet, times tables and how to read — can be as delightful to children as the world of Hans Christian Andersen. And by rights they should be, for they are inherently of the greatest fascination. But it takes thinking like a child to infuse the building blocks of knowledge with the golden glow of the child's imaginary world. However, since we've all been children, thinking like a child shouldn't be too difficult — and it's a great way to take a vacation!

HOW EXCITING THE BASICS COULD BE!

Our six year old who wanted to find out where the universe makes itself could have practiced his times tables by counting the stars in the night sky. He could have learned to read by studying books on astronomy. He could have essayed writing and literature by making and sharing his own stories about the origin of things. If he had learned the basics through exciting activities like these, he would never have developed learning problems.

A fourth grade class in Kentucky did a simple five minute exercise in order to learn about the planets. Within a month most of the children in that class were pestering the librarian for books on astronomy. This silly little exercise, (which I've hidden for your entertainment somewhere in this book), produced such remarkable results that the teacher said he was embarrassed to tell anyone about them because no one would believe it. Too bad our would-be astronomer couldn't have been in that class!

OUR TWO HUMAN INSTINCTS

Let's begin, then, where the learning process begins. You and I came into the world instinctively prepared to do two things. One was to suck nourishment from our mother's breasts. To accomplish this we used our sucking instinct. The other was to do everything else. To accomplish this we used our learning instinct.

The miracle of childhood learning is so remote from our awareness it must be studied scientifically to reveal what happens as the infant performs feats of intelligence that would stagger the most accomplished adult. Born with a mental structure that organizes the sounds of spoken words into complex grammatical forms, the child builds a language without anyone's instruction. All he or she needs is to listen to these sounds and then try them out. Obviously, the more listening and practice the better.

Born into a world in which the subtlest nuances of facial and vocal expression carry worlds of meaning, the child begins to distinguish between these nuances almost from birth. And while nearly all other animals perform the simple task of walking and running on four legs, the young human begins almost immediately to prepare for the much more difficult task of using only two for walking, running and perhaps ballet dancing. In the process the stage is set for the development of important intellectual concepts, like balance: concepts that can unify our understanding of all the different subject areas.

Along with all this developing skill goes a sense, expressed in chance comments, fantasies and questions, of the possibilities of the life that lies ahead. These possibilities are distinctive and unique to each individual.

EDUCATION IS . . .

The key to education is adapting teaching to the way we naturally learn. The Latin *educare*, — "to educate," is related to *educere*, which means "to lead out from." The task, then, is not to impose learning on the young, but to lead out from their infinitely resourceful minds those things that will best serve the emerging creative personality. And what are they? Sensitive listening and interpretation will discover them. Attend to your little one's babblings, behavior and wonderment as you would watch a spider weaving a web or an artist at the easel. Observe the emerging design. Try to make out the image this newly forming mind is offering to show you. Expect nothing — but await expectantly.

Young people reach for education in all sorts of ways. For it's a collaborative effort. The young in their earliest years will make observations and be influenced by your responses, will ask questions and be influenced by your answers, will do things and be influenced by what you do in return. From these interactions a unique destiny and quality of intelligence gradually reveal themselves.

The care, skill and sensitivity you bring to your interactions with children will, of course, depend on you. But it has been found that certain kinds of activities and interactions stimulate the imagination, the creative force and the intelligence more quickly than others. This book will show you ideas and activities which will help you make the learning process work better — perhaps hundreds of percent better — than it would if you chose to go it alone.

MAKING THE BEST OF WHAT WE HAVE

Today the crisis in the schools has grown to monumental proportions. Many parents complain that they cannot find the education they want for their children, or that the schools have stultified learning. It's not always that way. I have visited schools that are models of commitment to excellence. I have sat in classes inspiring for their quality of teaching and learning, and a little later I'll give you some glimpses of them. Such schools offer much of tomorrow's education today, cultivating in their average students performance that would seem superior anyplace else. But these are rare exceptions.

It would be nice if we could introduce high quality education everywhere right away, but unfortunately for the time being most of us have no alternative but to begin transforming learning opportunities in the home. You needn't worry about subject matter — that is the job of the school. Instead, focus on setting the stage for your child's reaction to the information and ideas presented in the classroom.

SCHOOLS CAN'T CHANGE UNLESS PARENTS DO

The long range goal is to get our educational system to accept and apply the most effective means of developing student potential. We know this can be done. It is happening in many isolated schools, public and private, here and in other parts of the world.

Your understanding, experience and commitment to better education are important, because only as large numbers of parents understand the nature of the learning process and begin to ask their schools to apply these principles, will we see a transformation of the schools, whether public or private.

The time is ripe, though. Public outcry to improve the quality of education is strong, and many federal, state and local programs are exploring new possibilities in education. More and more people realize that we must change our educational system or witness the erosion of the quality of life in our society and our hopes for a more equitable, brighter future. For example, a report published in *The New York Times* by the National Alliance of Business estimates that there are over a million school dropouts each year who represent $240 billion in lost earnings and taxes during their projected lifetimes. Other economic forecasters estimate that the additional costs in welfare, crime and other social costs add up to another $130 billion for each year's dropouts. That is nearly $4 trillion a decade, a cost which dwarfs what our government is spending on all forms of social service put together, including education.

Unfortunately, too many think improved education is achieved by more discipline, longer hours in school, more homework, and an environment that is even more likely to stamp out the child's instinctive desire to learn than what we've got now. This is like saying that if pulling on a plant doesn't make it grow faster, you should pull harder. The tendency has always been for adults to impose on children the kind of education they themselves received. The trouble is, we now know that fear in the classroom automatically inhibits substantially the rate and depth of possible learning. So, although discipline is essential in the schools, terrorizing students into good behavior is not the most effective way to improve the quality of their learning.

Some educators are skeptical of new ideas that claim to produce a transformation in the average person's ability to learn. But I know from experience that teachers who are given the chance to implement these new ideas almost always become their most enthusiastic supporters. After all, the teachers benefit at least as much as the students, perhaps even more.

AS THE WORLD CHANGES, SO MUST SCHOOLS

It is sometimes suggested that because for the first time in history a generation has failed to improve on the previous generation in test results, the undisciplined environment of the young has been responsible. Few have considered the possibility that scores have dropped because the world the young grow up in is so far removed from the one experienced in the classroom that student burn-out occurs more widely and at an earlier age than before. Young people today should not be treated the way their grandparents were, because their world is different. If they don't know things like the dates of the Civil War or the names of the Presidents, it could be because the environment in which such things were presented was so unpleasant as to make learning almost impossible for them. If the basic lesson of your school experience is that you are stupid, probably have no chance for significant opportunities in life, live in a culture that doesn't care about you, and are mostly perceived as a trouble maker who is not really wanted, then you're not likely to see much point in learning anything, at least not in a classroom.

But if school is a joyful experience, sort of like a cross between a good party and a first rate movie, then you're likely to want to learn a great deal and remember it for a long time.

THE STRUCTURE IS DIFFERENT, BUT IT'S THERE

I'm not suggesting the touchy-feely activities of the sixties, which produced so much chaos in thinking and so much undermining of the basic building blocks of education in many people's minds. I am suggesting a highly disciplined and structured kind of classroom — with high standards and high expectations. Recent investigation of the early growth process has revealed some important insights that need to be incorporated in educational theory — insights ignored or defied by traditional education. If we continue to ignore these findings in our schools, we can expect little improvement, no matter how many demands we make on students' time or productivity. So I'll point out what's true about our minds and how that differs from models of learning that currently dominate most educational practice.

THE ENVIRONMENT IS ALL-IMPORTANT

I'll also suggest what kind of home experience and environment helps a young person want to prosper intellectually, emotionally and physically. Most of us can't be much help to our children, though, unless we help ourselves first. Whether you're a Ph.D., a movie star or a factory worker, there's more to life than you've yet imagined, so start living more richly and fully right now. You owe that to your children — and to yourself. With the guidance of this book you can take the first steps toward treating yourself in the loving, sensitive way you've always deserved to be treated.

WAS SHAKESPEARE REALLY JUST ONE OF THE GUYS?

If you want to be successful in creating these new opportunities for yourself, you may need to change your attitude towards genius. Some people seem to think that geniuses should be looked upon as Acts of God, sort of like the Grand Canyon. No one knows for sure just how much of what makes up genius is an accident of heredity, but we do know that everyone's potential goes far beyond anything ever realized. The question then arises: just how far can you or I go in realizing our potential? It hardly matters, for each opportunity to become more aware, more sensitive, and in effect more intelligent, brings out more of the inherent genius in each of us.

Is it possible that people like Leonardo da Vinci, William

Shakespeare, Sir Isaac Newton and Mahatma Gandhi had essentially the same potential as the rest of us, but got more opportunities to develop it? That, at any rate, was Einstein's opinion, at least in reference to himself. Perhaps nothing happens to turn off a genius's ability to learn and perform well. Perhaps he or she is lucky enough to be influenced by people and events that stimulate learning in unique and powerful ways. Who and what makes the difference, we may not know; but the nature of genius is such that sparks of influence and appropriate challenges can have an enormous effect, as biographies often indicate.

So consider thinking of geniuses as people who had the opportunity to learn extremely well. And then seek to develop similar excellent opportunities for the young people around you. Meanwhile, reawaken the young whippersnapper in yourself and get acquainted with your everyday genius too.

EDUCATION CAN MAKE A DIFFERENCE

The geniuses of the past set high standards for us, but they are standards we should be able to meet. Incompetence in anything results from a lack of some specific relevant skill or skills which can be learned. By learning the missing ones, we should ultimately be able to build competence to the highest level. This so seldom happens because our educational system is based on the assumption that ability is more or less fixed from early childhood. This commonly held negative assumption strongly predisposes students to believe that little can be done to improve their overall performance more than perhaps a grade level or two.

It is not enough to identify and master the skills of geniuses of the past. We don't need more Shakespeares, Mozarts or Newtons, because their work is already done. We need geniuses uniquely different from them, whose work and contributions we cannot foresee. This means we can't precisely identify the skills they will need to learn, and therefore can't teach those particular skills in advance.

But a person who wants to accomplish something and is good at self-teaching can learn to improve his or her own performance to the highest level — assuming that he or she can control the learning process in the first place. And that's the important secret. Our educational system disempowers people by discouraging them from taking control of their own unique learning processes, but it can't stop them if they are determined enough.

MIDLIFE CREATIVITY BINGE

I know I may sound overly optimistic, so let's look at an actual case.

Gilbert Kaplan is among the world's most extraordinary symphonic conductors. When he conducted Mahler's Second Symphony at Carnegie Hall in April, 1983, New York critics hailed the performance as one of best ever heard of that symphony.

Two things set Kaplan apart from other orchestral virtuosos. First, he can't conduct anything except that one symphony. Second, in 1980 he couldn't conduct anything at all, and could barely read his way through a simple composition on the piano. He still can't read an orchestral score.

At the age of nearly forty, Kaplan, who was a New York publisher by profession, had become so enamored with the Mahler symphony that he decided to take a year off and study it. During that year he set out to learn conducting from scratch and memorized every single note and orchestral notation of the eighty-five minute work, one of the most complex in the symphonic repertoire.

Despite the fact that professional musicians discouraged him, Kaplan decided to master a new skill in midlife and pulled it off so well he now tours the world conducting this symphony with all the leading orchestras. When he first started, he never intended to do anything of the sort, never dreamed he could do more than learn the symphony and pay a group of professional musicians to let him conduct them. It was those musicians who proclaimed him a master of the art of conducting, plus critics from *Newsweek* and *The Village Voice*, who sneaked uninvited into his first private concert.

BUT YOU MUST BE KIDDING — MY CHILD ISN'T MOZART

This example of an adult mastering a new skill to a level comparable to the finest professional (even if only in a very narrow sphere) may seem a far cry from the question of bringing out genius in your child. However, most people are quite convinced they couldn't succeed at challenges like the one undertaken by Gilbert Kaplan, and that conviction gets transmitted to their children as a part of the deeply ingrained belief that permeates the whole culture. In contrast, those who achieve the highest excellence are often influenced from childhood by a quite different set of assumptions.

Unfortunately, examples of parents, teachers and theorists who proceeded on the assumption that children can learn anything from earliest infancy, also give us pause. From the nineteenth century English philosopher John Stuart Mill, who was subjected to an education of almost inconceivable intensity, to the 'superbabies' and 'hurried children' of today, the risks are clear: we must not sacrifice the child's development as a person to the development of a particular skill or intellectual prowess.

So where does this leave the parent or teacher of the seemingly average second grader, or the teen-ager who might be struggling to finish high school? To most people who consider the potential of these youngsters, it may seem that only those who are recognized as prodigies at an early age will grow up to be geniuses, and that lower expectations are appropriate for the rest.

SOME FACTS AND QUESTIONS ABOUT PRODIGIES

Examples of prodigies are often cited as evidence that unusual mental skill is something we are either born with or will never possess. However, observations recently made about prodigies show a noteworthy pattern of common environmental influences.

According to Roderick MacLeish writing in *The Smithsonian*, the scientific study of prodigies is comparatively recent. David Feldman, of Tufts University, and Rima Laibow, a child psychiatrist in Dobbs Ferry, New York, are two who are making a career of it. As a result of their efforts and others', a picture of the conditions usually common to prodigies is beginning to emerge. Here are some of the facts so far revealed, together with questions I have about them:

1. Most prodigies are boys — is this because throughout history boys have been expected to outperform girls, and they usually still are?

2. They tend to be first-born to middle class families — is this because the first-born get the brunt of most of the parents' attempts to experiment on their children, and because you try harder if you're only middle class?

3. Their parents are likely to be beyond the usual child-bearing age — is this because older parents are closer to the mid-life crisis, when they're pretty sure they're not going to fulfill their lifelong ambitions, and therefore are more likely to project these onto their children?

4. A high proportion of prodigies are born by caesarian section — is this because, (in addition to the fact that older parents tend to have more caesarians) there's a feeling of incompleteness in being born that way which seeks fulfillment through more intense self-expression?

5. A high percentage of the parents seem to be trying to realize their own ambitions through their amazing children — is this the crucial force that drives children to the fullest expression of their innate abilities?

IT'S CRUCIAL THAT YOU EXPECT EXCELLENCE . . .

For all the emphasis on inborn capacity, the relation between nature and nurture is still unclear. We still don't even know what it is about the workings of the brain — what we think of as nature — that leads to higher performance. The functioning of the brain itself may be susceptible to change in an enriched educational environment. What is clear, however, is that expectation on the part of parents can go a long way, particularly expectations expressed or implied early in childhood.

What we are left with is a combination of social expectation, parents with a high motivation to bring out the best in their children and, perhaps, some inborn capacity. For some reason, according to James T. Webb at Wright State University in Ohio, the statistical incidence of high intelligence in our society appears to be increasing. This suggests that if a society is receptive to the flowering of intelligence it will get a great deal more of it than if it is not.

At the individual level the story of Ezio Pinza, famous star of Broadway and the Metropolitan Opera, may be relevant here, for surely if anything is genetically determined, it is a great singing voice. Yet the story is told that when Pinza was born his parents held off naming him for nearly two weeks. Then one day as his father was walking through the streets he struck up conversation with a man who said to him, "Name him Ezio, and he will become a famous opera singer known all over the world." Could this incident have triggered expectation on the part of superstitious parents who then perhaps unconsciously prepared Pinza for the career that would make him famous?

... BUT DON'T DRIVE TOO HARD

Many prodigies had parents who clearly drove them too hard. John Stuart Mill had a mental crisis at the age of twenty from which he suffered for the rest of his life. Many others, perhaps driven too hard, burned themselves out too early ever to be heard from. William Sidis entered Harvard at the age of eleven, and amazed his teachers with a lecture on mathematics. Upon graduation, however, Sidis was so exhausted from the efforts to make him a genius, that he dropped out of sight into a shiftless life in which his main interest and achievement was collecting street car transfers from all over the world.

Those who remained successful as adults, like Mozart, Mendelssohn, violinist Yehudi Menuhin, and mathematician Norbert Wiener, may have had parents and teachers able to temper their own ambitions with enough humanity to make the child feel like more than just a freak to be put on public display. Certainly Mozart's letters reveal a very human family life, filled with fun and triviality side by side with fame and excellence. Indeed, Mozart's bizarre and off-color sense of humor, so disproportionately featured in the movie *Amadeus* is a quality he shared with other prodigies.

The moral is clear. Don't try to make your child a genius through the use of pressure or force. You might end up with a very intelligent person who deeply resents all your efforts. Genius, if it is to be fostered in the nursery, should be encouraged gently and in a context of the warmest nurturing and support. If human values get lost in an overweening emphasis on intelligence and performance, the result may be eventual psychological disaster.

High expectation should not be confused with specific goals and predetermined milestones which the child (and parents) are anxious to achieve. Remember that true learning is enjoyable, and when enjoyment ceases learning usually stops. Criticism, no matter how well intentioned, is never as supportive and productive as positive, patient encouragement. Each child develops differently; comparing one child's development to another's rarely has a beneficial purpose or effect. Pay attention to the children's own interests and allow these to guide you to the areas that will excite them most.

In this kind of supportive environment, you can trust the child to seek and find the challenges that will lead to the greatest growth and eventually to the highest performance of which he or she is capable.

2

HOW YOU AND YOUR CHILDREN NATURALLY LEARN

*And how traditional methods of teaching fail
to match the way we naturally learn.*

By now there's plenty of evidence to demonstrate the effectiveness of Integrative Learning, also known by such other names as accelerated learning, Optimalearning, Superlearning, Suggestopedia, whole brain learning, and holistic learning. These approaches share the assumption that **by changing the learning environment and the way information is presented, we can get substantially better results than are possible with traditional education**.

That doesn't mean throwing everything out and starting over, it means making better use of resources available now. Because Integrative Learning requires few expensive changes, it is the best bargain in education currently possible.

In today's atmosphere of crisis over schools, we tend to blame teachers, administrators, parents and the students themselves. The real cause of the problem, though, is the system, together with the limited understanding many traditionally schooled educators have of the learning process. Otherwise, most people are doing about as well as can be expected, hampered by outdated concepts of education and a bureaucratic organization that often brings out the worst in students, teachers and administrators.

This situation will not be difficult to change, but first we'll have to recognize what's wrong with what we've got. Rest assured, though, maintaining the status quo won't benefit anyone, so change is coming.

THE MYTH OF THE AVERAGE LEARNER

The problem in the schools begins with the expectation that teachers must follow pre-set lesson plans and courses of study. That would seem reasonable enough, but the difficulty is, most such plans require that you assume an average learner; and the average learner is a myth. As a result, nearly every classroom fails, at least in part, to meet the needs of any of its students.

The stresses and strains this situation inevitably creates are suggested in a Greek myth. Procrustes measured his overnight guests on his bed. If they were too tall he cut off their feet, and if they were too short he stretched them. Unfortunately, this is all too often how young people's minds are treated today: some are cut short, others stretched unreasonably. Occasionally a student's natural style of learning may happen to fit the class activities, but as long as the teacher sticks rigidly to a pre-set plan, this will occur only once in a while by accident.

Sometimes a student's particular interest may be the subject under discussion, but this, too, is largely a matter of chance. I remember five occasions in grades one through twelve when my interests were addressed or developed. I was introduced to astronomy in the first grade, when a parent came in to substitute for a day, and I immediately fell in love with the subject. But I had to wait until the eighth grade before I got another crack at it in school. At least this introduction provoked a great deal of reading and study on my own. Even with such infrequent stimulation, I think I was exceptionally lucky. At least *something* happened in school that aroused my interest.

THE TICKET TO NOWHERE

As far from ideal as the current situation is, many children learn quite a lot in school, because their minds are so hardy they can survive almost anything. Lots of them get excellent grades, some without learning very much. These are often the ones who suffer most. They've bought the system at the expense of becoming alienated from themselves. This is particularly true of children who have not been intellectually stimulated enough for them to sustain it in their own free time during and after school.

Haverford College psychologist Douglas Heath has conducted extensive research in private schools which not only points to the irrelevance of much school experience to life, but also clearly suggests that success in school does little to predict success in later life. Other studies indicate a similar lack of correlation between school experience and later success. Getting good grades may just mean a student has chosen to ape teachers, meeting their demands mechanically and without any sense of their importance or meaning. Since some of these demands may be unreasonable, a young person who gets good grades may be uncritical of unreasonable behavior.

I frequently talk to young people about courses on which they're currently spending a lot of time and energy. How often they're bored at the mere thought of discussing these courses! When it comes to material supposedly learned in the past, they'll often say, "I don't remember anything about that — we studied it last year."

Most young people are unaware how ironic it is that they spend so much time doing things they don't even enjoy thinking about. Because they see schoolwork as inevitable, they tend not to consider what it would be like if they actually enjoyed everything they did in school. Nevertheless, a few eventually become quite concerned about the waste of time, energy and sense of purpose that goes into doing well at something that has no value for them.

For example, I recently talked with an adult who always got straight A's in school, but paid a heavy price. "It was the only way I could get approval from my parents," she said. "They had no respect for my original, creative ideas, so by now I've taught myself to suppress those, even though creativity is essential in my work. I have to struggle all the time to overcome the results of learning to conform so well to someone else's standards that I no longer know what my own are. I want to find my special purpose in life, but I'm constantly fighting something inside me that tells me I'm worthy only to meet the demands of others."

THREE DAYS IN TWELVE YEARS

If you add up the amount of undivided individual attention most students get during their twelve years in school, it probably comes to about three to six school days' worth. You could pay a tutor ten dollars an hour to provide as much attention for $480. It costs the public roughly a hundred times that amount to accomplish those six days' worth of attention. Allowing for the fact that you can often learn a lot even when you're not getting individual attention, it still should be possible to produce an education ten times as effective as what we've got now — for not much more than what we're currently spending.

And an education of that quality really is possible. I have worked in schools where teachers whose approach to their classes had remained unchanged through three generations became eager to adopt the methods I suggested. I have seen the cynical and bored come to life and grow excited about their classrooms. I've seen large groups of teachers, originally skeptical, become so committed to Integrative Learning they're eager to go out and teach other teachers how it's done. So I know it's possible to make the necessary changes.

The least inspiring teachers can improve, and will be eager to, if given the right opportunities, support and information to make it possible for them to do so. There's a lot more teaching talent in the schools right now than we're using. So it's not only children's minds that are being wasted, it's teachers' minds as well. Which is certainly ironic, given the fact that teachers are usually the ones who have to take most of the blame when children don't learn.

Teachers are all too often the first victims of the skewed priorities of the educational bureaucracy, when they should be encouraged and rewarded above all for concentrating on teaching and on improving their teaching ability. When the bureaucracy places the highest value on good teaching, the quality of life in the classroom improves exponentially.

Unless this happens, students have to fend for themselves much of the time. Those who tune in to what class plans demand of them often do better than those who do not, but few even approach the full use of their potential. Many students just give up and become academic derelicts.

TIMES WHEN YOU REALLY DID LEARN

But instead of griping about the current situation, let's consider for a bit how things might be improved. If you take stock of the times when you really learned something, you may notice that these often involved the use of your whole body. Perhaps you can recall when you first learned to ride a bicycle, when you played a musical instrument well, or when you first caught the excitement of a game, whether badminton or chess. You can probably also remember the total intellectual and physical involvement you experienced if you have visited another country.

Of course, it is possible you number among your memorable learning experiences an unusually stimulating lecture, an insight into mathematics that occurred in a classroom, or some time when a teacher explained a subject particularly well and you got it. But if you can remember many times like that, you're rather unusual. Lots of us have to think long and hard before we can remember any good learning experience that happened to us in a classroom. But most of us probably can remember having to sit still, pay attention, stop moving around the room, avoid speaking out of turn, and so on. Most of these restrictions don't contribute to an environment in which human beings naturally learn.

HOW OUR ANCESTORS GOT BY

The reason is simple: You were born to learn with your whole body and all your senses. You were not born to sit in a chair eight hours a day and listen to someone talk, or to pore over books year in and year out. Our ancestors learned by moving through the forests or tilling the fields, riding horseback, or sitting around the fire telling stories. Until recently (only minutes on the evolutionary scale) there were no books, no classrooms and no lecturers.

CAUTION: BABIES AT WORK

If we pay attention to the learning of babies and young children, we can see how similar it is to the way our ancestors learned throughout their lives. Children learn by doing things. They are almost constantly active. Sometimes, though, they will sit still long enough to listen to a story. And they like to hear the same story over again until they can repeat it back word for word. Children love music, dance, games, sports and other forms of play. They love to paint, work with clay and make up fantasies of their own.

Babies and little children also need people to assist them with their learning, or they cannot progress. But they don't sit still while an older person lectures or drills them on verb forms. They respond to interest in them with delighted imitation. When their actions and thoughts are guided and shaped by a really attentive and sensitive older person (sometimes only a couple of years older) they can learn to build rich and unique patterns out of self-initiated behavior. That's how Annie Sullivan taught Helen Keller, and how Leopold Mozart and the crowned heads of Europe raised one of the finest geniuses in music history. The technical term for what I'm referring to here is "mediated learning experience."

Reflect on how you learned your native language — by doing the things children love to do, and by happily interacting with people around you who were excited about your learning. In that environment and with loving and supportive help you also learned to communicate non-verbally, to use your body, to understand people, and to make sense of the world.

THE IMPORTANCE OF TEACHING SUCCESS AND SELF-ESTEEM

The attitudes we develop toward learning — from earliest infancy —

have a profound impact on how well we can learn later. A few years ago, some fascinating research performed by Drs. Klein, Weider and Greenspan at the National Institutes of Mental Health, applied some of the ideas of Reuven Feuerstein to pre-school learning experiences. Feuerstein believes that impairments in the ability to grasp certain concepts can be corrected at any age if the right kind of teacher-pupil interaction is created to build the necessary conceptual base for whatever has to be learned.

In observing mother-child interactions, the researchers discovered it's possible to predict a child's cognitive abilities fairly accurately by observing the way the mother interacts with the child during the first year of life. Several different types of interaction were studied, one of which, the sense of self confidence in relation to tasks, instilled in a child by teachers and parents, is called "mediated feelings of competence."

"Through mediated feelings of competence," the researchers wrote, "a child may not only learn that he or she has been successful, but also what components of . . . behavior produced the desired outcome."

It was interesting to note that mothers from low-income groups of the type sometimes regarded by bigots as less intelligent than middle or upper class people, "were found to mediate very little feeling of competence and regulation of behavior." In other words, a major reason why competence does not develop well in low income groups is that children do not receive the same clues about it from their mothers during early childhood that middle and upper class children do.

Based on experiences working with such individuals, I believe that this situation is relatively easy to correct. A child's self-image and expectation of success can and should be developed and improved in the classroom. When this is not done, we can expect that children will continue to operate on the basis of clues they received early in childhood, which were instrumental in forming their original self-image.

DEVELOPING SELF-ACTUALIZATION AMONG THE POOR IN COLOMBIA

Glendon Nimnicht, an educator who has studied the effect of environment on learning, argues rather strongly for the importance of developing human potential through encouraging self-actualization, or the realization of one's inborn drive for excellence, even while dealing with the most basic problems of survival.

In a study of four impoverished and isolated Colombian communities he found that "the development of human potential can be an integral part of overall development. An environment that supports human potential also has the ability to fulfill basic biological needs."

In other words, it doesn't do much good to try to help people overcome poverty unless you also help them discover ways of seeing themselves as successful and potentially able to deal with the world in a positive and effective manner. These attitudes can be easily taught, but only a tiny percentage of the population will learn them if they are not taught. All teaching, in other words, should encourage and reinforce the learner's belief in his or her innate capacity to learn and succeed, at the very time it provides knowledge and skills. And this can be done only by making the learner feel good about the learning process. The kind of put-down and negative critical evaluation so often found in traditional education militates against an optimum learning experience. Above all, fear must be banished from the classroom, replaced by hope and a constantly reinforced experience of success and self-worth.

HOW THE INTELLECTUALLY SUPERIOR GOT THAT WAY

Beginning about 1950, a Bulgarian psychotherapist named Georgi Lozanov set out to investigate why a few individuals are able to perform mental feats that outdistance the rest of us to such an astonishing degree. Is this because they are inherently smarter, or because they were allowed to learn in a different manner? Does it have anything to do with the fact that geniuses so often display a childlike quality? Lozanov came to believe that everyone is capable of learning at a rate two to five times as fast as our present system considers normal, and that probably this rate of learning can be speeded up even more.

The secret of accelerating learning, Lozanov found, is to recreate the natural learning environment of the infant: to structure the classroom so students alternate between the passive state of listening attentively to a wonderful artistic presentation of their lessons, and actively involving themselves with the material in song, dance, drama, other sorts of physical movement and discussion.

As a result of his studies, Lozanov proposed that classes be conducted in an atmosphere similar to a living room or a child's playroom, that the teacher should take on a nurturing role, reinforcing the learner's own attempts to learn with affectionate and positive responses, while downplaying and ignoring mistakes or reinterpreting them as meaningful attempts to communicate. Over and over Lozanov accomplished a rapid and permanent increase in the rate of learning. He did this through the process he called *Suggestopedia*, one aspect of which was infantilization, which means recreating in the maturing learner the receptivity of mind of the infant.

As the term Suggestopedia implies, suggestion was the cornerstone of Lozanov's theory. The mind is extremely pliable and, when in an infant-like state, will often take suggestions literally and act on them. That is why it is so important, as Nimnicht and the researchers at NIMH found, to create an atmosphere focused on self-actualization and success orientation. This is because we tend to succeed at those things we believe we can be successful at, and to fail at those things we believe we cannot do. "Give me a long enough lever," said Archimedes, "and I will move the world." In a similar spirit we might say, "Give me the right set of suggestions and get me to believe them, and I will do anything." Of course, the most basic way to teach a person to believe in success is to provide learning experiences that lead logically and necessarily to success. That's much more effective than just telling people they ought to believe in themselves.

LOZANOV'S THREE CONDITIONS FOR ACCELERATING LEARNING

Lozanov maintains that when people are learning to their fullest potential the learning experience has three essential characteristics. First, true learning is inherently **joyful**. Second, it unites the conscious and the **paraconscious**. Third, it draws upon the **reserve complex**. Let's consider these one by one.

As to the matter of joy, it isn't just that we enjoy the feeling of accomplishment at having learned something — rather, the learning process is joyful in and of itself. So naturally, if we're going to learn something, we must begin with joyful anticipation, and end with regret, or at least nostalgia.

MATCHING WORDS AND SIGNALS

It is a fundamental mistake to ignore the inseparability of conscious and paraconscious experience. By paraconscious, I mean background thoughts you're not focusing on at the moment, but could attend to if you chose. This is a particularly important concept for parents to understand, because children are influenced by their paraconscious sensitivity to the attitudes behind words. These are communicated unconsciously with tone of voice and gestures — it's maddening that whatever we're trying hardest to hide is the very thing we most assuredly reveal to the paraconscious sensitivities of children.

So it's important when you're with children to communicate your excitement about what you think they'll be able to accomplish in life. You might also get excited about how life for the whole family is a joyful adventure. Of course, you'll need to believe what you're saying, or they'll just pick up the message behind your words which, according to some analysts, is 93% of what they'll pick up.

Just as parents — by making sure their non-verbal communication reflects their words — can help children anticipate a successful and fulfilling life for themselves; so teachers, when they meet their classes, should harmonize the content of the course with the non-verbal components of the presentation. Lozanov called this harmonization process *double planing*. The teacher should not suggest, by even the faintest hint, that the subject is boring or difficult, or that the student might not succeed. Also, the teacher should constantly reinforce an attitude of joyfulness about all that is to be done. For example, the comment "Recess is over — now it's time to get back to work," creates the impression that study is not fun, while recess is.

THE RESERVE COMPLEX

When Lozanov speaks of the reserve complex, he is referring to our underutilized capacity to think, create, solve problems, and challenge ourselves to the highest level. In contemporary society, the reserve complex tends to be tapped only under extraordinary conditions, because most of us are convinced we're inferior, or at least ordinary, and quite incapable of being outstanding at much of anything. But the reserve complex is present in everyone, waiting to be tempted into the open, once the environment becomes safe for excellence and the everyday sort of genius. It's best supported by a parent's consistently expressed belief in the child's ability to meet the highest level of challenge — though this must be a valued and realistic challenge, relevant to the child's own purposes.

THE THREE BARRIERS TO LEARNING

In order to help identify what might be interfering at any given moment with the apparently universal inclination to learn, Lozanov invoked what he called the **anti-suggestive barriers**. These barriers are erected when a student feels something offered by the teacher is deficient in logic, ethics or enjoyment. In other words, for a thing to be learned easily it must be logical, ethical and enjoyable.

For example, many of us have trouble with arithmetic. We might not think it's fun, because we learned it under conditions that frightened or bored us. We might not think it's logical, because the explanation the teacher gave didn't make sense, or wasn't clear. And we might not think it's ethical, because it doesn't seem relevant to our personal value system.

If you think math is totally irrelevant to your life, you need to learn how vital it is — not by lecture, but by insight or experience.

The ethical barrier may also appear in the guise of prejudice against oneself. Some people feel guilty if things go well for them, because they assume they don't deserve prosperity. Perhaps they feel they can get it only by taking something away from someone else. Guilt about money is often expressed this way. But there may be similar attitudes toward knowledge or skill, even though you're not depriving someone else of knowledge when you gain it yourself. The idea, though, that learning makes us somehow "better" than others can sometimes lead to guilt feelings. Some children, for example, think it's wrong to learn things their parents don't know about. The parents may actually encourage this attitude in occasional cases.

THE BARRIER OF INTERNALIZED OPPRESSION

Mostly, though, self-oppression occurs in wholly irrational forms. For example, girls may believe only males can learn math. Or black students may believe only white students can learn it, that being black makes them unworthy or incompetent.

This phenomenon of internalized oppression, or prejudice against oneself, may develop as a result of culturally implanted self-images, and is widespread among groups that have been oppressed by society as a whole. Oppression, by the way, is mostly non-verbal. When people of color are overwhelmed with media images of white people playing most of the important roles on the world stage, that has a more insidious effect on their consciousness than direct expressions of prejudice — more insidious because it is affecting them paraconsciously, and it is harder to identify, deal with, and combat.

THE EFFECT OF SOCIAL PRESSURE

A further extension of these barriers on a large scale is the effect, conscious and unconscious, of social pressure. Lozanov referred to this as a negative **social-suggestive norm** — a belief shared by the whole society that learning is usually difficult and painful. Anyone who wants to have a good learning experience must first overcome this deeply ingrained societal belief. Using the classroom or home to establish more positive ideas about learning prepares the ground for new beliefs and, is the essential first step to cultivating these values in the society at large.

IT DOESN'T HAVE TO BE DIFFICULT

So powerful were Lozanov's concepts that adventurous educators around the world wanted to give them a try. When his instructions were rigorously followed, remarkable results were achieved. Students learned faster, better and with more depth of understanding than had previously been believed possible.

So can you, and so can your family. If you understand the conditions that favor learning, you can teach others of all ages how to continue growing intellectually, even though their school experiences may do little to encourage the learning process. In later chapters we'll explore Lozanov's work in greater depth.

But before you can successfully stimulate the intellectual growth of others, you may have to make some changes in your own attitude toward learning. While joyful challenge with some degree of temporary frustration is natural and desirable, painful stress for its own sake is not. So, if you were brought up in an educational system that encouraged you to think of study and learning as difficult, you may have been sold a bill of goods.

"No pain, no gain" — a slogan popularized by body-builders — does not apply to learning. But some people unconsciously seek to make suffering part of the learning experience. All too often that's what happens in school. And what they come away with, in the long run, is less learning and more suffering. Allow me to illustrate with an example.

THE ART OF LEARNING TO BE STUPID

Your brain is naturally adept at understanding and using grammar. You can make a sentence easily without having to figure out where to put subject, verb, adjectives and adverbs. You can handle a gerundive phrase without batting an eyelash. It ought to be easy to name the parts of speech and the structures they form — no harder than, say, distinguishing your nose from your mouth or your arms from your legs.

And yet after twelve years of studying grammar most of us end up feeling it's too confusing to bother with, or perhaps not worth remembering. If the thought of having to diagram a sentence makes you faintly suicidal, you have that in common with some of the brightest, most successful people around. Thus a whole population who intuitively understand English grammar are transformed into confused and awkward bumblers on the subject. In the interest of taking the simple last step of teaching them to name the structures they are using in their everyday speech, we manage to get them so confused that even if they spend many hours studying, they never quite figure it out. In fact, we ought to be able to teach them everything we want them to learn in a few hours.

GRAMMAR CAN BE FUN

It is not hard to teach grammar by getting students to engage in enjoyable activities that do not seem like drill or study. My own approach is to have them diagram sentences with their bodies. To do so, they make up humorous sentences, each person adding a word. The grammatical relationships between the words can be vividly established without any grammatical terms. For example the "subject" shakes hands with the "verb," the "verb" stops on the foot of the "object," an "adjective" touches the shoulder of a "noun," an "adverb" touches the shoulder of a "verb," and so on. This is great fun, and the sentences that result from the combined efforts of everyone in the room are often quite amusing.

If you name a part of speech and try to describe it outside of the context of its use in an actual sentence, it's almost impossible for students to connect what you're describing with what they've been doing for years. That's because we learn best by doing first and then naming, or by doing and naming simultaneously, but seldom by naming first and then doing. A name without an action or object to attach it to is like a grin without a cat. It doesn't make sense. Yet teachers persist in writing the word "noun" on the board and saying, "Now children, a noun is a name of a person, place, thing or idea."

LOVE AFFAIRS WITH COMPUTERS

You've probably noticed how many young people are entranced with computers and will sit in front of one for hours. To them this machine is an ordinary part of the environment. Perhaps their first contact with it was through a game. Then, as they got the feel of it, they wanted to know it better and so figured out more about its operation, much as they previously figured out how to crawl around their living room without anyone telling them. Through games, children experience mastery of a new concept, plus the association forever after with an experience of fun.

Such mastery may be a mystery to you, because for the initiate the computer is a set of experiences while for you it might be associated with words and symbols that don't mean anything, like "digital," "on line," "spreadsheet," "ram," "rom," "wraparound" and so on. You either associate these words with familiar experiences, or they are part of a foreign and vaguely threatening system.

If you don't happen to like computers at the moment, don't give up on yourself. You can still learn to understand and love them. That might happen as a result of your having fun playing with one before you get too much abstract explanation. When you've had some experience (or while you're having it) you can apply words to what you're doing, and they'll make sense.

NOW LET'S ALL MAKE A FAN

I'm going to ask you now to do a thought experiment that will get to the essence of what I'm talking about. Fold a piece of paper to make a fan. When you're finished, decorate it and make it beautiful. Next, imagine you have to follow a page or two of instructions on how to fold the paper to achieve the same result. You would probably take as much time making the second fan as it took to make *and* decorate the first, just using your innate sense of how it's done.

This little exercise is often performed with students. Asked to make a fan, they can all do so. Told how to make it, most of them fail, or get confused.

HOW TEACHING INSULTS THE MIND

This is the root cause of most of our problems with learning and teaching. Schools do not draw excellent performance out of people — they tell them what to do and how to do it. Telling not only insults the intelligence, it also creates confusion.

Often, the best way to teach is to begin by drawing out of the student whatever he or she already knows about the subject. You can teach just about anything that way, provided the learner is prepared to learn. Preparation to learn can be taught as well, for the strategies of successful learners have been analyzed and can be taught to unsuccessful ones. Nonthreatening involvement with fun and games is often helpful. In any case, the necessary background concepts must be taught, so as to provide a background for the anticipated new learning.

For example, when I present the concepts of Integrative Learning to a group of educators, I usually begin by leading them through a series of experiences. Then I ask them to describe what we have done. They then generate a list of the basic principles more relevant to them than any I could supply, because the list is in their own words, based on their own experience. Should they be lacking concepts necessary to help them understand the principles of Integrative Learning, that will be revealed in the discussion, and the necessary clarification can be supplied.

GETTING STARTED AT LEARNING SOMETHING

If I want you to learn something, the best way I can support you is by surrounding you with experiences from which to structure your developing knowledge or skill. The process continues as I provide you with additional guidance and feedback. If I am skillful enough, you will eventually get the impression you are doing everything yourself. My role will become less central as I function less to give information or develop skill, and more to facilitate. Thus my objective is to help you, the student, become independent of me, the teacher.

It's not hard to conduct classes this way, it's just that we're not used to doing it. Our traditional educational practices have misled us into doing most of our students' thinking for them. After depriving them of the most fruitful opportunities to use their brains, we complain that they don't know how to think.

THE ROOTS OF TRADITIONAL EDUCATION

You might well wonder where the traditional educational practices that cause so much trouble came from in the first place. I could give you a lot of answers to this question. I could lead you through the development of educational practice from Egyptian times and speculate about the relationship between school and society. I could explain that through history most societies have not wanted the majority of their citizens to function intellectually, they've wanted them to be workers, capable only of carrying out orders literally. Elitist thinking has always assumed the majority were not capable of anything better anyway; and short of revolutions, the majority have usually responded to this vote of no confidence by doing what was expected of them.

Or, I could point out that our public school system was mainly designed to produce factory workers who would show up for work on time, understand and follow oral and written instructions and not rock the boat.

But I'll content myself with giving you an analogy.

YOUR CHILD IS NOT A COKE MACHINE

So, let's perform another thought experiment. Imagine you've put some quarters in a Coke machine, and nothing happens. You don't get your money back, and you don't get any Coke either. What do you do next? If you're like most people, you kick the machine. This might work. Badly shaken machines sometimes get jiggled into action. If kicking the machine doesn't suffice, you probably look around for an expert — someone with a key who can open it and get your money back. Or someone with the authority to refund your money and reprimand (or possibly even fix) the machine later. If none of these succeeds, and you're rich, you might continue feeding in quarters, hoping eventually a Coke will emerge.

That's more or less the way the educational system drives teachers to deal with children. They present information, and if the students learn it, well and good. If they don't, one of four things happens: They punish them (equivalent of kicking the Coke machine). Or they call in an expert to fix them. Or they report them to an authority (a parent, or an administrator) who can be counted on to deal with them later. And if none of these is effective, they make them do everything over.

Most actual school practice doesn't vary a whole lot from this. It's true there are some enlightened theories of education, and some teachers are able to motivate children by loving them or making their classrooms unusually appealing, or by excellent teaching. But the educational system as a whole mostly treats young people the way you and I might treat a Coke machine. It puts in the facts and gets back the test scores. If the test scores are not satisfactory, it punishes, refers to experts, or calls in authorities. When all else fails, it cries in rage and anger at the poor confused child, "There's no excuse for your not being able to do this — do it over again!"

This would all be fine if a child were just like a Coke machine, because the way we deal with Coke machines is usually appropriate. But since children are intelligent living beings and not Coke machines, it's not appropriate to treat them as if they were.

WHAT IS A STUDENT?

The secret of educating children is about as simple as the secret of dealing with Coke machines, but it's seldom tried. The poet Robert Frost put it this way: "A student is someone who is somewhere and is trying to get somewhere else." That statement assumes two things: knowledge and motivation.

If you happen to have a child who has no knowledge at all, the only thing to do is keep it in bed and feed it intravenously. The moment you discover any kind of intelligent response, you are ready to take the next step: find out how the child would like to increase his or her knowledge, and why.

A GOOD START LASTS A LIFETIME

This collaborative relationship between parent and child can be delightfully rewarding for both. One of my most positive early memories is of the time I told my mother I wanted to write a book. She immediately went to the typewriter and started pounding out the words I dictated to her. Imagine my sense of power as I uttered thoughts that would be immortalized by her typewriter! Though I could barely read at the time, she handed me a typescript which I could immediately identify as the first book I had ever written.

Another excellent thing she did occurred when I was eleven. I had been given one of those books with cutouts in it for making a marionette theater complete with marionettes. Soon I was presenting little shows for the edification of my mother, the maid, and any of the neighbors who could be corralled from the street. This successful impressarioship led my mother a few months later to build a larger marionette theater with dolls suspended from thread, an incomplete collection of settings and a thorough but unfinished dramatization of my favorite story, *The Wizard of Oz*, all of it obviously intended to be completed by me. It was homemade makeshift, but I shall never forget the magic it bred in my imagination. It was probably the main reason that a few years later I founded a theater with live actors that eventually grew to be a major summer event in Washington, D.C.

When my own children came along, the idea of writing books was not forgotten, though I handled the matter somewhat differently. My children were introduced to the opera before they were old enough to go to school. Since they already loved having stories read to them, I would write and illustrate books for them, telling the story of the opera, filled with the sort of emotions that children really understand. This made it easy for them to follow and enjoy the complex music. My ears are still alive with a four year old little voice saying, "Mimi died, and that made Rudolph very sad, and he cried," or after sitting in complete silence through three and a half hours of Cavalli's *L'Ormindo* (a difficult work even for the opera buff), "Daddy, when can we see it again?"

When children show sparks of interest in things, the proper response is to share their interest without taking over or dominating their approach to the subject. Surround them with opportunities to learn. Ask them if they want to try things you think might interest them. Show excitement in the things they are interested in.

The excitement you feel models the joy of learning for your children, making them feel it's all right for them to be vitally interested too, even if not in the same things. If you communicate with them and share your joys, they will want to tell you theirs as well. The important thing is that this kind of parent-child communication be a two-way street.

Give them as much information as they want, but always in appealing and delightful forms. Listen carefully to their questions and give the best answers you can. If you don't have an answer, admit it and invite the child to help you make one up. Remember, there are no stupid questions, only stupid answers. By responding to your child's real interests, you can help a challenging and powerful mind take its first eager steps toward mastery.

TEACHING LITERACY TO ADULTS

Here's an interesting example of good teaching that happens not to involve children, though the technique I'll describe is often recommended for working with children as well as adults in teaching literacy. Unfortunately, many teachers find it too demanding of their time, and so don't bother to use it. I first heard about it from a teacher who had been unusually successful teaching functionally illiterate coal miners to read. He approached the task as follows:

The first day of class he asked the miners to talk about themselves while he tape recorded what they said. That night he transcribed their remarks, and in the next class gave transcripts of the remarks to those who had spoken them, asking each man to read his own words of the day before. The man would labor over the first few words before recognizing them. Then he would usually exclaim, "Well, now, these are *my* words." After that, the words would begin to flow from his mouth and take on some of the cadence of a man speaking, not just an awkward reading.

This is step one. The teacher started by asking the miners to read only words they knew and could use. Furthermore, he made them aware they were working with what they already knew. He did so in a supportive way, saying in effect, "The words you spoke were so important I've typed them for you to read."

Now we come to step two, for the teacher had helped the miners be aware where they were, in Robert Frost's terms. He next needed to help them get somewhere else. How could he best do that?

He had already let them know he was on their side and wanted to help them. He had done so through actions, not just promises. Because he had taken the trouble to type out their words, they knew he respected and cared about them.

ON LEARNING THE HARDEST THINGS FIRST

But he wanted to establish a motivation for them to learn to read, so he said, "If you could make out the words of anything written, what would interest you the most?" The answer was the instruction manuals for their equipment. So he brought in copies of the manuals, which the miners learned to read remarkably quickly. Of course instruction manuals are not the easiest reading, and that is why teachers often think they have to start out with books like *Dick and Jane*. But *Dick and Jane* has nothing to do with miners. It doesn't relate to where they are or where they are trying to go, so it is not effective for teaching them to read. To be honest, it's not really effective for teaching anyone to read.

This leads quite naturally to one of the most important principles of Integrative Learning, which is: Get a view of the full scope of the subject first, and then allow the details to fall into place.

FREDERICK DISCOVERS ALGEBRA

Let me illustrate with a story from my own teaching experience. Frederick was labelled as having a severe learning disability. I had been hired to teach him English skills, but after we had been working for some months with good progress, I brought him an algebra book and suggested we explore it together. Frederick was fourteen and had heard of algebra, but knew nothing about it.

I turned to the end of the book and told him we would start with the last problem. This I proceeded to do while he watched. As I worked, I explained every step, showing him the mathematical concepts involved. This took about forty-five minutes. When it was finished I knew he could not have done the problem himself, but he understood, in general, what I had done. I then paged through the book from back to front, pointing out and reminding him of the various processes we had used to do the problem. About 80% of the book was familiar to him from this point of view. Then I asked if he had any questions.

"Yes," he said, "why does anyone think algebra is difficult?"

The next time we were together, we started with the first sentence in the book. Its meaning was not clear to Frederick, so we talked about it for two hours. This took us into such fascinating matters as the nature of the fifth and sixth dimensions, and we had a thoroughly good time. There was still an hour left of our lesson, so I asked Frederick to start working the problems in the book. He was to work as many on each page as he needed to to understand the process involved, and then go on to the next page.

He did all the problems he attempted correctly, and by the end of the hour he had reached page fifty-three.

Since that experience with Frederick, I've repeated it, with some variation, with a number of other students. I've also talked to several teachers who told me they'd tried essentially the same thing with similar results. And one teacher, to whom I told this story at a teacher training midway through the school year, said he immediately introduced the technique to his algebra class. They finished the book a month early, even though in previous years he usually could not finish the book at all.

All of which illustrates how it is easier to understand something if your first exposure to it reveals its richness and complexity. Knowing you can follow and understand all the different processes, even though you might not be able to remember and reproduce them, leads to a feeling of familiarity with the subject that makes it easier to anticipate mastery. In approaching a new subject, the mind feels more comfortable knowing its full shape, and likes knowing what the hardest things are. In the earliest stages of working on something, you can take in a lot of new information rather quickly. After that you tend to get more bogged down with details. If the earliest exposure lays out the whole scope of the subject, you have a structure to which you can relate everything else, so the remaining details fall into place more easily.

THERE'S NO NEED FOR PABLUM

Perhaps we can agree by now that spoon feeding isn't the best way to approach the mind, which prefers to learn whatever it's interested in at a fairly advanced (but unconfusing) level from the beginning.

Can you imagine a classroom in which the teacher proceeded by finding out where each student was, and where that student wanted to go? Would it be chaos? Would the pupils become estranged from each other? Would it be too much for the teacher to handle? Or could there be a way of tying activities together for teacher and students alike?

That's what it was like in the one room schoolhouse, where teachers had to instruct all twelve grade levels in the same room. It wasn't possible to present very much to the class as a whole, so the teacher usually taught the most advanced students, who would in turn teach those at the next level down. Meanwhile, everyone was aware from the first grade of the levels of information yet to be learned, so all the material seemed familiar when it came time to study it. Many who received their education in this environment said they learned their subjects very well that way.

If you still think a teacher confronted by a class of thirty-five children can't possibly adapt to all their needs and desires, consider how the problem is solved by communications experts. Anyone who works in advertising or writes a popular book, mass-marketed film or TV show has to appeal to a wide range of interests and abilities in readers or viewers. This is usually accomplished by an orientation toward basic human needs or interests in a rich enough aesthetic context so most people are drawn into the experience. There's no reason a classroom teacher cannot arouse and develop interests using the same kind of artistic techniques writers, artists and communications specialists use.

We must not, however, lose sight of what can and should be done at home. What happens there is fundamentally important to your child's education. Many studies such as the Coleman Report have shown that success in school is not much affected by traditional school experiences. These studies suggest that children's learning is determined more by the home environment than anything else. Only an unusually outstanding school can make much difference in how children learn.

A series of interviews with successful people revealed there was always someone in their background who took a special interest in their education. In other words, a major factor in helping a young person become successful is modeling and sharing your understanding of excellence and how to achieve it. That's why the biographies of famous people so often emphasize childhood influences.

WHAT'S IN IT FOR YOU

You'll probably want to undertake the challenge only if several conditions are met.

1. Everything in this book should be read with the assumption that you're already a good parent. Feelings of guilt about what you should have done or didn't do are counter-productive. Use the ideas here as they fit comfortably into your family life. You don't need to do everything in the book — in order to provide variety and choice, I've included more here than any one family can use. So keep reminding yourself you're a good parent, and each thing you do, however small, is making you an even better one.

If something does go wrong and you feel guilty about it, remember that all parents sometimes fall short. Your children will rise above your mistakes as you rose above those your parents made. So there's no point in berating yourself over whatever went wrong, or feeling that if you're not the perfect parent you're no good at all. (I've found many parents do feel that way.) Be proud of the mastery you've already demonstrated in guiding a young person toward adulthood. You're doing an outstanding job, considering the unusual demands parenting makes on one's intelligence, patience, sensitivity and ingenuity. If that weren't true, you wouldn't be reading this book.

2. You'll do the things recommended in this book much more readily if they benefit you as well as your children. Most of us are too busy to devote much time to helping our children grow, except when we are faced

with an emergency. But this book is not about emergency situations. It offers you and your family a chance to live a fuller, richer and happier life. You can plan family activities so that what helps your children will also help you, and what is fun for them will be fun for you as well.

3. Most people are too busy to do more than they're already doing. So this book is designed to fit in with your already existing schedule. Do the activities around the dinner table or at bedtime, or during special family times or occasions like birthday parties.

REMEMBER, IT'S FOR THE WHOLE FAMILY

So right now resolve to start a new chapter in your family life, one that will bring you and your children closer in a more loving and rewarding relationship. In this new experience you will learn as much from them as they from you. You can apply what you learn to your practical needs and be thinking about how to get more fun out of life at the same time.

3

THE BUILDING BLOCKS OF LEARNING

*An explanation of the three components of the learning
process: input, synthesis, and output.
How Georgi Lozanov's innovative approach speeds
learning, and makes it more enjoyable.*

Two phenomena which have been the bane of educators during the last generation — television and video games — deserve a second look. Both, of course, have similar technology, but their impact on the mind is different.

TELEVISION VS. VIDEO GAMES

The effect television has on its viewers could be of outstanding educational value, but most often it's trivial, or worse. Each week there's probably enough information on the airwaves to equal a college education (if you compare all that's programmed with all the information a typical college graduate can recall). So if content alone were the criterion, it ought to be possible for your child to stare at the tube night after night and walk away with the equivalent of a B.A., or better.

One reason this doesn't occur is the tube provides only one of the three necessary requirements for learning: **input**; and lacking the other two, **synthesis** and **output,** it may actually decrease the usable intelligence of the viewer. If the second and third components of learning were added, the result might be a significant increase in learning skills.

By contrast, the video game supplies all three of the requirements in an almost ideal ratio. So video games can dramatically increase skills in a short time. What they lack is meaningful cultural impact, as well as human interaction.

Consider how a video game affects you, the player. You're trying to control the movement of images on a screen. To do so, you must have input (the first stage of learning). That is, you must observe the changing configurations on the screen moment by moment. But as every beginning player knows, that's not enough. The maze and jumble of visual information suddenly thrown at you is difficult to sort out. It takes the second stage of learning, or synthesis, to acquire comfort in play.

HOW THE MIND PROCESSES NEW INFORMATION

Synthesis occurs when you compare what you observe each moment (the new input) with previous experience recorded in your memory. While practicing the game, you store up a fund of experiences, on the basis of which you evaluate new input. Gradually, as you acquire familiarity with the game, your ability to relate new input to past experience grows.

Output is the third stage. You can't just passively watch, you've got to respond whenever anything happens on the screen. If your response is good enough, you score. Gradually, as a result of the coordination of input and synthesis, responses improve — and so do scores.

The most valuable attribute of the video game is its immediate feedback on performance. Whereas children in school usually have to wait days or weeks before finding out how they did on a test, video games tell the story instantly. This instant **feedback** is one of the most important factors in speeding up, and generally improving, learning.

THE AUTOMATED TEACHER OF THE FUTURE

So when the cultural complexity made possible by television has been combined with the structure of the video game, we'll have a powerful new learning tool. This will allow us rapidly to acquire, synthesize and output information. Nevertheless, we'll still lack the human interactions so vital to learning — in the home, in schools, and in other educational and training enterprises.

In school, these interactions will have to be provided by classroom teachers. Relieved of the burden of drill, repetition and boredom, teachers will then be able to help us enter a new age of excitement about learning, an age which may make teaching once again one of the most honored of professions — and one of the most widely in demand.

For when machines handle the presentation of information, providing students with rapid evaluation and feedback, teachers will be free to engage in activities and discussions which help their students humanize what they have learned. Students will have increased opportunities to develop and use the linguistic and artistic skills on which good communication depends. And teachers will enjoy their work more and have a chance to make a greater impact on students than most of them can now.

Because the interactive video-computer will bring rich new possibilities to the classroom, most people will desire to continue being students, at least on a part time basis, all through life. This will create new job opportunities for teachers, who will also be better paid than they are now. Indeed, education may become the biggest growth industry of the next half century. For there's nothing that can benefit people more, provided it actually works.

But there's a lot to do before we can achieve this ideal, so let's consider a little further why television doesn't currently do much to educate children, and see what we can do to supplement it.

HOW TV CONFUSES CHILDREN

The role of the television viewer is passive. Television programming makes no distinction between the sublime and the ridiculous. It leaves it up to the viewer to evaluate what has been seen and put it in perspective. This can be confusing to children who spend a lot of their time in front of the screen. Because they can't relate what they are seeing to their own lives, the information they acquire isn't rooted in experience, and therefore they can't interpret it properly. For example, one child who had lived through the John Kennedy assassination, as seen on TV, interpreted the Robert Kennedy assassination as a re-run.

Because television seems so much more dramatic and fast-paced than real life, it tends to make school (and the rest of life) seem boring by contrast. As a woman friend recently pointed out, "I got a very distorted view of relationships between women and their competition for men from watching soap operas with my mother." The tendency of television to dramatize an inaccurate picture of reality increases a child's difficulty in relating effectively to life in general, as well as to the classroom.

WHY TV CAN MAKE YOU MISERABLE

We are all hungry to synthesize and activate everything we learn, so the passivity of the young television viewer is stressful. Children who spend long hours in front of the TV may tend to feel a vague dissatisfaction with life, without knowing where it comes from. This is aggravated by the fact that whereas families used to sit around and talk by the fire after dinner at night, often raising questions and problems that had to be dealt with, today many of them simply watch the tube and no longer interact personally. Thus many children are missing out on the personal interactions and problem-solving opportunities their parents or grandparents took for granted.

This double deprivation may partly account for the appeal of drugs and other extreme forms of sensory stimulation to the generations influenced by television. The drug experience might be interpreted as an attempt to make up for some element missing from one's life.

Watching television all day long is a way of building relationships with pictures. So let me ask you to perform another thought experiment. What would it be like if everyone you cared about were available to you only as a photograph? You could look at the pictures as much as you wanted; but could never talk on the phone with those dearest to you, or have any other sort of live contact with them. How frustrated would you feel under such conditions? The essence of a relationship is continuous contact with another person through a changing series of circumstances. We relate by active participation, not by passive absorption. Similarly, to be an effective learner, you must participate in experiences with your teacher.

The implications are profound. Properly conducted, even without the ideal technology, classrooms can be much more exciting and fulfilling than television sets, because they can involve children in active learning with plenty of chance to synthesize and dramatize their experience.

A MODEL FOR SUCCESSFUL TEACHING AND LEARNING

When educator Georgi Lozanov sought to analyze successful learning and teaching he turned to the study of language, a development I will discuss in the next chapter. Eventually, he found a way to teach languages more quickly than they've ever been taught before. What he discovered lends itself to many applications.

Lozanov defined three essential steps in teaching: **decoding**, **concerts** and **activation**. These correspond roughly to the three components of learning just examined, though input, synthesis and output are interwoven throughout the learning experience, while Lozanov's learning cycle is presented sequentially.

For the purpose of teaching languages, the decoding phase of the presentation is a once-over-lightly on the material. The teacher does this part in a dramatic, almost ham-acted way, like a charades game. The object is to give students a chance to guess the meaning of the word or concept represented. This brief decoding process is not meant to teach the material by anchoring it in the memory, but only to make it familiar.

HOW TO APPROACH A TEXTBOOK

Consider the application of decoding to your personal learning activities. We usually omit this phase. Instead, we're prone to plunge into a new subject without an overall notion of what it will involve. The way to decode a biology textbook, for example, is first to study the table of contents, to determine what general categories of information will be presented. Then read the summary of each chapter and look up any words you don't understand. Finally, draw a diagram representing the different kinds of information you find in the book. (See Chapter Twenty-four.) This will make the material more familiar, so as you read the book, or take a course in the subject, you will know where it is taking you. After you've tried this process yourself, you'll be able to teach it to your children.

USING MUSIC TO ENTER THE LONG-TERM MEMORY

Lozanov's second stage of presentation, to help synthesize the information, is the concert session. This introduces new material quickly and painlessly to the long-term memory. During this phase the teacher or parent reads a fascinating story or play containing the core concepts, or most essential information to be learned. The reading is matched to the musical structure of a work of baroque, classical, or romantic music, so the words follow the rhythms and emotional qualities of the music. If you want to know how this is done, I suggest you listen to a recording of *Peter and the Wolf*, noticing how the actor's voice interweaves with the music. When speech and music interact, it's as if the speaker has become an instrument in the orchestra. Thus, a concert session is an artistic process that allows you to make a piece of music into a concerto for speaking voice and orchestra, with your voice becoming like a musical instrument, even though it never utters a note of actual music.

Sometimes, when working with students individually, I like to teach them to read concerts themselves, because the process of matching the voice to the music helps develop better reading skills. So you might try having a family reading time when everyone takes a turn, while music plays in the background, and each person tries to match the musical patterns with the rising and falling of the voice. Or you might have a dinner time ritual in which each night one member of the family presents for all the others a short, prepared concert reading. If you do this, I think you'll find everyone's reading skills and interests spurting ahead.

This approach was used by one of my associates, June Sasson, to remove a friend's foreign accent. When she first drilled him on pronunciation, he made little progress, but when she played music in the background while they worked, he could hear the sounds he was supposed to produce more clearly, and thus produce them more easily. It took about three weeks, she said, for him to remove completely a thick Arabic accent he'd had for many years.

SAVING TIME WITH MUSIC

When the concert presentation is used in a classroom, much less time needs to be spent reviewing and drilling on the material. Lozanov has asserted that, properly used, the concert session can do 60% of the teaching in about 5% of the class time. It is this element of his work that most clearly distinguishes his contribution from those of other educators, for he was able to accomplish far more in his classrooms than many other innovative educators who did not know about this powerful gateway to the long-term memory.

Works such as Pachelbel's *Canon*, Handel's *Water Music*, or Beethoven's *Emperor Concerto*, are chosen for the concerts. When you use dynamic vocal patterns to match the text to the music, the long-term memory is immediately tapped.

In addition, because one part of the brain processes linguistic information, while another processes music, the harmonization of the two may generate feelings of euphoric relaxation, sufficient to lower still further the barriers to new information. This euphoria may induce healthy bodily responses. The result is to create in learners a state of mind similar to the intense involvement baseball fans may feel while memorizing World Series scores, or creative dancers while improvising in the presence of an admiring audience. We learn and create best when the whole personality is pleasantly focused on a single activity. If you've ever been so deeply involved in something you lost track of time, you know what I mean.

The concert session doesn't necessarily make the information it contains available to the learner directly. Rather, it usually stores information in a part of the memory just below the surface of consciousness, so with the aid of a little additional activity it can be brought back into consciousness and remembered for a long time. Lozanov's research on concert sessions demonstrated that material learned this way is not readily forgotten. Also, if it does slip away, relearning is easy.

This response differs significantly from the so-called Ebbinghaus curve of forgetting that follows more traditional methods of study. It's that kind of forgetting you experienced when you crammed for an exam, did well, and three weeks later couldn't recall much of what you'd studied. Teachers who use concerts, on the other hand, are surprised to find their students highly conversant with the material months after it's been studied. Most have never witnessed behavior like that before. Also, I've seen remarkable examples of bits of information, which had been presented in concerts years earlier, plucked from the memory, even when there was no intervening review.

ART IS INHERENTLY EDUCATIONAL

Another factor contributing to the effectiveness of the concert is that it is easier to remember material when it is presented in an exciting and artistic way than when it's encountered in a boring or threatening context. In my opinion, certain types of classical music enhance this process, because the structure of the music itself stimulates neurological responses in the brain to a high level of intellectually integrative activity.

Perhaps the effectiveness of classical music in aiding memory has to do with the origins of this type of music. Many baroque, classical and romantic composers specifically dedicated themselves to spiritual values, and those who did not were writing in the traditions and forms created by those who did. Tracing its lineage back to the medieval church, much music of these periods never lost contact with its spiritual origins. This kind of music typically moves the listener through a series of aesthetic responses, involving continual tension and relaxation, which achieves a complex resolution of thematic elements, much as a spiritual, meditative state helps bring to resolution conflicts that may have troubled the mind.

This resolution and artistic unification of the thematic and harmonic materials stimulates a condition Lozanov called *concentrative psycho-relaxation* — an apparently relaxed response in which, he believes, the subcortical (emotional) awareness of the brain supports the intellectual functions of the neocortex in actively processing new information. Since the subcortical portion of the brain, or limbic system, contains the entry point to the long-term memory, information presented in a way that stimulates this system can be memorized instantly.

Perhaps Lozanov's concert sessions will one day become a more elaborate ritual than merely sitting and listening to words brought together with music. Researcher Don Campbell, a leading expert on how music affects both body and mind, believes the relation between sound and balance in the ear is crucial to the development of intelligence. Consequently, he sees combining music and movement as an important element in early learning. "Music is not a frill," he maintains. "It can actually orchestrate the way we learn. It organizes patterns of vibrations in sound and movement. I don't agree that children should be taught to read at an extremely young age. We need to develop a child's imagination first with imagery, storytelling, myths, imitation, patterned breathing, relaxed movement." And in his book, *Introduction to the Musical Brain*, he envisions a setting where a student may ". . . dance a discovery, act out a mini-tragedy like a Greek actor, and sing answers to important questions."

LIFE'S UNFORGETTABLE MOMENTS

In order to explore a little further the relationship between intense feeling (sometimes with the whole body) and long-term memory, let's do another thought experiment. See if you can recall some things you learned after only one exposure. For example, if someone you loved had died, would you need to hear that more than once to remember it? If you'd just won a million dollars in a contest, would you be likely to forget the fact unless you'd gone over it several times? Do you have difficulty remembering the first time you fell in love, the first beautiful thing you created, or the first sight of your child after birth? Events like these impress themselves on our memories instantly, and generally remain there throughout life. We forget less interesting, less relevant events and experiences. Or we forget experiences so traumatic our minds suppress them.

SONGS MY MOTHER TAUGHT ME

You probably can also remember the nursery rhymes and songs you learned when you were little, even if you haven't consciously thought of them for years. Songs like "Twinkle, Twinkle, Little Star" and "Mary Had a Little Lamb" never leave us. No doubt you can recite "Thirty Days Hath September" any time you want to know how many days there are in each month. And when you recite the alphabet, do you do it to the tune of the Alphabet Song? How often do you think "*i* before *e* . . ." when you're trying to remember how to spell a word?

If we succeed in remembering anything for five years, we will probably remember it for another fifty. Wouldn't it be nice if the facts in our biology text could be recorded in the memory this same way?

Well, they can. It's only necessary to put them into a dramatic, artistic and rhythmic context as exciting, as powerful, as simple, or as reassuring as the examples I've given above. If you know the song "Dry Bones," you can probably remember that the head bone is connected to the neck bone. If you learned similar songs about biological facts, you'd remember them just as easily. In fact, Don Campbell instructs teachers in how to present all basic information in rhythms, rhymes and songs, often using the rap as a primary vehicle for classroom instruction.

I once had to substitute teach in a class on Chinese history, a subject about which I don't know very much. So I asked the students to tell me what they knew. Like clockwork I got in perfect sequence the dynasties and something important about each of them. This information was coming from all over the room. The students were having a wonderful time showing off what they knew. I discovered they'd learned all this the first day by memorizing a song that was essentially an outline of Chinese history. The teacher later told me they hadn't been enthusiastic about learning the song, but by the time I met them, they were certainly enthusiastic about the results of having learned it.

THE TEXTBOOK AS A WORK OF ART

The insight from which Lozanov developed his use of concert sessions and musical activations — the mind's tendency to absorb and remember beautiful, rhythmic, artistic experiences — has other practical implications for education. It also suggests the importance of transforming textbooks into works of art. They should present and develop inter-relationships between elements of the subject matter, so one can absorb a variety of clearly related facts easily and quickly. Precious few textbooks are designed with this brain patterning approach in mind. Most present their material linearly, with little of the richness of contextual development characteristic of art. Just decorating the book with pictures, however attractive, is not enough. The entire subject should be conceived and presented globally and integratively.

PRACTICING CAN BE MORE FUN THAN A GOOD PARTY

The third stage of Lozanov's learning cycle is the activation. This is usually lengthier than the preceding two. It consists of games, songs, skits, discussions and other activities designed for practicing use of the material. It replaces the dull, routine drill and rote memorization standard in most classrooms. It makes it entertaining and easy to review the material in a number of different ways, removing almost all stress and strain from the learning process. Of course, the same activities would not be as much fun if a concert session didn't precede them. Half the fun is discovering how the right answers pop into the mind almost magically.

Most of the activities in this book are activations designed to help you retrieve from your memory what you already know, and to use or develop it in new and different ways. Their purpose is to help you take a flying leap toward more flexible and enjoyable use of your intelligence. If you use your imagination in creating concert sessions to precede them, when it's appropriate to do so, you'll find these activities will work even better.

WHEN SCHOOLWORK BECOMES PLAY

Let me give an example of a simple activation I saw in a school in Chicago. Joan Pilot, who teaches at Hinton Elementary and is one of the finest, most stimulating teachers I've seen, developed this activity for her class of young learning disabled students.

Think about your experience of learning to read in school. Most of us sat in little reading groups waiting for the teacher to call on us, one by one, often in a pre-established order, so we knew when we would get our turn. It might have been a boring, painful, or maybe even humiliating process, stumbling over words and having the teacher correct us. The rest of the students, meanwhile, probably allowed their minds to wander as they waited their turn. Sometimes the teacher had to deal with disruptions, interrupting the flow of the class.

When I visited Joan's third grade class, it was just after Thanksgiving vacation. On the board was a list of more than a hundred words or phrases the children had thought of to express what they were thankful for. The first three on the list, by the way, were "mother," "father" and "Hinton School."

Joan told me the idea for an exercise called "Read Till You Miss" had just come to her one day, and had been very popular with her students. As I watched, she called the students to the board. Because they knew what was about to happen, they ran up to her excitedly, each wanting to be first. So Joan, standing at the table next to the board, shuffled papers with their names on them and pulled one out: "Sarah." A little girl jumped up and down screaming with delight. Everyone else was excited for her. It was almost like watching the crowd at a football game.

As Sarah began to read the list of words, all the others had their eyes glued to the board and followed along, many whispering the words as she read them. She got through about thirty of them before she paused and stumbled. Her classmates wanted to help her. But Joan said, "We'll give someone else a turn now." She pulled another name from the pile, and the game continued. The third name she pulled, "John," belonged to a little boy who was noticeably much slower than the first two. He labored over each word, while his classmates squealed with excitement whenever he would get closer to being right. When he paused and stumbled, they were eager to help him, but Joan in her motherly way kept him working on his own. "He's my slowest one," she whispered to me.

Later she told me John had been completely non-functional in the class until they started playing a learning game that involved tossing a ball. John turned out to be the best one with the ball, and so gained status rapidly. Since then he had been working hard at other things, which led, Joan noted, to a lot of improvement in his achievement.

"Read Till You Miss" is one of the most effective ways of teaching reading I have witnessed in the classroom. Each student was involved and excited. All seemed to be practicing their reading skills, and also learning from each other. It scarcely mattered what their ability might be to start with: it would improve as long as Joan continued the game.

This game illustrates the importance of taking advantage of that natural love, common to all of us, of testing and improving our abilities — provided we can do so safely, enjoyably and without humiliation.

THE JOY OF TEST-TAKING

When you think about it, the widespread and agonizing preoccupation with test scores is indeed paradoxical. Many of us anticipate with terror taking a test that will determine our achievement level or competence. Each year high school juniors and seniors find the anticipation of SAT's creating a knot of fear in their stomachs. "Your whole future career may hang in the balance, based on how well you do on this," many are told (whether or not it's true.)

At the same time, we're also a nation of insatiable test-takers — provided, of course, we don't call them tests, and they don't have any serious consequences. Many of us give high ratings to tests of skills and intellect. Most of the games we participate in, or watch on television, provide such tests. When our football team is playing, we feel as if the whole city is being tested. The day after a championship game, millions are either elated or depressed, depending on how the game went. When Doug Williams triumphed in the Superbowl, it was as if everyone in the nation had won along with him. He'd triumphantly passed a test not only of athletic ability but also of character. Speaking at Howard University afterwards, he said he felt as if he came from all black colleges, as if he were a sort of Everyman figure. He became a superstar because he had been tested and won, and we all won with him. No culture that *really* hated testing could react this way.

You can also see this mania for test-taking at carnivals, where almost every booth provides another opportunity to be tested. And what of one of the best sellers among games, "Trivial Pursuit," which is nothing if not a test? In fact, it's so similar to some of what we encounter in school that one might wonder why children don't look forward to exams as they do to Christmas. The whole nation is partying around the opportunity to be tested on what they know. While TV quiz shows are among the most popular forms of entertainment, many of us prefer the more intellectually aloof activity of working our own crossword puzzles, or playing Scrabble in bed with our spouse.

SCHOOL SHOULD BE THE BEST PARTY IN TOWN

How sad that classrooms should pervert this fierce enjoyment of test-taking into a dreaded rendezvous with fear and harsh judgment. How easy to turn the routine of drilling on the three r's into the liveliest activity one could wish for! Suppose school were a place to have fun watching your knowledge and skill increase. Would it not then be more attractive than television, movies or rock concerts — offering opportunities for participation in a loving and supportive environment in what amounts to a party with treasured friends?

That's what it's often like at some of the schools I've worked with, where students may complain if they have to stay home for a day. "I usually have more people in my classroom than are enrolled in my class," says Chris Owens, a teacher at the Robeson High School in Chicago. "The hall proctors let them come in, provided they're not missing someone else's class. They get here early in the morning and stay as long as I let them in the afternoon." Looking around her classroom, I don't wonder. She's created an environment you can learn from just by walking through the door. And it makes you feel inspired to learn — and capable of learning — just to be there. Her class? Teaching the classics to students diagnosed as slow learners.

Before she used Integrative Learning Chris Owens had 50% of her students leave school by the end of the first semester. The very first year she used Integrative Learning, none of her students left school by the end of the first semester. Teachers like her agree it's not really so difficult to change the atmosphere of classrooms to make them places where students have fun — and succeed.

MOTIVATING A CLASS IN A HURRY

Let me give an example of how quickly this change can occur. One of the teachers I was working with at the Hinton School in Chicago said to me, "The trouble with my class is they're all slow learners, and only three out of seventeen have any motivation at all. The others just sit there. What can I possibly do with them?"

"I'll bet the problem is they have a poor background in verbal skills," I said. "They've been raised in homes where people don't talk to each other very much. Then they go to school and all they hear is talk. One thing they're sure of is they don't understand what's going on. What can they learn in that situation, except how inadequate they are? Wouldn't you be unmotivated?"

"I understand," she answered. "But what can I do about it?"

"Your students are street wise," I said. "They're good with their bodies. They know how to fight and show off and run and dance. Get their bodies involved in the learning process, and you'll see a big difference."

Then I went into her classroom and watched her, at my suggestion, direct her students as they acted out a concept they were studying in science. It was simple: They were to be molecules and show the difference between solids, liquids and gases. As solids, they scrunched their bodies together, as liquids they moved freely in a limited space, and as gases they ran all over the room. Not a very demanding exercise, really, so everyone could do it. It was pretty far from ballet. They moved awkwardly and hesitantly, not being used to such shenanigans in school. But the important thing was, they were moving.

Then their teacher quizzed them on the three states of matter, and everyone was immediately involved. Nearly all hands went up, and many who had never responded before were doing so eagerly. Afterwards, the teacher said, "That wasn't my class. You didn't see my class. Those children have never been like that before. They all wanted to answer the questions. I couldn't believe it!"

That was all it took — involvement of their bodies in the learning process — and they came to life. We didn't solve everything, but in a few moments we got a process going that can change learning behavior significantly and, perhaps, permanently.

4

THE BACKGROUND AND DEVELOPMENT OF INTEGRATIVE LEARNING

*The development of Integrative Learning by Lozanov and
his followers, and my experience adapting it
to a wider range of applications.*

In order to reap the benefits of Integrative Learning you don't have to know a great deal about its background and development. In fact its background may be of no real interest to you until you have tried it for yourself, in which case, you may want to skip this chapter for now. However the development of these ideas and methods — the false starts and detours as well as the successes — is certainly relevant to the present and future applications of Integrative Learning.

Take a notion about learning, turn it over, and what you will see on the other side is a notion about teaching. That's because any attempt to understand learning usually derives from someone's effort to teach something. And in practice, any theory about learning worth its salt will be based on the desire to teach and the practical experiences of teaching.

So the history of Integrative Learning necessarily involves an account of various attempts to develop successful methods of teaching. Having been directly involved with methodologies related to Integrative Learning since 1972, and indirectly for years before that, my account reflects my own experiences, some frustrating and some, in retrospect, amusing. Teaching is an art, not an exact science, and just as I continue to learn about it both in and out of the classroom, I hope my experiences will help others.

I trust this will be interesting and valuable to a broad range of parents and teachers, for they and all those who aspire to teach, are the backbone of our civilization and our hope for the future, and whatever we can do to make their role better understood and more successful is worth the effort.

HOW LOZANOV GOT STARTED

Georgi Lozanov's interest in developing a new approach to learning was aroused, as I mentioned earlier, by curiosity in the seemingly astonishing mental feats that a few people are able to perform. In particular he was intrigued by the accomplishments of the Indian Brahmans, who committed the Rig Vedas to memory. He wondered how it was possible to develop such excellent memories. His own experience with hypnosis confirmed that the average mind has resources far beyond what's considered normal. It became clear to him that under ideal conditions information can be memorized after a single exposure. This was sometimes possible with hypnosis, but hypnosis was not practical for use in classrooms.

Then he discovered it was easier to learn under the influence of suggestion than hypnosis, if the learning environment supported the suggestion, because the full conscious cooperation of the learner helped the learning process to be effective. He discovered it was possible to produce the necessary mental relaxation by using concert music instead of the breathing or meditation exercises usually used by groups with highly developed powers of memory and concentration. He felt a European culture would find concerts more acceptable than breathing exercises, because many people who dismiss meditative processes are quite comfortable listening to classical music.

Partly because of his association with his chief trainer, Evelina Gateva, a former star of the Sofia Opera, he came to understand that the principal composers of baroque, classical and romantic music had used melodic and harmonic patterns that help the brain to relax and develop receptivity to new experience, in a way particularly suited to his purpose.

DEVELOPMENT OF THE LANGUAGE TEACHING PROGRAM

Lozanov decided the best way to demonstrate the speeding up of learning would be by teaching languages, because the results could be measured more easily with language than any other subject, since language students continually demonstrate in the classroom how they are progressing, and additions to the vocabulary are easy to quantify.

The Institute of Suggestology and Suggestopedia, which he established in Sofia (but which he is no longer connected with), was soon offering classes enabling students to attain independent competence in a foreign language in twelve weeks with only three hours of study per day, and with no homework. And what's more, the classes were fun.

SUGGESTOLOGY

Lozanov used the term Suggestology to mean "the study of suggestion." Scientific understanding of how suggestion works was applied in his classrooms. Remember that suggestion goes on continually in all classrooms — where the paraconscious mind takes in more information than the conscious mind — but if it's not understood and controlled it can have negative, possibly disastrous effects. So rather than allow teachers to unwittingly destroy the learning process in children, we need to teach them the rules whereby it can be kept alive and nurtured.

Lozanov understood how important it was to keep in mind the fact that if you believe strongly enough you can learn something quickly and easily, you'll find it a snap, whereas if you believe it's going to be difficult, you'll probably have trouble with it. So the teacher who begins the first class by saying, "You're going to find this subject difficult and boring" is actually helping to create the condition described.

How well I remember my freshman year in college, when I found out I would have to take physics, and other courses I had not counted on. "Is the freshman year pretty cut and dried?" I asked a passing sophomore. "That's right," he answered. "They cut you up and they dry you out." Small wonder, then, that I was failing freshman physics all the way up to the last two weeks of the year, when I discovered quite unexpectedly that it was actually one of the easiest courses I had ever taken. That final two weeks of A work enabled me to pass for the year.

The obverse of this is that if the teacher knows you will love studying the subject, pretty soon you will know it too. Buying a love of math from an enthusiastic teacher isn't all that different from buying real estate in Florida from a charismatic sales person. The difference is, when you've bought the love of math, you've really got something, whereas the Florida property might turn out to be offshore fishing rights.

At any rate, under the influence of sufficient conviction and enthusiasm from your teacher, you can hardly restrain yourself from loving whatever it is you're studying.

TRANSFORMATION OF THE TEACHER

So, the most important feature of Integrative Learning is not any of the techniques associated with it, but the parent's or teacher's personal acceptance of and belief in it. For those who have not absorbed these principles probably cannot, simply by using techniques, do much to accelerate learning beyond the results achieved in traditional education. Integrative Learning is not just a method or system, it is also a philosophy — guiding parent or teacher to act always out of belief in the limitless capacity of all human beings to learn, provided they have the right opportunities.

THE TEACHER AS HEALING ARTIST

People who use Integrative Learning are also healers. They heal the injured learner in the student — that part of the mind that long ago capitulated to the oppressive command to shut down and accept limits. This healing happens so subtly, the student is scarcely aware of it. For the healer uses the technique of a performing artist. Performers do not tell their audience what they intend, they just move us to tears or laughter. Through them the arts are allowed to speak for themselves. Parents and teachers should let the subject should speak for itself in the same way.

In such a learning environment, the students usually feel they have learned independently of the effort to teach them. That is because the teacher does not find it necessary to point out what is happening in order to reactivate their infinite capacity to learn.

And this healing effect of learning can be quite striking. Lozanov early noted that people who took his classes seemed to be experiencing improvements in their health. Recent research indicates that stress-free learning, particularly when it is spiced with humor, stimulates the immune system, and thus helps heal even serious illnesses. Norman Cousins has argued this philosophy at some length.

RECONDITIONING OUR THINKING

Good teaching reverses the conditioning which most of us, adults and children, have received as a result of discouragement, fear and other negative emotions associated with learning in a formal school setting. The resulting new attitudes and experiences make us feel confident of ourselves, so we want to stretch our limits and trust our ability to think and create. Progress comes not by some indirect theoretical means, but in the only way possible: through direct experience, or re-experience, of the natural joy and ease of learning. The teacher cannot impose anything, but guides the student into experiences that precipitate new insights.

The teacher's behavior helps foster release from tension, ease about approaching new subject matter, a sense of the totality of the learning process and a complete trust in the intelligence of the learner. Most people feel they have many latent talents and are relieved and stimulated when someone else notices this and tells them how smart they are.

One of the comments I hear most frequently after someone has received instruction in Integrative Learning is, "I feel better about myself as a person." This reaction may last for years. It seems that having our natural learning process affirmed (particularly through direct experience of its effectiveness) removes some of the deepest doubts and regrets we have experienced in life. Recently a participant in one of my training sessions said at the end of the week, "I have lost my fear of math and science." In that particular session we had barely mentioned either subject.

GETTING YOUR PAPER BACK CAN BE TRAUMATIC

I recall an experience during my freshman year in college. I had committed to paper some of the ideas closest to my heart (many of which are contained in a more developed form in this book). Unfortunately, the writing in the paper was atrocious, because my ideas were still in such a raw and undeveloped state I was unable to create a logical context for them. When I got the paper back, it was filled with marginal notes condemning my reasoning, and concluded with the comment, "This is one of the most bizarre and poorly reasoned papers I have ever read. See me."

For the next year, whenever I noticed an original idea tip-toeing into my consciousness, I would sadly put it aside, determined not to allow myself to engage in undisciplined thinking. The emotional trauma of having my ideas so scornfully received took a long time to heal.

When I became a teacher I soon discovered most of my students had been exposed to similar rejections. Sometimes I was lucky enough to receive a paper like the one I had written, in that it seemed to want to say more than it was able to express clearly. When that happened, I would meet with the student, communicate respect for his or her ideas, and help put them into a more satisfying form by asking questions and reserving judgment about the responses. The first student for whom I did this learned so much that when she attended college they found her too advanced to take any of the English courses offered to freshmen, so they created a special poetry tutorial for her.

"WHAT HAVE I MISSED?"

Experiences of having our most cherished ideas rejected by someone we respect can sometimes shut down our thinking for long periods, or even permanently. Because of the extensive readjustment that often must follow such an experience, it may be difficult to reawaken an interest in the full use of the mind. It may be too painful to have to accept the fact that if the shut-down had not occurred, everything in life could have been different. Far easier, some seem to feel, to leave the status quo undisturbed and go on feeling inadequate, but safely adjusted to a low level of performance.

I find some of the teachers I've trained have to struggle with the implications of Integrative Learning for this very reason. The pain of facing the fact of missed opportunity can be profound. One has to decondition one's own negative experiences, and this may mean re-experiencing some of them. That's why Lozanov held that de-suggestion can actually play a more important role in the classroom than suggestion. We have to get rid of a lot of misinformation in the student's mind, so we can proceed with a clean slate, ready to learn freshly. The best form of de-suggestion, by the way, is finding you can learn something you always thought you could not.

MY OWN RESISTANCE TO THESE IDEAS

In my search for Integrative Learning, I suffered this same kind of deconditioning and emotional rejection; though for me it lasted not a few hours or days, but several years. Almost from the beginning of my teaching career I had been committed to the search. But I wanted simple, concrete means of helping people learn faster. I was not prepared to accept the complexity and ambiguity required to get in touch once again with how I learned as a child. I had come to believe that a certain level of pain and distress was necessary in order to make learning happen.

So when, in 1972, I read about Lozanov's teaching languages in Bulgaria, I was at first fascinated by what seemed like an automatic system for speeding up the learning process; and then, after I met the man himself, appalled by his speculations about infinite potential. These seemed to me both impossible and wrong. I believe I went through a long period of not wanting to hear his name mentioned ever again.

LOOKING FOR THE QUICK FIX

There was a frustrating lack of specificity in what he had to say. What's the magic formula? I kept wondering. I was looking for a quick fix that would transform people and cause them to learn faster. I wanted a mechanical process, and imagined it would produce successful students like wind-up toys. I wasn't alone in that. We'd all like to go to a doctor and get a pill to make everything better.

Therefore, it wasn't surprising that many would be looking for just such magic in Lozanov's work. When information about his method was first brought to this country, rumors circulated that he had used some long hidden occult process ultimately suppressed by his government, that political pressure prevented him from telling us how he had achieved his remarkable results.

EACH TEACHER DOES IT UNIQUELY

It was only later that I realized the key element in Lozanov's approach is excellent teaching, which of course varies with the style of the individual teacher. The teacher must begin by learning and then practicing the philosophy of education that Lozanov developed, using the Suggestopedic process to present information. While the teacher is still learning, pre-designed lesson plans may be used to establish the pattern in detail. However, so long as correct principles are adhered to, it is better for the teacher to work class plans out individually. Also the teacher must be prepared to make instantaneous adaptations of the plans, based on the response of each particular class. All classes, of course, have their own unique personalities, and what will keep one group going for half an hour may wear out after forty-five seconds with another.

There are several essential components to the process the teacher may develop. Appendix Two is a summary of my own adaptation of Lozanov's language teaching methods into Integrative Learning. Most of what you'll find there is consistent with his work. The differences are occasioned by additional insights coming from other sources, and by the need for adapting Lozanov's philosophy to fit our somewhat different culture, as well as to the teaching of many subjects beside languages.

THE FUNDAMENTAL BELIEF

For all the technical information Lozanov conveyed in his books, articles and lectures, the most important thing he was saying amounted to this: People can learn much faster — and with greater depth of mastery and enjoyment — than ever before thought possible. If you act on this belief, you can accomplish results of a different order of excellence. Stop believing in limitations, and recognize that natural learning should proceed five times as rapidly, or more, than previously accepted standards would prepare us to anticipate.

The virtue of communicating this as a philosophy instead of a methodology is that it acknowledges the infinite variety of ways to teach, so long as the general principles of learning are understood. In reality Lozanov is no more comfortable giving precise instructions to teachers than he would be outlining a step-by-step approach to finger-painting. I feel the same way.

I do not believe I can tell you how to raise your children, or how to structure their learning. Instead I can acquaint you with principles and examples of successful results, plus suggest some activities to increase the probability you'll discover something you can use effectively with the whole family. **But the most significant thing I can do is encourage you to believe that you and your children have unlimited learning capacity.**

STARTING A SCHOOL BASED ON SUGGESTOPEDIC PRINCIPLES

In the early 1970's, I was associated with a businessman named Carl Schleicher, who knew Lozanov personally. I told Carl I would start a private school in which the Lozanov method could be taught, if he would make arrangements for teachers to be trained by Lozanov. Together with my wife I founded a school within a school at Sandy Spring Friends in Maryland, where we had both previously taught. This ultimately became Thornton Friends School, an independent high school in its own right which, under other but compatible leadership, is still operating.

In recent years state officials have praised and studied it, and education experts have hailed it as a model of effectiveness and success. But during the early years we had to struggle for accreditation with the State Department of Education, because no other school in the state had ever come into being the way ours did. In a single classroom together with twenty-four students Nancy and I revived the one room schoolhouse, teaching all subjects, and trying as best we could to make our teaching fit the philosophy advocated by Lozanov. That experience is described in my published paper, "The Sandy Spring Experiment."

OUR STUDENTS WERE WELL-RESTED, BUT . . .

That first year of operation we were unable to arrange to have anyone trained in Bulgaria, so we developed a home grown variety of Suggestopedia. For five hours a day, students lay on the floor listening to music while I read Latin to them. At the end of six weeks their skills in English had improved an average of six months, though no English had been taught during that time. When I tested their vocabulary, I found they were learning it faster than I had when I took Latin. I later learned that lying on the floor for five hours was not the best way of learning Latin, however, so I don't suggest you try this with your children.

Although this process had some interesting effects, it had little similarity to Lozanov's practices. We still did not have the information essential to activate the learning process. So far, only the concert sessions had been reported in published documents available to me, probably because they are the most dramatic and unique part of the instruction process — albeit one not usually effective in isolation. It was two more years before we learned the full sequence of decoding, concerts and activations that Lozanov recommended, for only then did we have the opportunity to use in our school teachers actually trained in Bulgaria. And still there were difficulties, for the teachers we sent for training were not flexible enough to adapt their style to the students we offered them.

LOZANOV'S WORK IN THE UNITED STATES

Up to that time Lozanov's work was not well known, and certainly not well understood in North America. One experiment in language teaching had been attempted in the early 1970's by the Canadian government. Unfortunately, it got bogged down in politics, and Lozanov's directions were not adequately followed. As a result, the experiment was not successful. Nevertheless, the Canadian-Pacific Railroad, one of the largest corporations in Canada, has used Lozanov's philosophy of instruction in training its employees for more than ten years.

A number of experiments in the United States with an adaptation of the Lozanov method called Superlearning encountered similar pitfalls. This process focuses on the use of music to absorb information into the long-term memory, but not so much on the form in which the information is to be presented, or how it is to be processed later. Furthermore, it prescribes complicated breathing and counting exercises, which Lozanov now says he never used. When asked where this idea came from, he said that probably he had discussed his tentative plans for trying such an approach with a journalist, who confused his speculations with the methodology he was using. Finally, in 1974, Lozanov did come to the U.S. and began instructing language teachers. This instruction, as practiced in Bulgaria, requires that in addition to learning the philosophy, the teacher also learn a new language and teach a language class. Only when all three have been completed can the teacher's work be properly evaluated.

However, Lozanov's busy schedule and the economics of training teachers did not allow for the complete process to take place in the U.S. The result, a not very satisfactory compromise with necessity, was a forty hour training course I was eventually to teach myself.

ADAPTATIONS OF TEACHER TRAINING BY MYSELF AND OTHERS

The teacher training first offered was designed for language teachers only. In response to the need for adaptations to other subjects, I developed a modification of Lozanov's training, which I first used in the Chicago Public Schools with results discussed more fully in Chapter Six. It also appealed to leaders in school systems in Detroit, St. Paul, Syracuse, St. Louis, New York City and elsewhere, as well as to corporate trainers.

Meanwhile, others in this country have been making similar kinds of adaptations, notably John Grassi, who has developed forty complete curriculum plans for elementary level instruction in the Boston Public School system. In California, Charles Schmid worked in the Paradise School District, which also achieved outstanding results. And Ivan Barzakov, a former associate of Lozanov in Bulgaria, has provided excellent training for schools and other organizations.

At the college level, Ron Herring at the University of Wisconsin produced a flood of excellent results, as did Lynn Dhority, who used Lozanov's approach to teach languages and other subjects at the University of Massachusetts and Harvard. At Southwest State University in Marshall Minnesota, Professor Charles Reinert has developed a complete introductory physics course based on Integrative Learning. He reports this has doubled the rate and depth at which students learn physics. Professor James Quina has been instructing future literature teachers at Wayne State University on how to use Integrative Learning in their courses. His book on instructional techniques, *Effective Secondary Teaching, Going Beyond the Bell Curve*, incorporates Integrative Learning along with traditional instructional techniques. Integrative Learning has also been tried at a summer teacher training program at Hamline University in St. Paul. It is used extensively at the Detroit Center for Professional Growth and Development at Wayne State University. And the Department of Health and Human Services has funded a project to make the nursing department at Prince George's Community College in Maryland an Integrative Learning program.

Some of the most promising and effective work at the college level is at Syracuse University College where, under the direction of Laurence Martel, Integrative Learning has been used in the Higher Education Opportunity Program. Here adults with weak educational backgrounds are brought up to a level that enables them to succeed in college subjects. A course called "Activate the Genius Within You," developed by Jerry Perez de Tagle, has been taught by Perez, Kay Farrar and Marilyn Herr, and has significantly lowered the dropout rate for students in this kind of program. Meanwhile, Martel is also supervising an Integrative Learning Mathematics curriculum that Elena Levy is developing.

On the corporate scene, David Meier, at the Center for Accelerated Learning in Lake Geneva, Wisconsin, has made important inroads in applying Integrative Learning concepts to corporate training. After a slow start, the demand for accelerated learning is spreading very rapidly in the business world. The Bell Atlantic telephone company adopted his methods for some of their training courses and saved themselves $624,000 a year on student costs alone.

My former partner Bernard Saunders is breaking new ground in corporate training in Minneapolis, using Integrative Learning techniques applied to management training and the workplace. His introduction of the Option Finder, a new process for corporate decision making, has had powerful results at many corporations, including IBM.

It has thus become evident that Integrative Learning can be applied to virtually any learning situation, pre-school through graduate school, literacy through training in advanced technology, science or the arts, at school, in the workplace or at home.

ADDITIONS TO LOZANOV'S WORK

Some of the people Lozanov originally trained later incorporated into their teaching additional methodologies compatible with Suggestology. One is the Total Physical Response method, which involves having students perform a physical action before naming it (which recapitulates the childhood learning experience), thus integrating the language learning process into the neuro-muscular system. For example, the teacher says, "sit," and all the students do so without saying the word until they have performed the action several times.

A second is neurolinguistic programming, a widely practiced approach to integrating information about the neurological system into learning theory. It is from this source that much insight into how best to deal with the different learning modalities comes. In addition, one of the techniques used in NLP is "reframing" — that is, interpreting in a positive light an event which had previously seemed negative. An example of reframing goes like this: "The dog ate my paper last night, which at first upset me because of all the work I had put into it. But then I realized that this gave me the chance to do it again, and I could do a better job the second time, as well as learn the material much better."

Interest in the split brain work of Roger Sperry has also led to a spate of exercises in so-called right brain thinking, with excellent contributions from teachers like Tony Buzan, Betty Edwards and Gabrielle Rico.

More recently, the breakthrough research of Howard Gardner at

Harvard's Project Zero contributed additional new insights on learning. His Theory of Multiple Intelligences has created a healthy stir in the educational community, because it expands the notion of I. Q. beyond the single measurement of logical process, to seven different intelligences. He has provided what may be the best framework within which to design classroom procedures, making sure that in each class we educate all seven of the basic human intelligences, instead of just the two that have been traditionally taught (mathematical-logical and linguistic). Lozanov, who was able to educate virtually everyone who attended his courses to about the same level of excellence, was using classroom procedures that activated all seven intelligences in roughly equal proportions.

So it is no longer appropriate to speak of much of the work in the United States as being pure Suggestology or the Lozanov Method. However, Lozanov's language teaching results have been equaled or exceeded by a number of educators in this country, including, in addition to those already mentioned, Allison Miller in Minnesota, Ocie Woodyear at the Lozanov Institute in Silver Spring, Maryland, and instructors at the University of Houston, Howard University and the University of the District of Columbia.

Adaptations of Lozanov's work have been legion, and have merged with various alternative learning systems and philosophies from other sources. Many of the adaptations have been channeled through the Society for Accelerative Learning and Teaching (SALT), whose journal published under the editorship of Don Schuster has preserved the best academic papers on the subject. SALT came into being when Lozanov selected Iowa State University as the official academic center for Suggestopedia in the United States. Much of its research has been coordinated and evaluated by Lyelle Palmer, chief researcher in the general field of accelerated learning, and responsible for much of the credibility in academic circles SALT has been able to achieve. Each year SALT holds a conference drawing together leading experimenters and practitioners in this field from all over the world.

Another organization that has provided excellent leadership in developing and circulating new information is Seattle-based New Horizons for Learning, led by Dee Dickinson. She has put together excellent workshops around the country, which have attracted educators from all over the world, both as presenters and participants. Dickinson also publishes information about new developments in the field.

In Minneapolis, Kaia Svien and her associates, who have done excellent work applying accelerated learning principles to helping learning disabled children, also publish a newsletter on new developments.

WHAT SHALL WE CALL IT?

With this ferment of activity and cross-pollination of ideas, there has naturally come some confusion of technical terms and jargon. To reduce the confusion, it might be useful to review some of the terms that have replaced Suggestopedia, and what their implications are.

Accelerated learning is a widely used blanket description of many of these methodologies. Unfortunately its focus on the speeding-up process ignores the fact that depth of understanding and increased ability to think well are more important than the speed of learning, and these are also achieved with Lozanov's work.

Superlearning, already mentioned above, is really an adaptation based on the use of the slow movements from baroque concertos. As the name suggests, it emphasizes more the dramatic, quick fix aspects of Lozanov's work than its philosophical implications. *Optimalearning*, an apt descriptive term coined by Ivan Barzakov and his wife Pamela Rand, has had successes both in education and business. Another widely used term, related to Suggestopedia, but not originating among Lozanov's followers, is *whole brain learning*. This focuses on the balancing of right and left brain, but not the body's role in learning. The same criticism may be leveled at the term *whole mind learning*, also in wide use.

INTEGRATIVE LEARNING

I chose the term *Integrative Learning* (originally suggested by my colleague, Jerry Perez de Tagle), because it describes the way infants learn. They observe their environment freely, responding to any and all aspects of it without erecting barriers between them. As they move comfortably from one piece of the environment to another, they form patterns that create original and unique interactions among many different things. Gradually these patterns are refined and take on useful meaning as, during the infant learning process, experience reinforces some and extinguishes others from memory.

This describes the approach to subject matter Lozanov used. He taught that all elements of language structure should be relevant in the classroom from the beginning, not gradually introduced in linear sequence.

Integrative Learning is an approach that is infinitely expandable and can assimilate other methodologies, provided they do not contradict its fundamental principles. The principles may be revised as well, as new information about learning becomes available. For we are dealing with a compendium of learning activities involving the whole personality. They are based on the common assumption that learning is unlimited, and they focus on complete affirmation of the learner's capabilities.

Coincidentally, the term Integrative Learning is also used by California educator Barbara Clark, whose book *Optimizing Learning* has much to offer that is consistent with the philosophy of this book.

Techniques for eliciting Integrative Learning from students are still relatively primitive. Anyone who becomes involved with this new approach to education will be able to make innovative and effective contributions to this growing body of knowledge. Indeed, a great deal is already being done, and there is now a need to make it easy for teachers to pool their insights and experiences through newsletters and other forms of communication. The SALT organization at Iowa State University has done an excellent job of publishing academic research, but less formal communication is desirable as well. In addition to those already mentioned, Patrick Rohan in the Field Superintendent's Office of the Chicago Public Schools welcomes successful classroom strategies, which he will publish and circulate among networked public school systems. In addition, I welcome letters from teachers and parents are seeking information about programs and materials or who have had successful experiences, and will find some outlet for publishing and circulating information about them.

CHANGING THE PARADIGM OF EDUCATIONAL RESEARCH

There are solid grounds for optimism that the benefits of the work done by Lozanov and so many others will soon be spread more widely in our educational system and other sectors of our society. The need for change is certainly recognized, and political pressure for it is growing.

But I remember that when I first read about Lozanov's work in 1972, it seemed self-evident it should be imported into the United States and applied in schools here. I put a lot of energy into looking for a financial or governmental commitment to accomplish this. But I discovered that although our schools were in crisis, no one seemed able to help. Bureaucracy, I discovered, does not make it easy to solve problems, even when solutions are at hand.

The problem is deeper than bureaucratic caution and inertia. It has to do with how we think about learning and education, and where we look for answers to our questions. Paul Messier, in the research division of the U.S. Department of Education, has addressed the notion that it's time for a paradigm shift in educational research.

Because of a long tradition going all the way back to the middle ages, educational policy, research, practice and reform have been viewed within the paradigm of developmental and cognitive psychology and behaviorism. These largely ignore recent neurological research on the function, structure and interaction of the brain, (which we'll get to in the next chapter.) This more recent research expands the context for understanding teaching strategies and learning environments.

The problem is this: if you add anything to the knowledge of learning that doesn't fall within the existing paradigm — a paradigm which is designed to filter out everything outside its narrowly defined range of scrutiny — no one in the Department of Education, and consequently in educational research laboratories all over the United States and the rest of the world, is likely to hear about it. In theory, this would seem to mean that no matter how many solutions one might find for the current educational crisis, as long as they fall outside the paradigm, none of them would be used in the public schools. In practice, there are ways to circumvent the paradigm, as I did — mainly by finding leaders in the school system adventurous enough to risk trying something new.

By shifting the paradigm of investigation, Messier hopes to make it possible to fund a great many more research projects having some common ground philosophically with Integrative Learning. "Unless we change our standards of evaluation," he says, "we'll just continue recycling the same old stuff — which we know doesn't work."

IT'S SPREADING IN THE PUBLIC SCHOOLS

Finally, it is encouraging to report that as this book goes to press numerous federal and state officials are showing keen interest in Integrative Learning as perhaps the one viable solution to the current crisis in the schools. As Jack Mitchell, the Field Superintendent in Chicago, told me, "We're looking for solutions, but we're not finding much that works except this system."

Others who have expressed strong interest in getting Integrative Learning into the schools as quickly as possible include members of the New York State Board of Regents, as well as leaders at the White House, plus the commissioners of seven states and additional superintendents and principals around the country. It is interesting to note that in the North Syracuse School System, impetus for forming a pilot project came from a handful of teachers, who in a matter of months managed to interest people all the way up the line to the Superintendent's office.

AN IDEA WHOSE TIME IS HERE

Pessimists sometimes try to persuade me that Integrative Learning, no matter how good it is, will take a very long time to penetrate the public school system, which they say is too mired in bureaucracy for anything to help. Education, they argue, must be taken out of the hands of professional educators and entrusted to people who can make it work, such as members of the business community.

I don't believe that. While the process of getting started has been slow, there's a momentum now that cannot be stopped. I no longer meet resistance when I tell teachers, superintendents and government officials about Integrative Learning. Instead of arguing and giving me a chance to demonstrate the effectiveness of what is possible, they get right to the point of expressing eagerness to make it happen as soon as possible.

Perhaps that's partly because the public school community is threatened by criticism and therefore looking for an immediate solution to the problem. But more important, and more dependable in the long run I believe, is the deep desire on the part of educators and parents to do their best for our children. So I think I can promise you Integrative Learning will become an option for your child's school in the foreseeable future. If you want to make it happen sooner, though, consider visiting your principal and giving him or her a copy of this book.

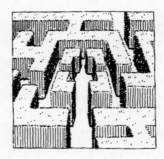

5

ADJUSTING LEARNING TO THE BRAIN

Recent research on the brain is yielding a better understanding of paths — and obstacles — to learning.

The human brain is the most marvelous object we know. Its mysteries have not yet yielded to the probings of scientists more than a tiny glimpse of their true complexity. Many basic questions about it remain unresolved, or perhaps even undreamt of. Nevertheless, recent research has given us insights, suggestions and hints as to how our brains function. Some of these insights and conjectures — when applied with appropriate restraint and always with reference to actual experience and observation — are proving useful in understanding how we learn, and how we may learn better.

For those of us concerned with enhancing learning, the value of these new insights into the functioning of the brain is more indirect than direct. Brain research is not giving us 'keys' to use, 'switches' to turn on to make our brains more efficient, at least not yet. Most of the conclusions drawn by researchers are tentative at best, or expressed in metaphors we would be unwise to take too literally.

What these new observations do point to is the great variety of ways in which our minds function, and the necessary interconnectedness of mental functions and activities. This encourages us to explore a rich variety of approaches to learning, and to be aware of a much broader range of legitimate teaching and learning activities in even the most formal settings.

And the very depth of the mystery of how the brain functions serves as a healthy reminder of how amazingly vast and varied are the mental capacities and potential of *every* human being.

THE MYSTERY OF MEMORY

Among the greatest of the brain's mysteries is memory, for we do not know precisely how it is stored, though we know something of the pathways to storage. It is certain that memory is not stored in a purely linear fashion, because there are many routes to a particular memory, most of them through a variety of associations, analogies or generalities.

For example, we may access the memory of an apple through the concepts of fruit, redness, sweetness, roundness, doctors, teachers, food stores, diet plans, computers, New York, and so on, encompassing perhaps hundreds or thousands of different routes to that one memory, or idea. A single memory of an apple will, in turn, lead to other specific memories. In fact, if enough attention were fixed on the idea of apple alone, one could probably access, through free association, virtually every experience one had ever had (or even thought of having) with apples.

Two tiny regions in the brain are important in moving information from the short- to the long-term memory. The short-term memory serves you for a few days and enables you to recall recent experiences. The long-term memory provides more or less permanent storage of information you need to call upon frequently. The two organs providing the bridge between them are the hippocampus and the amygdala.

The hippocampus moves conceptual material into long-term storage, while the amygdala is now thought to perform the same function for emotional material. If the two work together, it's easier for a memory to move into long-term storage than if only one is involved. That's why it's so much easier to memorize things in an emotional context. In fact, it's hard to see why anyone would want to teach information in an atmosphere not intensified with positive emotion. It's just too inefficient.

THE HOLOGRAPHIC QUALITY OF OUR MINDS

Central to our puzzlement about the brain's mysteries is the general ambiguity concerning the location of particular functions or activities. Though specific areas, and indeed cells, can be identified with precise functions, when these are destroyed, the lost functions may sometimes be recreated in other parts of the brain. So while the brain does have some of the characteristics of geographical location in its memory storage system, it also seems to operate holographically. It's a little like the problem in quantum mechanics, according to which light sometimes behaves as if it travels in particles and at other times seems to travel in waves. No one has ever been able to explain or conceptualize this ambiguity.

It is largely due to Karl Pribram's path-breaking research that we know everything stored in a part of the brain is in some sense stored everywhere in it. Perhaps this is why all our memories seem so interconnected. Understanding and developing this interconnectedness of human thought patterns is a major way of activating the reserve complex of the mind, and thus releasing previously unsuspected skills, talents and abilities.

The conceptual model Pribram developed is inspired by holographic photography, which reproduces a three dimensional image of an object not by replicating its image, but by recording a set of wave-interference patterns from two laser beams focused at the object. When two similar laser beams are later passed through the photographic plate, the result is an image of the object in three dimensions. If you look directly at the plate, you see only wavy lines. If you cut the plate into pieces, each piece contains the whole object — it's just less clear than in the original.

This holographic view of the brain provides an interesting basis for critiquing other models of neurological organization, such as those discussed below. However much certain functions may initially seem to be limited to particular areas of the brain, exceptions can usually be found; so for every new theory of brain geography that emerges, critics arise to point out neurological anomalies occurring in large enough numbers that they seem to invalidate a given theory. In the light of such criticisms, it is useful to keep in mind that whether or not these theories can be taken literally, as models they provide valuable insights for understanding the educational process. It doesn't really matter precisely where in your brain something happens, what matters is that it happens at all, and that different and distinctive brain functions can be identified.

THE TRIUNE BRAIN

One of the most useful models of the brain to come out of recent research was developed by Paul MacLean at the National Institutes of Mental Health. According to this "triune brain theory," our organ of abstract reasoning evolved in layers. The oldest, or reptilian portion (located in the brain stem), is rigid, instinctive and automatic in response, and controls the vital functions. It takes care of our most basic needs, and when we are in a life-threatening situation, we tend to downshift into this area. Automatic responses may be useful in a moment of immediate crisis, but they don't serve us well when the crisis is more imagined than real.

Unfortunately, many classroom situations tend to cause downshifting. Although a student's life is not literally in danger, he or she may feel so threatened at the thought of being called on, humiliated, or tested, that automatic responses replace thinking ones. If this happens frequently enough, merely entering the classroom may eventually produce down-shifting. Thus the place where the student is expected to function intellectually is transformed into the least favorable environment for such behavior. "I have a little switch in my brain," a student once told me. "And I turn it off whenever I enter a classroom."

That's why Lozanov placed such emphasis on eliminating fear from the classroom by maintaining a positive suggestive atmosphere at all times, and by dealing with mistakes in a non-threatening manner. If you're feeling threatened, you can't access the neocortex, and therefore can't think. Some students feel threatened all the time, with the result that they may test as having a low level of intelligence. When they've learned to overcome fear, they perform better, and their brains start to function differently.

THE INTERPLAY OF THE RATIONAL AND EMOTIONAL

In MacLean's model, the next higher part of the brain is the limbic system. Situated beneath the rational neocortex, it is the seat of emotion. Here feelings are activated. Here also the hippocampus and amygdala are located; as I've noted, the limbic system must be actively involved when the long-term memory is accessed.

It seems likely that the proximity of the neocortex to the limbic system facilitates interaction between them, so the rational neocortex keeps the emotional limbic system under control and gives it perspective. In turn, the emotions give life and motivation to the rational. It's an easy and normal kind of interplay, sorely stressed by pressure to keep feelings and ideas in separate compartments.

Many philosophers and mathematicians have written of their passion for thinking. When ideas are presented in a way that ignores this component of passion, students are not only cheated out of the drama of discovery; they are also subjected to a subtle trivialization of the material, likely to decrease their capacity to appreciate it.

Separation of feeling and conceptual thinking causes both brain levels to operate in extremes, producing on the one hand the kind of cold ratiocination that isolates itself from reality; and on the other, the wild irrationality of emotions finally breaking through after too much suppression. How ironic that those who seek to suppress their emotions are most susceptible to having them run amuck and provoke wildly irrational statements and actions when they feel threatened or insecure. The Stoic ideal of a mind above emotion is simply not a viable option for anyone gifted with an actual human brain, because the neocortex and limbic system do not function well as alternating systems. They prefer to work as a team. It follows, therefore, that a classroom which is coldly rational and logical without room for appropriate forms of fun and feeling — while it might work for educating computers — is no place for humans.

Integrative Learning functions best with just such comfortable interplay, particularly between intellect and emotions, so each gives direction and shape to the other. When positive emotions are evoked, downshifting to the reptilian brain doesn't happen. If downshifting has become a habit, it's still possible, in a sufficiently relaxed and joyful environment, to shift back up again.

EXPLORING THE WEAK TO STRENGTHEN THE STRONG

That's just one example of how important it is for the various portions of the brain to work together in harmony. All the ideas, skills and operations we have learned are in communication with one another, though we often learn to see them as separate, and do not make the best use of the possibilities of their interconnectedness.

Sometimes, after strengthening one of our weaknesses, we find our stronger abilities have been strengthened as well, since the improvement of one ability influences others. One example of this phenomenon has been the approach of Mona Brookes, an art education specialist who founded the Monart Schools of Southern California, and wrote *Drawing with Children*. She found that by giving young people a vocabulary of skills to increase their drawing ability she not only enabled them to make better pictures, she also helped them perform better in other subjects, such as math.

SPLIT BRAIN RESEARCH

Another focus of recent attention in brain research has been the relationship between the left and right hemispheres. This "split brain" theory is based on the Nobel Prize winning work of Roger Sperry, who cut the corpus callosum, or connecting link between the two brains, as a means of treating epilepsy. When he studied the effects on personality, he found the result of cutting this connection was to alienate important brain functions from each other, so the part of the brain that could understand music, for example, had no direct communication with the part that could understand language. Having lost communication, the two hemispheres developed separate personalities.

By using experimental techniques enabling him to communicate with each of them individually, he was able to determine what kinds of tasks each performed. The left hemisphere, we have learned, is logical, dealing with language, mathematical and sequential learning. The right is imaginative, intuitive, musical and creative. Your left brain, concerned with logic, language and analysis, prefers to break ideas and information into sequential bits of information, to give them logical structure. Your right brain, the synthesizer and map maker, explores relationships holistically, relating ideas to emotions more easily than does the left. It is also the seat of musical intelligence.

Though some researchers have since questioned the validity of Sperry's research, deriding the popular interest in these ideas as "unscientific," the distinction between "right and left brain thinking" is at the very least an important and useful metaphor. However, one distortion of this theory that is not only unscientific but perhaps malicious as well is the attempt to classify people with dominance in one hemisphere or the other according to racial, sexual or national type. Such categorizing amounts to little more than stereotyping.

While this specialization of the two hemispheres is indeed interesting, the interaction between them is far more important than what either accomplishes alone. Education, after all, should not be directed either to the right or the left brain, but toward the goal of synthesizing their actions into a harmonious whole.

ENJOYING THE BRAIN IN HARMONY

When the two halves of your brain are separately engaged, you probably experience conflict. When they purr together in harmony, you experience euphoria. There are few more pleasurable sensations than having the left and right brain in synchronous states of electrical excitation. When material to be learned is processed by both hemispheres simultaneously, students feel relaxed and comfortable.

Learning to get the two sides of the brain operating in harmony makes it easier to process information of all types. Anyone who can sense the integrative structure of what is being learned, while at the same time breaking it down and analyzing it in a linear format, can absorb information more rapidly and enjoyably. Concert sessions and other brain-harmonizing activities train the learner to operate this way more of the time. It's a return to the childhood experience of learning.

According to researcher Ned Hermann, if we include the left and right limbic system in our calculations, there are four different brain dominance preferences possible. A person whose left limbic system is dominant, seeks security and regularity in life. This need is satisfied in the classroom by regularly anticipated rituals associated with learning.

The right limbic system, when dominant, predisposes a person to group process. The needs of this dominance are satisfied by the kind of positive interaction between classmates that usually happens only in good family situations.

The right neocortex likes to think synthetically. It prefers to evolve ideas and information from experience, rather than absorbing them from a predigested format. This dominance prefers experiential learning.

People whose dominance is in the left neocortex like to analyze things. For their sake, learning experiences that teach how to pin down information and experience in specifically structured formats and categories are important.

In a larger sense, these four approaches are important for everyone, so a learning system that provides them in equal balance will help satisfy the needs of differing brain dominances, while developing proper balance among them in all students.

THE LEARNING MODALITIES ARE IMPORTANT TOO

Another recent area of concern among educators is the different learning modalities. Five have been identified: visual, auditory, kinesthetic, print-oriented and group-interactive. Each of us is likely to prefer one above the others. In traditional classroom situations, auditory and print-oriented learners tend to be more comfortable than those with a preference for the other modalities. Visual and interactive learners have a more difficult time, but there are at least some opportunities for them to learn through their favored modality. Kinesthetic learners have the least chance of being able to function comfortably and meaningfully in school.

Understanding and diagnosing the different learning modalities is a major interest of some leading educators. However, unscientific and downright racist attempts have been made to link these preferences with racial groups, despite the fact that all races exemplify all the preferences. This has led to a regressive "separate but equal" mentality. Fortunately, the whole issue can be avoided by creating classrooms in which all the modalities are served equally, and all can learn from each other. Since each of us must use all the modalities, it behooves us to strengthen all of them.

VISUAL LEARNERS

Visual learners like to have things presented in pictures or diagrams. What they hear, they translate into visual images. When they talk, their figures of speech are visual. They often learn more by watching than by talking, listening or doing. They may doodle while listening, which assists their memories more than words.

In classes in which I've asked students to use words to communicate visual experience, I've found that, after some initial resistance, they tend to improve their intellectual capacity, sometimes carrying their changed perceptions over into everyday experience. "I see the world differently," one student said after a unit based on developing his interpretation of what he saw. "Even when I walk down the halls, it's a new experience."

What's the difference he's talking about? Basically, I think we learn to see in clichés by applying language to so much of our visual experience. This means we can safely ignore much of what we see. As these clichés are challenged, our minds and brains tend to reevaluate visual input and consider new possibilities for it. This reevaluation process can be a powerful new opening to the world of ideas and experience. Thus the habit of relying almost entirely on words as a means of communication in classrooms does not challenge thought in important areas of experience.

Let me offer a couple of examples of how to strengthen one mode by strengthening another. Robert Persig tells the story in *Zen and the Art of Motorcycle Maintenance* of the girl who could not write at any length until he got her to describe a wall, brick by brick. This enabled her to unleash thousands of words.

I've used that insight in a number of cases. One in particular was with a student who believed he completely lacked any creative ability. I asked him to describe in detail a random series of lines, and found it almost impossible for him to do this. I suspected he was not really seeing the lines except superficially. So I mentally took him by the hand and led him through a bit of my own description. Once he saw what I was doing, he was able to do it too, and soon experienced a profound improvement in his ability to think creatively. I won't sketch out the conversation. It's similar to one you'll find in Chapter Fourteen.

If you'd like to develop your visual modality, though, I recommend you try several books: *Visual Thinking* by Rudolf Arnheim, *The Natural Way to Draw* by Kimon Nicolaïdes, *Drawing on the Right Side of the Brain* by Betty Edwards, *Drawing with Children* by Mona Brookes, and *The Zen of Seeing* and other books by Frederick Franck.

Beyond that, Amiel Francke's work in developmental optometry has forged new areas of understanding in vision as a dynamic process, engaging the whole body, and developed throughout the neuro-muscular system. By changing the way the eye functions in perception, Francke is able to help students open up new, more powerful brain functioning. I was able to benefit from this approach when I started working with him in 1956. At that time, as a junior in college, I was at a fourth grade level of visual coordination and reading comprehension. A few years later, I tested in the top one percent of college educated adults.

AUDITORY LEARNERS

Auditory learners like to have things explained to them. They can follow ideas easily, and like the sounds of words. They would rather listen to a story than look at pictures while being read to.

For auditory learners, the world of sound may have special meanings it does not have for others. They may or may not be musical, but sounds in and of themselves contain a rich variety of meanings for them.

An exercise that heightens auditory sensitivity is to list all the sounds you can hear by listening closely to everything that's happening. Such sounds as the clock ticking, the traffic noises outside, the fan, bird songs, and so on, come into consciousness then. As a further step, construct a fantasy or story from just these sounds.

Auditory learners risk confining themselves to words as their sole source of learning. Such an exercise in listening can open the mind to additional possibilities. Practice in translating auditory experiences (including musical ones) into words can expand the ability to think creatively and reveal the limitations of words as a means of communication.

Researcher Don Campbell, as I've pointed out, believes the seat of intelligence is in the ear, with its connection between hearing and the delicate activity of balance that enabled us to stand on two legs millions of years ago. By fully activating the auditory potential of the mind, while linking it with kinesthetic experience, we can stimulate the growth of our intelligence. Alfred Tomatis, a French physician and audiologist, has done important work in developing new understanding of how the ear works in language, speech and thinking. It seems that it, like the eye, can fall into clichés of perception which, when they are challenged, may unleash new intellectual power.

KINESTHETIC LEARNERS

Kinesthetic learners want to feel action in their bodies before they're sure they've understood a new concept. They express themselves well through gesture, dance or posture. They are often "street wise" and do well in sports. Getting the "feel" of something means they have internalized and mastered it. They may be well coordinated, skillful with their hands and good at using tools. They would rather do a thing than talk about it.

Because kinesthetic sensations translate poorly into language, we sometimes lose contact with our awareness of them. That's why expressing verbal concepts and ideas in the form of dance can be so powerful. By seeking new ways of communicating with our bodies, we may become more sensitive to how our bodies are trying to communicate with us.

An associate of mine was responsible one year for the English and social studies program for all the ninth graders at a well known private school. She relied heavily on movement as a means of instruction, asking students to translate their ideas about literature into dance, having them beat out the rhythms of sentences, and so forth. Though the program was discontinued the following year, that group of ninth graders proved, when they were seniors, to be the most outstanding graduating class many in the school could remember.

As a drama teacher, I noticed powerful changes occurring in students' ability to communicate after they practiced exploring different postures. Our posture reflects much we have experienced: the acceptance or rejection we've felt from others, for example. By becoming aware of what different postures tell us of experience, we can better understand our own non-verbal processes, and this can lead to improved verbal communication. That's why in Part Three I've included a number of exercises designed to inspire such insights.

Paul Dennison, developer of Educational Kinesiology, has designed a series of exercises called *Brain Gym* to help students focus their energy before undertaking academic tasks. With only a few minutes a day of easy exercises designed to harmonize brain and body processes, he shows them how to get a lot more out of their studies.

PRINT-ORIENTED LEARNERS

Print-oriented learners love to read because they store ideas from the printed page easily. They would rather read the book than see the movie, and prefer reading about things to having them explained. They easily remember what they have read and can verbalize it well, either repeating it back or writing about it on a test.

Just because they read so easily, however, they may have assumed a stereotyped response to the printed page. The better a person is at reading, the more important it becomes to explore a variety of different approaches to the printed page. Asking questions of the text and developing a dialogue with it are two of the most powerful routes to greater success for a print-oriented learner.

Because print is so linear, it may sometimes seduce the mind into exclusively linear thinking. Print-oriented learners need to exercise more global, holistic thinking skills, and can do so by learning to manipulate ideas originally expressed in words through images and diagrams, gaining a more fluid view than print by itself makes possible.

It also seems to make a difference what colors we're looking at. Reading ability can be improved, immediately in some cases, by placing an appropriately colored gel over the printed page. Readers especially sensitive to color may also benefit from taking notes in a variety of magic markers. And it helps them if the teacher uses colored chalk for writing on the board. Color, it seems, can be a great help to the memory.

GROUP-INTERACTIVE LEARNERS

Group-interactive learners are at their best when involved in discussions or other activities that require the participation of others. They like to exchange ideas; and if they're not outputting as well as inputting, they may fall asleep. Since they understand things better after experiencing them as part of a group process, they are likely to be social beings, sometimes learning more from a dinner table conversation than a formal class.

There are any number of possible styles of interaction, from being leader, to being "the life of the party" or an effective follower. Since many are uncritical of the ways they choose to interact, their associations may become addictive, as in the case of social cliques or gangs. Teachers and parents should refuse to give any acceptance to gangs, and work together to create environments in which healthier forms of group activity will take their place. It may be extremely important for this type of learner to experience good group process techniques in the classroom. Since they often take their cues from the crowd rather than from their own sense of what is right, group-interactive learners need to be in groups that will help them set high ethical standards.

DISABILITY IN THE PREFERRED MODALITY

Everyone makes some use of all the modalities, but the preferred one dominates learning. Unfortunately, it may also be the one that is most learning disabled. A print-oriented learner may develop visual problems and be unable to read well. A kinesthetic learner could have coordination problems and be ineffective in dance and sports. An auditory learner might have a language difficulty, and thus be unable to follow linguistic sequences. In other words, the preference for a learning modality does not guarantee skill — it just means that, all other things being equal, the student would prefer to learn that way.

Since this is the case, it's all the more important to challenge each student to develop all the modalities as fully as possible. It would not be desirable to teach students exclusively in their dominant modalities, because this would fail to give them much needed exercise in developing the others. Instead, we should focus on providing balanced learning experiences.

THE SEVEN INTELLIGENCES

To further complicate — or enrich — our appreciation of how our brains function in learning, researchers have identified a variety of "intelligences" as well as learning modalities. There are at least seven different intelligences to be developed, only two of which, the logical-mathematical and the linguistic, get much exercise in traditional class-rooms. Indeed, most traditional pedagogical theory is based on the mistaken assumption that these two types constitute all there is to intelligence.

The seven intelligences identified by Howard Gardner of Harvard University are discussed in his book *Frames of Mind*. Though more recently Gardner has come to believe there may be a large number of additional intelligences, these seven deserve recognition in the classroom and in all learning experiences. They are the logical-mathematical and linguistic, as well as the spatial (visual), bodily-kinesthetic, musical and personal (both inter- and intra-). In any individual these seven are likely to be developed to different degrees. So a person who is poor at logical reasoning may be excellent at music, or at inter-personal relationships.

Gerald Grow asserts that Gardner's work leads to three important conclusions: "(1) Human beings have evolved to have several distinct intelligences and not one general intelligence; (2) Each intelligence is relatively independent of the others; and (3) Any significant achievement involves a 'a blend of intelligences'." The theory of multiple intelligences, Grow believes "could be the beginning of a revolution in the way we understand and train human potential."

The seven intelligences seem to be neurologically isolated in the brain. Sometimes one is present in a highly developed form, while the others are virtually missing. It is possible to remove each one surgically and leave the others intact. A brain injury might, at least for a time, render someone unable to talk, but leave that same person able to compose music.

When making class plans, we should try to strengthen all seven of these intelligences in about equal proportions. That is in fact the focus of Integrative Learning, which may be described as an application of the theory of multiple intelligences, because it aims to balance them effectively in classroom experience.

THE ROLE OF THE GLIA

When Albert Einstein died, much was made of the fact that his brain had been willed to science. Nothing more was heard on the subject for nearly thirty years. Then it was revealed that Einstein's brain had about twice the glia found in that of the average person. These are the cells surrounding the neurons, providing a buffer between them and the blood vessels, nourishing and carrying off wastes. Some think they also amplify electrical impulses traveling through the neurons.

Experiments with rats have established that frequent and varied exercise increases the number of glia in the rat's brain. Rats with more glia respond to stimuli more intelligently. Could it be that the right combination of mental and physical exercise will stimulate the production of these cells? This research suggests how important the body-mind relationship may be in thinking. There is no suggestion, of course, that merely strengthening the muscles will stimulate the brain. But perhaps systematic fine motor exercise coordinated with intellectual input, such as occurs in practicing a musical instrument, may provide valuable neurological enrichment. Einstein, by the way, was a competent amateur violinist.

THE INTEGRATIVE BRAIN DESERVES THE INTEGRATIVE CLASSROOM

When functioning well, the integrative brain is a kaleidoscope of interactions between neocortex and limbic system, right and left hemispheres, all five learning modalities, and at least seven intelligences. Insofar as possible, Integrative Learning keeps these in balance and appeals to all of them equally.

Integrative Learning, properly developed, nurtures this interactive quality of the brain, providing a variety of experiences that, taken collectively, stimulate all the different areas of brain activity, allowing students to exercise their strengths, and strengthen their weaknesses. Those who are particularly talented in only a few areas will nevertheless receive the support and stimulation they need when their favored area is called into play. But all minds will be stretched in each area of development — weakest, as well as strongest. Only thus can we hope to educate truly well-rounded and capable students.

6

HOW INTEGRATIVE LEARNING WORKS
IN THE CLASSROOM

*A first-hand look at a public school where Integrative
Learning is changing the lives of students and teachers.*

So far we've considered the theory and principles of Integrative
Learning. Perhaps it's time now to venture into the classroom and see what
it looks like in action.

When I arrived at the Guggenheim Elementary School in early 1984 to
train the entire teaching staff, I found myself in a neighborhood where cars
are routinely robbed and murders are not unusual.

During the thirty hours of instruction I gave the faculty on Integrative
Learning I was pleased to hear such comments as, "This is the best training
we've ever had," and "I can't wait to go on 60 Minutes and tell the world
about what we're doing here." At the conclusion of the training, a couple of
teachers said they had been planning to retire, but had changed their minds.

I didn't see any of those teachers again until nearly two years later,
and while they received some follow-up from a colleague of mine, he was
not given nearly as much time as he would have liked. So when I returned
for a day recently, I wasn't prepared for what I heard. Wandering into the
science lab, I greeted teacher Sharon Bean. For the next twenty minutes she
spoke in superlatives. "I can get my first graders to do anything the sixth
graders can do," I particularly remember her saying, "and my second
graders to do anything the eighth graders can do."

Later the same day, Nancy Ellis, who heads the Superlearning Lab (where I'll be taking you in a moment) said, "For five years before I took the Integrative Learning training I had been teaching a Mastery Learning unit on outlining. It took four weeks, and I had to follow all the directions precisely. At the end of the four weeks of instruction, everybody always failed.

"So the first thing I did when I got back from the training was boil the whole course down into one week and teach it by Integrative Learning methods. At the end of the week I gave a test and everybody passed."

Nancy is one of the teachers at Guggenheim who truly exemplify everyday genius at work. (She's not alone, however. The general level of instruction at Guggenheim is outstanding, and getting better all the time. It's an excellent demonstration project for Integrative Learning, and has had visitors from all over the country.) Filled with enthusiasm and commitment to her teaching, Nancy went on to tell me that before experiencing Integrative Learning she had planned to look for some other profession.

Not that she hadn't been successful already. As an eighth grade teacher, she made sure most of her students graduated with reading skills at grade level, a rare accomplishment in an inner city school such as this. Now, however, if she were to use Integrative Learning techniques to do the same job, she says she'd have them pretty close to college level. Meanwhile, the students she's currently teaching are selected from the bottom three of the ten stanine (achievement) levels. But when visitors come to her class they think they're watching a gifted and talented group.

"At first when they asked me if they were gifted and talented, I would say, 'No, they're my first, second and third stanines,'" she says. "But after a while I decided they *were* gifted and talented, so I started saying that."

A VISIT TO THE SUPERLEARNING LAB

At Guggenheim they've established the Superlearning Lab for students who are in trouble in their regular classes. In other schools it might be the special education class, not exactly a group that students are clamoring to join. But here it's considered the place to be. I asked a youngster sitting in the principal's office what he thought of the Superlearning Lab. He almost leapt out of his chair. "I LOVE that class!!!" he said.

Visiting it, I soon understood why. Nancy had about fifteen students seated comfortably on deck chairs in a rather small room. Since there wasn't much extra space, I had to squeeze into a corner behind the desk.

Before class, Nancy told me that the night before she'd composed a dialogue for the day's lesson. Entitled "The Root of it All," it presented basic concepts of plant physiology. However, since she had not yet learned to use her new typewriter very well the handout had numerous mistakes. "Why not have the students correct them for you?" I suggested. What had been a problem became an opportunity.

Watching the students enter, I could hardly believe these were the intellectual dregs and discipline problems of the school. Seldom have I seen a group of young people come into a room in better order: smiling and spontaneously cheerful, they took their seats, eagerly awaiting the day's adventures. There weren't enough chairs, so two boys shared one, sitting together without embarrassment.

There's nothing of the martinet about Nancy Ellis. She keeps perfect order just by holding everyone's attention. Since she knows how to be with her students, speak their language, understand their experience, and then bring them to where she is, she's a living monument to the idea that getting tough is NOT the answer to today's educational problems. She is energetic, motherly and full of fun.

The class I visited seemed more like a birthday party than school. As the students took their seats, Nancy passed out signs for them to wear. These identified them as great scientists — Galileo, Kepler, Einstein, Madame Curie and George Washington Carver — personalities they would take on for the next forty minutes.

CORRECTING THE TEACHER

Nancy began the class by explaining she'd written a dialogue, but had made some mistakes and needed help in correcting them. When she gave out the papers, the students eagerly began looking for and correcting errors. "This is fun," I heard someone say — the only comment in the ensuing silence of concentration.

Thus the class began with practice in spelling and English usage. Soon the students would be able to see how well they had corrected their teacher, as the proper form of the dialogue was clarified by acting it out — so it didn't matter too much whether everything was correct from the first. Wherever I could catch a glimpse of a paper, though, I noticed the changes all seemed correct.

QUIZZING THE SCIENTISTS

When that particular "assignment" had continued long enough, Nancy tossed a ball to each of the assembled scientists in turn, asking each to give an autobiographical fact. Some had consulted the encyclopedia and could report to the class, while others had not yet done so. There was no remonstration about homework not done, but I'm told those who remain uninformed soon busy themselves to gather information and clarify their role in the unfolding drama. Meanwhile, Nancy made sure to give at least one fact about each scientist, so no one would be left speechless. Then she had the students throw the ball to each other, so each could say something about the scientist who threw the ball to them. This was a great success.

BEING IS BELIEVING

Next it was time to act out the dialogue. There was a lot of competition to be one of the five characters. I'll never forget one little girl jumping up and down, screaming "I want to be a SEED!!!" Those who were chosen rushed to the center of the room and began to perform. As Nancy took the role of drama coach, the performance improved. The class was learning about the parts of a flowering plant by acting or watching their friends act out those parts.

NOTICING THE BENEFITS

As the class progressed, the effect on the students' self-images was clear. Nancy's way with them consistently made them feel in charge of what was happening. She gave information only as needed, asking questions everyone seemed eager to answer. About eighty percent of the time the answers were correct, and when they weren't, someone else would provide the correct answer. By starting the class correcting the teacher's mistakes, by performing in the drama, by having a good time, by identifying themselves with eminent scientists, and by discovering how much they knew, the students were learning self-respect at a rapid pace. How important this would surely be in motivating them to work toward a position of respect in their communities!

I also noticed the number of approaches Nancy had taken to the written material in one short class period. First, the class had read silently with an editorial eye. Then it had read the dialogue aloud as drama, naturally identifying with and making an emotional commitment to the subject. Soon the whole group would chant related material. And finally, they would spontaneously create a musical composition to bring the material to life in another way. Skill in reading and writing requires that written language be approached in a variety of ways, that it be a tool for thinking, not just words on a page.

Stage directions, of course, were not meant to be read aloud, but to be translated into action. The students were interested in this distinction, and thereby explored the difference between information and action.

I noticed a remarkable amount of teamwork in the room. Despite the competition for leading roles, there was no leftover rancor: The ones who didn't perform today would get another chance tomorrow. They all seemed interested in each other's progress. There were no put-downs.

The learning process is powered as much by questions as by answers. Nancy had remembered this in writing her dialogue which, like those of such masters as Plato and Galileo, was in questions and answers.

CREATING A MUSICAL ACCOMPANIMENT

For me the most exciting part of the class was watching the young people become composers. Nancy had chosen a chant about plant physiology from John Grassi's excellent science text, designed for Integrative Learning classes. The class did a choral reading of this. Then Nancy suggested they do it as a rap, everyone together creating a rhythmic background while individuals took turns reading the text.

This was the most popular and delightful event of the period. Everyone began making rhythmical noises. The group shared a strong sense of musical design — tossing rhythmic and sound ideas around without apparent leadership. Each wanted a chance to read the words, which they approached with interesting rhythmic configurations, the way a composer experiments with rhythms while setting words to music.

Noticing one boy's problem getting the words in the right order, I realized he was dyslexic. I also noticed he was solving his reading problem himself, by fitting words to rhythm, so eventually every word was in place. Though this was a challenge, he seemed to be having a wonderful time. Others struggled in similar ways, but no one gave up.

MULTIPLE LEARNING EXPERIENCES

Toward the end, Nancy had the students summarize what they'd learned. This they did clearly and eloquently, focusing on the main ideas with remarkable skill.

During the progress of the class I noted seventeen different types of learning experienced in a forty minute period. Though varied, these held together as a unit. This class accomplished in a few minutes what elsewhere might not be attempted in years.

OTHERS COULD DO IT TOO

Though Nancy Ellis is remarkable, I believe others can easily learn to do this kind of teaching. It's not so much the complexity of her methods as the assumptions she works from that make the difference: she believes her students are capable of excellence, and can enjoy learning. With enough resources to keep things moving, she usually asks questions instead of giving out information. These modifications of the traditional classroom behavior are simple and inexpensive to achieve. As Sharon Bean observed, such changes don't cost much, but they make an enormous difference to what can be accomplished.

HOPE FOR THE INNER CITY

The problems of inner city education seem unsolvable to some. Schools graduate illiterate students who remain on welfare throughout life and have a shockingly high probability of violent death before middle age. Integrative Learning could transform this situation.

For example, Kanya Vashon McGhee wanted to teach basic skills to illiterate adults in Harlem. Finding his students interested in astrology, he taught them to cast horoscopes. You can't do that, of course, unless you can read, write and do mathematics, so he had to teach those skills as an entré to the secrets of astrology. The result was accelerated literacy training.

Starting with one student at a time, Kanya taught them to teach each other, and before he was through he had hundreds of students coming to his Tree of Life Center every month. His students were replacing their commitment to drugs with a new interest in being educated. He told me, incidentally, that under pressure from real estate development interests the city of New York responded to this by evicting him and tearing down the building in which his center was located.

He also told me the average thirty year old black man from Harlem has lost an appalling percentage of his friends to violent death. That brought me up hard against the realities we're dealing with here. Whether it's Nancy Ellis working with elementary school students or Kanya working with adults, the impression that it's possible to get people beyond the violence orientation of the inner city will not go away.

READING IMPROVEMENT FOR ALL?

In Waldorf, Maryland, at the Lifetime Learning Center run by David Finsterle the average person who attended in 1987 — including children and adults — progressed two or three grade levels in reading ability in thirty six hours of instruction. A typical adult who couldn't read would progress to a twelfth grade reading level by gaining about one grade level for each ten hours of instruction. Twelve grade levels in one hundred and twenty hours isn't bad, when you consider that the same people probably spent thousands of hours failing to learn to read in school. Unfortunately, the excellent record of this center was not sufficient to keep it alive financially, so it has now disappeared.

I was prepared for such statistics because I had previously talked to Coletta Long, who helped design the Evelyn Wood reading program. Coletta designed her own reading program for learning-disabled children and once took a class of eighth graders from a third grade reading level to college level. It took her twenty-four hours of instruction time to accomplish this in a normal sized classroom. Coletta and I calculated that the cost of significantly improving reading skills in schools would be tiny, considering the results that could be achieved. I once reported this information to the proprietor of a school that specializes in learning disabilities. "Your information is incorrect," she told me. "What you say cannot be true. If it were, we'd all be out of jobs."

Possibly that attitude has something to do with the fact that Coletta's experiment has never been repeated. It's a misguided attitude, though, for Integrative Learning is sure to increase the numbers of jobs for teachers substantially, if only because reducing the drop out rate will increase the need for them.

INSTITUTIONALIZED INTEGRATIVE LEARNING

Here and there schools have adopted one form or another of Integrative Learning. In Minneapolis, the Clara Barton School uses Whole Brain Learning, which focuses on innovative approaches to problem solving. Students there score normally on most academic tests, but in problem solving ability they're almost always in the stratosphere.

The Barton School is a lovely place to visit. One gets educated just by walking through the halls, and the esprit de corps in classrooms and among teachers is excellent. This school was converted to Whole Brain Learning with funds provided by the State of Minnesota. Such funds are available to other public schools in the state that wish to convert to whole brain learning or similar forms of education.

In Connecticut there's a school based on the principles of brain compatible learning as explained by Leslie Hart in his book *Human Brain, Human Learning*. Reports are that students there progress three times as fast as would be considered normal in other schools.

Some of the best work in public schools is being done in Boston by John Grassi, whom I mentioned earlier. His self-published text books in elementary school science and geometry are among the best resources elementary school teachers now have. Grassi has adapted Lozanov's work to many different subjects, with outstanding results.

The SpeakEasy language school in Minneapolis, based on Lozanov's theory of instruction, has offered very successful accelerated foreign language classes in a number of private schools in the Twin Cities, such as Mounds Park Academy, Visitation and Woods Academy. All of the teachers at Woods Academy, by the way, have themselves been trained in Integrative Learning.

And the Thornton Friends School in Silver Spring, Maryland, which I co-founded in 1973, continues to provide an outstanding opportunity for young people to discover in a school environment values that are worth internalizing and acting on so they become central in their lives.

TOWARD A NATIONAL VISION FOR EDUCATION

As these and many other examples of successful applications of Integrative Learning become better known, the question will soon be whether they will be emulated on a wide scale — particularly in public school systems. The alternative is to continue to waste the natural learning abilities of our children, with all the lost opportunity and increased human suffering that ultimately implies. The issue is survival.

The time is ripe for politicians of every persuasion to display leadership by helping create a vision of what can be accomplished with the educational, technological and creative resources we now have. But empty political promises aren't enough. A specific program is needed, one with details worked out as to how it will be implemented.

I don't mean to understate the political power of short-sightedness and fear to delay or hamper positive changes. During the days of the War on Poverty in the 1960's, many localities deliberately made it impossible for federally funded adult literacy programs to work. They were too threatened by the political clout a more literate population might be able to develop.

Now, however, the consequence of poor education threatens not only the underclass — it's a menace to everyone. The National Alliance for Business estimates that we have a three or four year window of opportunity to correct this problem. Responsible and thoughtful observers see a possibility that the underclass could cripple the society as a whole if it continues to develop along present lines.

PREPARING FOR ECONOMIC CHANGE

The type of school system we've had for a couple of generations was designed to keep people in line, not to encourage independent thinking. It can no longer meet the needs of a time in which most of us will have to become more flexible than ever before.

This is even truer of our children, who are inheriting the most rapidly changing social environment in history. Merely to survive, they must learn far more than the basics we found necessary. Above all, they will have to grapple with the unfamiliar and unexpected. Tolerance for ambiguity will be the *sine qua non* of their existence. This can be learned relatively easily, but unfortunately it is a mental ability traditional education generally discourages.

We have scarcely begun to realize the economic value of improving education. Voters do not yet understand, for example, what their tax dollars are buying when they buy education of the type I am advocating. When educational needs are met effectively, the value of money invested can be increased by somewhere between 4 to 1 and 1,000 to 1. That is, in the long run every dollar spent on schooling could earn or save as much as one thousand dollars. This has been shown to be true in business situations, but it should be clear in all cases.

For example, if a person who might spend a lifetime on welfare were to be educated well enough to earn an average yearly income of $20,000, that would be a major saving for society each year ($20,000 saved from welfare expenditures, plus whatever additional amount is earned from taxes and multiplier effects on businesses).

Since it should be possible to make this change in a person's lifetime productivity for an investment of about two thousand dollars beyond what is now being spent on schooling, the return on investment here is better than 10 to 1 per year. If we assume a lifetime income of 40 years, the return on investment could be 400 to 1, or more. This figure goes up, of course, as the lifetime income of the individual goes up. And that's only the direct monetary value, not taking into account indirect costs or gains, and such intangibles as happiness.

As these figures suggest, what I am advocating is not just a luxury, it is a necessity. Education as we have known it in the past cannot prepare us for the changes we must inevitably face. That's why the Departments of Labor, Education and Health and Human Services have made it a top priority for our nation to discover the most effective educational programs now in use and make them available to everyone. Otherwise the work force needed by the year 2000 will not exist. Large numbers will be on the welfare rolls because they lack the skills needed for employment. The robotic, production line skills suited to the factories of the past will no longer be adequate. Future workers will need to grasp current information, make independent decisions, be creative, demonstrate thinking ability, take responsibility, and originate new behavior in response to unpredictable situations.

EDUCATION FOR THE REAL WORLD

Integrative Learning can be a significant factor in solving these economic and social problems. It reactivates the individual's natural desire to be in charge, think clearly and act decisively. Thus it provides the education that a strong-minded and competent citizen needs.

At the Thornton Friends School we developed what many considered an ideal but somewhat utopian atmosphere for learning, one in which most students got along with each other extremely well, faculty-student relationships were excellent, the student-teacher ratio was extremely favorable, and students would often rather be in school than anywhere else. Some worried this might render our students incompetent to deal with the realities of life in a hostile world.

On the contrary, we found that skills learned in a supportive, comfortable environment can easily be applied in challenging situations. The confidence that comes with learning them well in the first place will carry students through later difficulties. It is not true that children learn best in a setting of constant difficulty and stress. Contrary to the beliefs of some stoics, such an environment is not good preparation for the "real" world. A properly supportive and yet challenging environment is, and will help the average person become a powerful and creative leader, able to meet the current need for innovating new solutions to global problems.

THE HUMAN RACE ISN'T AS STUPID AS WE THINK IT IS

But there's a popular impression that the average person is powerless and uncreative, and couldn't possibly think of new approaches to problems. As I recently learned, for example, the president of a top international corporation seriously believes that no new business idea can come from inside his company, because no one who works for it could be smart enough to think of one. The waste of resources caused by this man's belief is obscured because his company couldn't bankrupt itself if it tried. Its name is a household word, and its products are on your shelves.

The popular belief that most people are not very smart is far more of an obstacle to developing genius than anything of a practical nature. Merely knowing that something is possible is usually half the battle in making it happen. Once you know your whole family is made up of geniuses, anyone who is interested will be able to see that they are. Then you'll be paving the way for others to help themselves and their families in similar ways.

THE ATHENIANS NEVER HAD IT SO GOOD

Anyone who doubts whether we have the resources to transform our culture in the way I am suggesting might ponder the accomplishment of a small city twenty-five hundred years ago. This city (the size of present day Toledo, Ohio) was Athens, which in a mere century laid much of the foundation for Western culture.

Why is it that at certain special times and places excellence spreads throughout a culture or society? I believe this phenomenon occurs when there is sufficient agreement among the majority that creative brilliance is really important and possible for almost anyone to achieve. Then expectation of excellence becomes a shared cultural vision. Those who already understand it find plenty of students willing and eager to learn how to produce it. This expectation of excellence was one of the hallmarks of Athenian culture.

But even the Athenians wasted their most valuable resources, because nine-tenths of their population were slaves, and thus could not participate; women too were excluded. This left only five percent of the population as candidates for publicly recognized high achievement. Imagine the potential of a true democracy.

In our time and culture, excellence is not a priority. Because we have been primarily interested in the futile search for security, we have spent our private funds on the accumulation of property and wealth as opposed to experience and education, while public funds have maintained the economy and the defense industry. They might instead be used to develop the highest possible level of cultural excellence.

Indeed, a relatively small group could bring about the beginnings of a major cultural transformation by demonstrating that excellence is truly important and, given proper education, within the grasp of everyone. Thus, you ought to be able to organize in your own neighborhood an effort akin to that of the Athenians. After all, everyone can participate, not just the five percent who are neither slaves nor women. You need only persuade your neighbors how easy and enjoyable it is to discover new realms of intellectual possibility.

If this sounds idealistic, it's because our culture collectively does not believes in its possibility. Things will change as soon as enough people realize we already have the tools needed to solve many of the world's problems. This will happen naturally as we collectively activate the integrative intelligence everyone has a right to experience.

Some tell me I'm simplistic or idealistic when I say things like this. I've discovered the words "simplistic" and "idealistic" can quite usefully save one the trouble of trying to understand or correct all sorts of problems. What I'm saying, however, really isn't simplistic, it's just simple. That's because once we start doing things in accordance with human nature, what used to be complicated really does become simple.

EVEN IF YOU ONLY DO A LITTLE, IT WILL BE WONDERFUL

Because of the stranglehold I know the social belief system has on the national consciousness, I'll be a little surprised (though very pleased and impressed) if you take my suggestion and try to turn your neighborhood into a community devoted to excellence. Even if you are aware of your own genius, you'll find it takes some doing to persuade your neighbors they will enjoy becoming aware of theirs. So perhaps you'll prefer to wait until the possibility of using education to reform national priorities is a recurrent theme on talk shows.

Meanwhile, there's no need to put off enjoying the benefits of Integrative Learning — for your own family (or classroom), and yourself. How you can put Integrative Learning into practice in your life right away is the subject we will turn to next.

PART TWO

SETTING THE STAGE
FOR INTEGRATIVE LEARNING

We have seen in Part One how the secret of Integrative Learning is to be found in the natural learning environment of the young child — an atmosphere of fearless and active enjoyment, of affectionate and positive responses, which create expectancy of success both in learners and in parents and teachers.

Part Two explores attitudes and behavior that will help create an environment in which learning can thrive. For adults this may require some changes in attitude.

We can't be much help to children if we're not in good shape ourselves. Indeed, one of the joys they bring is not so much the opportunity to educate them as to rethink our own values and experiences. Take, for example, the joy of reliving happy memories while reading them stories we left behind when we grew up.

Beyond that, we want our children to have advantages we missed. Some of these are material, some psychological. The material ones are easily supplied if we have the means. The psychological ones are more complex: because we often unconsciously treat children as we were treated, we risk driving them to the same bad habits we'd like to be free of ourselves.

For this reason, it's essential to improve our own psychological strength in preparation for realizing more of our potential. We can't, for example, expect children not to smoke or swear if we do. In these and other ways we can prepare ourselves to assist another's growth by attending first to our own.

Here in Part Two, by giving you a chance to think through some of the cultural influences that could be standing in the way of your own development — influences you may tend to pass on to your children unless you first take steps to minimize their effect on you — I'm setting the stage for the exercises in Part Three.

So let's abolish the negative effects of misguided attitudes towards work, learn what it means to function productively within limits, reach out for the best that life can give us, practice dealing wisely and effectively with feelings, and replace negative competitive drives with positive cooperative ones. Setting the stage for learning in ways like these should add joy to life, while improving the quality of the family's time together.

7

HOW TO FIND HAPPINESS
IN THE PURITAN WORK ETHIC

Many of us believe in work for its own sake.
This is a questionable principle when applied to learning.
Making learning more enjoyable makes it more successful.

You and I are victims of a chronic cultural affliction often called the Puritan Work Ethic. Its most familiar symptom is the nagging feeling that we're no good except when we're working. People who have advanced cases of this malady tend to believe that the more arduous and awful the task, the better they can feel about themselves. But if they fall into the sinful pastime of enjoying their labors, they risk attacks of guilt.

This chapter is primarily about working and the different meanings and values we assign to the notion of work. It is only secondarily about learning. The reason is that much of our attitude toward learning is based on the role we think work plays in our social and ethical frame of reference. So, often we cannot really change our attitude toward learning until we first change how we think about work: what it is, what value it has, and what role it should play in one's life. If you want to help your children learn better, examine the notions of challenge, difficulty and delight you're communicating to them. Consider also what you can learn from them by observing how they approach life instinctively.

I won't elaborate on the source of the confusing and frustrating pressures of the Puritan Work Ethic. It stems from events and beliefs a few centuries ago that are mostly unrelated to present social conditions. But these beliefs, religious in origin, were transformed during the industrial revolution into a code of ethics that proved useful in forcing factory workers to grind out profits for the robber barons who owned the factories.

WORKING CAN BE A REALLY POINTLESS THING TO DO

Today the Puritan Work Ethic is out of date and should be scrapped. It isn't true that work itself necessarily makes you a better human being. And it certainly isn't true that any and all work is valuable for its own sake. A friend tells how in the Army he was required to mow lawns that didn't need mowing with lawn mowers that wouldn't mow. Presumably the idea was to develop unquestioning obedience — no more useful purpose seems to have been intended.

You're probably not involved in anything quite so pointless, but how much time do you spend on chores that don't need doing? And how many hours or perhaps years are your children struggling at school to learn things they ought to be able to learn in minutes, or maybe should not even learn at all? Work that wastes our time, energy and resources is useless and intellectually crippling.

BOREDOM DOESN'T MAKE YOU BETTER

Recently I made a presentation to students at a medical school about how they could learn required information more quickly. They protested that the material they had to study really was boring, and nothing could make it more appealing to them. Afterwards one of the professors told me that in her opinion too little of what medical students are forced to learn is of use to them. "The way things are presented in classrooms doesn't reflect the type of experience medical practitioners actually have," she said. "They need to learn things in the context in which they'll be used, not just to collect a headful of abstractions. Real learning seldom starts before internship. There on the hospital floor they begin to acquire knowledge and skills they can use. And they learn them integratively. As you say, it's the way infants learn. What is observed one day in an operation may be picked up again two weeks later when working with another patient. What you've told us about learning applies precisely to the way interns function, but little of it is employed in the medical school curriculum, most of which is tedious, irrelevant and soon forgotten, since it is useless to practicing physicians."

WE INSTITUTIONALIZE TRIVIA "FOR OUR OWN GOOD"

And so it goes. The inquiring student who asks "Why do I need to know this?" is often told, "You'll find out later." But that "later" may never come, as the student goes through life wondering what all the fuss and hard work was about. What it was about was the Puritan Work Ethic.

The fundamental problem with this useless anachronism is that it fails to distinguish between productive and non-productive activity. It values work primarily *for its own sake*.

THREE WAYS TO DIG A HOLE

Let's take a look at the consequences of this value system. Imagine three people digging a hole. One of them uses a blunted wooden shovel. Another uses a sharp spade. A third uses dynamite. If the object is to feel good about how hard you're working, the first is a saint, the second an Illustrious Citizen, and the third a ne'er-do-well. But if the object is to dig a large hole, the third wins over the other two hands down.

I know that's hard to accept after being brought up on misleading and guilt-producing fables like "The Ant and the Grasshopper" or "The Tortoise and the Hare." (Let's simply rewrite that last one so the hare takes a nap *after* winning the race. *Now* what's happened to all those self-righteous feelings of victory exemplified by the tortoise? Being able to do things quickly and easily doesn't necessarily condemn you to indolence, does it?)

The fact is if one person can get something done more quickly and efficiently than another, it doesn't matter how much work went into it. When I went to college I discovered that the student who had the highest grade point average seldom studied, while the student who worked harder than anyone else didn't even have a B average.

IS LAZINESS A FAULT?

Over the years it's become clear to me that nothing troubles parents more than the possibility their children might be lazy. I'm not certain, though, that laziness actually exists. I think it's really a cloak for some hidden emotion, perhaps fear. But there was at least one famous person whose laziness was legendary. Gioacchino Rossini, composer of the opera *The Barber of Seville*, was said to have been composing in bed once when a sheet of music he had written slipped to the floor. Rather than get out of bed and pick it up, he composed the piece again. He may have been lazy, but he was one of the most popular and admired composers of his day, particularly noted for his speed of composition. Many of his greatest operas were written from start to finish in less than a month. So if, indeed, Rossini was a lazy man, perhaps laziness isn't so bad after all.

There are some situations in which we actually reduce our productivity by working harder. This is particularly true at school, where students are often asked to put long hours and lots of effort into tasks that produce little actual learning. If we were a bit lazier, we might devote more energy to figuring out how to avoid such situations, and thus achieve more with less energy. Such a habit of mind could improve our lives, save money and reduce the drain of natural resources. So, in the end, perhaps laziness properly developed and cultivated may prove to be a virtue.

RESULTS ARE MORE IMPORTANT THAN BEHAVIOR

In situations where particular goals are desired and understood, it is clear that behavior as such is far less important than results. Yet frequently parents, teachers and managers are more interested in how something is done than in what end results it achieves. The point is, we shouldn't have to do a thing any particular way, provided we get the results we want. Left to develop our own methodology, we're more likely to find some joyful and uniquely personal route to our destination.

Emphasis on behavior instead of performance can have unhappy consequences. When we choose a physician, for example, we seldom ask for statistics on what percentage of patients have been cured. Instead, we divert our attention to such matters as degrees earned, bedside manner, and whether or not we like the doctor personally.

Many teachers of arithmetic place more emphasis on solving the problem in what they think is the correct way than on getting right answers. Children who want to develop their own way of solving problems should be encouraged to explore the consequences of their own approach and to evaluate its effectiveness in producing useful and correct answers. Instead, they are more likely to be rapped on the knuckles and told to do it the teacher's way.

WHAT'S YOUR POSITION?

So one thing I'm going to ask of you as a parent is to reexamine where you stand in relation to the Puritan Work Ethic. Do you prize work for its own sake, or for the results it accomplishes? If you prize it for its own sake, you will tend to criticize your children when they are not working. This will only confuse them. They are smart enough to know the difference between work that does and does not produce results.

HOW TO MAKE CHILDREN DISLIKE WORK

It's probably all right for you to do useless work if you want, but it isn't all right for you to insist that your children do so as well. The reason is not that children shouldn't learn to work. Quite the contrary, doing work for the sake of working, rather than achieving results, only convinces them that much work is pointless; doing genuinely productive work, on the other hand, can be one of life's greatest joys.

People who spend too much time doing meaningless work tend to become aimless and unproductive. Whatever the goal, there are more or less effective ways to achieve it. Hard work may be warranted, or it may not. Note that some people confuse challenge with stress and difficulty. Children, of course, *should* be challenged. Some children can challenge themselves and should be left to their own devices to do so. Those who cannot need creative guidance in finding challenges that excite them.

In general, enjoyable ways of doing things are more productive than unpleasant ones, because they are more likely to be pursued voluntarily. Children who are pushed into valuable experiences often learn to hate them, but those who are led to them in a creative and joyful way may embrace them for life. I must qualify this with a personal example. One of my daughters had to be pushed into studying the violin, but now would as soon give up her leg as her violin. So, better to have forced her than deprive her of the experience at all. Still, it should have been possible to lure her into a delightful association with music from the very beginning.

MATHEMATICS: CREATIVE CHALLENGE OR BUSY WORK?

One of the reasons so few people learn math really well is they never get a chance to find out why they are learning it or what they can use it for. It wouldn't be difficult to include in the curriculum a sense of where mathematics came from and why and how it is used, but most of us grow up without any exposure to such things. As a result, there are many who see mathematics only as busy work needed to earn a diploma, and who consequently may refuse to have anything further to do with it once they have met the requirements for graduation.

ON IGNORING IMPORTANT THINGS

There are many other pointless tasks we impose on children, often at the expense of the things they really should do. This leads to a confused sense of values. Children who are experts at diagraming a sentence, but have no idea what a sentence diagram is for may lack the practical skills necessary to earn a living. If they ever wondered why they spent their time in school the way they did, they would have a hard time finding an acceptable answer. Most, though, never ask the question.

When we do meaningless things, we tend to alienate ourselves from nature, which seldom does anything without a purpose. All of a plant or animal's processes or activities are directed toward survival and growth. A kitten's play rehearses strategies for defending itself or attacking its prey.

THE SERIOUS NATURE OF CHILDREN'S PLAY

Children's play is also a way to practice strategies for survival and growth, and their fantasies are symbolic maneuvers to understand and interpret the world as they experience it. They love to rehearse adult behavior in order to prepare themselves to grow up.

Children differ from animals, though, because while animal play is rigidly dictated by the genetic makeup of the species, children's play helps them absorb their culture. As a friend remarked while watching a cat perform the elaborate ritual of washing itself, "There's nothing you can do about that." Because of its imitation of observed adult behavior, children's play can be considerably influenced by parents and educators. Seldom do we use our opportunity to influence play with anything like the effectiveness we could. Indeed one purpose of this book is to use this missed opportunity constructively, and have fun doing so.

THE MAN WHO CHANGED HIS LIFE BY LEARNING FROM HIS CHILDREN

I'm not kidding when I say you can learn a lot from observing children's play. Not long ago I struck up a conversation with a man who seemed very enlightened. He gave me a little lecture on learning that rather resembled the way I usually begin my seminars. "We can learn a lot," he said, "by observing the way children learn. It's useful information."

I asked him how he had come by this remarkable insight.

"From my own experience," he replied. "I am a lawyer and an artist. I think I am a creative lawyer and a creative artist. I think the two forms of creativity are quite different, but I learned them both from my children. I was at one time an uncreative lawyer. I worked full time at my job and would hardly have considered myself an artist at all. But as my children grew and I observed them closely, I began to apply what I learned. This led to my changing the way I practice law. Now my practice takes only half my time. The other half I work as an artist."

WE CAN ALL LEARN THIS WAY

What this man told me was remarkable primarily because he had thought of it himself. It's even more remarkable that more people don't think in similar ways. After all, it takes a lot of your time to raise a child, so why not turn the experience to your advantage and learn what the child has to teach you? What you can learn is the extremely valuable skill of turning work into play. Play, after all, is nothing other than effective learning combined with effective work. Successful people love what they are doing and regard it as play, while people who struggle to get a day's work done are seldom successful.

TWO WISE SAYINGS THAT CAN RUIN YOUR LIFE

So your first assignment is to find opportunities to turn work into play. In the process I'd like you to consider revising two well known maxims for success. One of them states that you should never put off until tomorrow what you can do today. Now this is obviously nonsense, because almost anything you're planning to do someday you could do now. Why not, for example, Christmas shop five years in advance? The main effect of that old saw is to make us feel guilty because our work is never done.

How I suffered from that one as a youngster! I would come home Friday afternoon knowing I should do my homework immediately. But instead I would steal time, doing something I wanted. By Sunday night I still hadn't gotten to what I was "supposed" to do, and so Sunday evenings were always ruined as I wallowed in guilt over having finally to confront the dreaded pages of textbooks. For years after I grew up I regarded everything I wanted to do as being done on stolen time. If only as a child I could have congratulated myself on the wisdom that led me to engage in productive play instead of forcing myself always back to the treadmill of useless labors. For I now do nothing with those pages of biology I memorized and soon forgot, whereas I daily use the skills I was practicing Friday night and all day Saturday.

One thing I've noticed is if I refuse to do today anything I can put off until tomorrow I get more done, because many of the things I put off end up not having to be done at all. How many times I have labored at something in order to finish it early, only to find out later that my efforts were wasted.

Not doing today what I can put off until tomorrow enables me to do more of the things I enjoy. Since I do mostly what I choose, I've formed the habit of enjoying all my activities. When I do get around to the less desirable tasks I find it easier to enjoy them, too, — out of habit, if nothing else.

The other maxim which needs to be revamped is "If a thing is worth doing, it's worth doing well." This is one of the most wasteful and destructive sayings I know. In theory it sounds good, but it makes people feel guilty every time they can't do something well. ("Well" is often defined simply as being better than they can do it.) So they avoid many activities they would otherwise enjoy and might eventually master.

This, too, was a bugbear of my existence. When I had piano lessons I knew I was producing awful sounds and that an almost infinite distance stood between me and soloing in Carnegie Hall. If instead of requiring myself to play well I had simply been able to have fun with joyful little tunes of use and amusement to no ears but mine, I might, indeed, have eventually found my way to soloing for someone else.

I think we should change this one to say that "if a thing is worth doing, it's worth doing badly." That doesn't, of course mean it can't or shouldn't be done well, it just gives us permission to go through the cumbersome process of being awkward at it for a time. I have found that when people remove the blocks to learning, they usually do most things about as well as they can at any given time.

HOW ABOUT A DAY IN BED?

Leonard Orr, a popular seminar leader, gives delightful lectures on the subject of money. He suggests that if you want to double your income, you should spend a day in bed. I don't know whether this always works, but I do know that lots of people find it almost impossible to take that kind of advice. They work so compulsively that depriving themselves of work for a whole day would be pretty close to self-torture.

Spending a day in bed would give you a chance to look closely at your feelings about work. As your mind idles, it will begin to play with some possibilities you've long denied yourself the leisure to think about. How much do you do compulsively, and how much really needs to be done? If you remove the compulsion from your life, you'll have time to do some exciting new things that might turn out to be valuable. The result could indeed double your income.

GET A SECOND OPINION

If you have some doubt about whether or not a particular job needs doing, ask around and get other opinions on the subject. In particular, ask your children. You may discover they've been wishing you would stop working on something they've always thought was pointless.

Once you're sure all your work really needs doing, transform each of your tasks into play. This is asking a lot, I know, but if you take it one task at a time, you may find yourself breaking the habit of unnecessary work. If you're such a compulsive worker that adding a dash of merry-making to your tasks seems impossible — well then, you've found a worthy challenge! Roll up your sleeves, push yourself, and don't give up until you reach the goal. This could be the toughest challenge you've ever faced, but you can do it! If you get really stuck, ask your children for advice. You can regard them as your live-in experts on having fun.

WASHING DISHES FOR FUN AND PROFIT

Before I had an automatic dishwasher, I had to do the clean-up tasks after every meal all by myself. At first I found this disagreeable, but I soon grew to love it. Sometimes I would put on my earphones and listen to music while I washed. I found I enjoyed the music more and remembered it better because I was physically active while listening. At other times I found the activity just right to allow me to retreat into reverie and explore new ideas. In any event, when I finally got a dishwasher, it was with a little sadness that I said goodbye to my nightly ritual. I might have continued, except that I had made up my mind to avoid useless work.

The dishwasher, however, needed loading. Here was a new form of play. I was fascinated to discover what it could and could not accomplish. I performed experiments to see how dirty a dish could be and still come out sparkling clean when it was finished. I have noticed that some people cannot do this. They feel such a compulsion to help their dishwasher that they wash all the dishes before putting them in the machine. The poor machine, then, has to do it all over again, and gets no satisfaction out of having its abilities challenged and fully tested. I found my self-image did not depend on helping my dishwasher do its job, and it seemed easy enough to re-wash later anything the machine wasn't equal to. Meanwhile, I have never ceased to be amazed at the achievements of this remarkable contraption. I have grown so fascinated and delighted with its powers, that now the first thing I do when I get up in the morning is unload it. As I look at each dish, I notice how clean and sparkling it is, and I remember what a mess it was the night before. This little exercise in appreciating technology gets my day off to a happy start.

So get started. Difficult as it may seem to transform drudgery into delight, you should be able to enliven even the most routine task if you really work at it. Once you finally succeed in making all your weighty and trivial chores enjoyable, getting rid of the guilt feelings about having so much fun in life will be your only remaining problem. But these too will pass if you labor selflessly to overcome them.

I know I'm asking a lot, and it may be impossible to accomplish these two burdensome tasks merely to make your own life more enjoyable. But remember — the welfare of your children depends on it!

8

WORKING WITHIN LIMITS

Children need structure and need to be taught the basics.
They learn best when they are helped to discover the
underlying principles for themselves.

History is sometimes portrayed as a series of pendulum swings between opposites. Periods of freedom verging on license alternate with eras dominated by a desire for law and order. These swings are caused by reactions that are too extreme, and by an inadequate synthesis of the opposite poles of a continuum.

Just such a synthesis or balance between extremes of freedom and structure is necessary for effective learning. It requires freedom and opportunities to receive individual attention, but cannot occur without a framework. We need to have starting points — structures we can engage our minds with. If we're going to enjoy playing a game, we need to master the rules. That's why it's sometimes an imposition to tell a child, "Do whatever you want today." The child might reply, "Do I have to?"

THE STRUCTURE BEGINS IN THE BRAIN ITSELF

But what do I mean by "structure" and "framework"? Integrative Learning shouldn't be compared to "structured" learning as if the two were opposites. Confusion may sometimes arise, though, because in some classrooms the structure comes from the teacher and the textbook. In Integrative Learning it comes from the brain itself. For the brain may be viewed as primarily an instrument for discovering patterns in experience.

These patterns gradually evolve into a total life structure, albeit one with many inconsistencies and unresolved conflicts. But the brain is really trying to make sense of life and wants to reconcile and resolve as many of these conflicts as it can.

When the patterns of personal experience and those of instruction are in conflict, the child is forced to choose between them or suffer confusion and conflict within. So if the child's internalized patterns, derived from experience, directly contradict the structures of the classroom, the resulting conflict could be seriously disturbing. Thus the "structure" and "discipline" of the classroom may disorganize the student, producing in the brain a lack of structure, or chaos, which may in turn lead to undisciplined, possibly destructive behavior.

All of us want to be inspired and directed in our learning. We want to be pointed toward the most rewarding experiences life can offer us. But we also want to be sure they are real and accessible, and we don't want the truths we've discovered to be randomly and illogically violated. Nor do we want to have to be bored listening to someone talk about experiences that don't connect with our own. It's not enough for me to listen to you talk about your little excitements. I want you to show me how they can become mine as well — or else how to discover equally exciting things for myself.

WE HAVE TO EXPERIENCE IT

Thus a cardinal rule for good writing applies equally well to teaching: "Don't tell — show." Since the student cannot learn what he or she cannot experience, learning must be experiential. But the experience must have value and importance. A teacher, like an artist, cannot command students to have a valuable educational experience. The teacher who is an artist understands artistic inevitability much the same way the film artist does. You do not sit through a movie because the director orders you to, nor should you have to sit through a class because the teacher says you must. Both the movie and the class are capable of capturing our imagination and leading us into a delightful, powerful and humanly inevitable experience.

The teacher seeks to elicit structure from the student's mind in the light of experiences offered in the classroom. Hopefully the student will spontaneously discover structures, rules, meanings and procedures as a result of many different kinds of thought-provoking activities. Structured perceptions will arise naturally enough when the brain is given a chance to examine and play with all aspects of the material under study, and to give its own order and integrity to that material.

Toscanini often said his only purpose in playing a piece of music was to bring out the composer's intentions as fully as possible. Once when preparing a Wagner opera he determined from the musical score alone the exact point at which the lights should be raised. (Later, on examination of the original manuscript, he found Wagner had actually written the lighting instruction in, just as he had imagined it.) Thus Toscanini did not think he was imposing structure on a score, he sought to elicit it from the music itself.

WE LEARN BEST WHEN WE DON'T KNOW WE'RE DOING SO

Learning occurs most effectively when we don't even know we're doing it. It's better to say "Shake hands with the racquet like this" than to say, "Watch me to see how you hold the racquet." It's better yet to create an activity that leads to holding the racquet exactly right without knowing it. Once I accomplish that, holding the racquet is something I feel I do my way, not someone else's. This lesson is dramatized in the film *The Karate Kid*, which should be adopted as a text in Integrative Learning.

So we teach by indirections, that the learner may not suspect learning is occurring. "You caught us with our pants down," one of my students remarked about a literature class I had taught. "We were all convinced we were just having a good time and not having to do any work. Then when we talked to our friends in other schools, we found we were way beyond where they were. That brought a new appreciation for what we were doing."

So, though the learners may not suspect there's anything but fun involved, the teachers have something up their sleeves, for they know what they want, and have determined to provide experiences that will make the structure of the subject second nature. This is not at all like saying, "Do whatever you want."

ALTERNATIVE SCHOOLS THAT WENT TOO FAR

During the 1960s a growing attitude that too much restriction had been placed on young people resulted in a rash of schools dedicated to freedom and experiential education at the expense of content. In the following decade it became clear that many of them had given their students too little sense of what learning was all about. Some grew up lacking basic knowledge of reading, writing and arithmetic, though they had been exposed to liberating ideas about life and their own feelings. Later academic challenges brought them trouble because of their poor background.

CHILDREN HAVE A RIGHT TO BASIC KNOWLEDGE

Much of the impetus for the Back to Basics movement came from a legitimate concern that not providing children with the tools on which learning has to be based is a serious deprivation, difficult to compensate for later. In addition, too little challenge can give young people the idea that whatever they produce is good enough, so there is no point in trying to do their best. Making learning delightful does not mean neglecting challenge. Standards of achievement should be much higher than they are now. We do not avoid unnecessary stress by ignoring what needs to be accomplished; we do so by structuring the task so it integrates with natural tendencies, desires and experiences.

THE PURSUIT OF HAPPINESS IS THE PURSUIT OF EXCELLENCE

One of life's greatest satisfactions is doing something uniquely well. Haydn, struggling in poverty, would sit at his clavier at the end of the day declaring he would not exchange the joy he found in his own musical ruminations for the riches of a king. Infants and young children often become similarly absorbed in some task that interests them. Roderick MacLeish reports the following story told by child psychiatrist Rima Laibow:

"A three year old was siting in a playground sandbox drawing the schematic design of a car he was inventing. The mother of one of his playmates came over and erased his intricate markings in the sand. 'Children shouldn't be allowed to do those things,' the woman said. 'It just confuses them.' The little boy had in fact been deeply engrossed in what was, to him, fun."

Children need tools so they can reach for higher achievement. At the beginning of life they build these for themselves. Obstacles develop as they grow older and accumulate unpleasant experiences. Their blocks must be overcome if they are to achieve excellence. Often they need the help of adults to discover the joy in reading, writing, spelling and arithmetic.

When we encounter a difficulty, we generally have three options. We can avoid it. We can do just enough to get by. Or we can meet the challenge fully. Our choice may consciously derive from our priorities, or we may choose without thinking. This is where parents can help their children significantly.

LEARNING TO THINK ABOUT WHAT YOU ARE DOING

Early in life children can learn to think about how they do what they do and how they can do it better. This doesn't mean taking the mystery out of their activities, it means giving them a chance to consider their actions so they can understand themselves better. This kind of guidance can make their choices in life increasingly joyful and meaningful.

In Chapter Seventeen you'll find an interview I conducted with a young man who is learning to use his mind creatively. He's picturesquely articulate about his thoughts, and by entering his world and asking questions about the applications he makes of his ideas, I'm able to help him clarify his thinking further. You'll note when you read the interview that I often ask leading questions, but the implications of these questions are not forced on him, and he's free to reject them. You'll see him working out a carefully designed and highly structured approach to creative thinking. Conversations like this can provide stimulation and enjoyment as we explore the making and unfolding of a new mind, a new consciousness, a new talent, a new genius.

OUR OWN, OR SOMEONE ELSE'S?

When structures are imposed from without, we may be less likely to make them an integral part of our thinking than when they are discovered from within. The structures we discover for ourselves give shape and meaning to experience. There's the sense of personal ownership that comes from the "ah-ha" sensation of discovery. It's not that we can't have structures pointed out to us; it's a matter of *how* they're pointed out.

I remember a math teacher standing over me, asking a series of gentle but provocative questions about the differences between the effects of squaring numbers and cubing them, and how that related to the structure of the universe. I've been fascinated ever since with discoveries I made as a result of those questions, with the physical consequences of these mathematical relationships — such as the pudginess of babies, and the heat of the sun — and the links connecting these phenomena. Both phenomena occur because as something increases or reduces in size its (cubic) volume increases or reduces proportionally much more than its (squared) surface. The mathematical structure exists in the universe itself, not just in my mind; but "seeing" it that way left me insatiably fascinated with its endless and kaleidoscopic manifestations.

What I discovered was not just an observation about the universe, it was also a limit on behavior — at least imagined behavior. Remember that childhood fantasy I mentioned in Chapter One about whether our universe is an atom in some giant's? I spent a lot of time thinking about that when I was a child, as I believe many people do. I kept shrinking and expanding my imagined universe, creating universes within universes endlessly. Now I realize that a tinier universe or a larger one would have to be indescribably different from the one we experience because the surfaces and the insides of things don't shrink or expand at the same rate.

This may appear to be putting a coldly rational brake on the freewheeling imagination of childhood. On the contrary, when the time came that I was ready to comprehend these structures and limits of the physical world, I was ready to perceive a whole new domain of wonders and mysteries. If we did shrink to the size of insects we'd probably have to have exoskeletons like them to keep all the heat and moisture from leaking out of our bodies too quickly. And if we were as large as the sun we'd have a terrible stomach ache because all the atoms in that region, crushed together by immense gravitational forces, would be smashing into each other and exploding like hydrogen bombs. So, out of respect for my lovely smooth skin and my comparatively calm digestion, I've disciplined my fantasies to conform a little better to the mathematical realities of nature.

Speaking of digestion, I've also found in the process of growing up that eating too much candy makes me feel awful. So I've learned to avoid doing that most of the time. In both instances discovery led to discipline — one mental, the other physical. The self-discipline in each case is more effective because I discovered it for myself than it would have been if the thought process or behavior had been forced upon me.

INNER VERSUS OUTER DEMANDS

The problem of juggling the demands of inner perceptions with those imposed from without is one of the most delicate balancing acts we face in growing up. Unfortunately, adults often treat children as if they had no priorities of their own. They think a child who does not immediately do whatever is asked has no sense of responsibility. The child, naturally, resents this lack of perceptiveness and wishes to rebel against it. When the inner and the outer demands come into frequent conflict, chaos may result, with the child unable to find consistency in either. When we grow up with this kind of conflict, we may come to feel that something other than our will is in control of our life.

LEARNING COMMITMENT TO YOUR OWN ACTIONS AND VALUES

Children who have insufficient opportunities to discover structure may experience anxiety because they do not know what is expected of them. Some parents let their children off the hook repeatedly, thereby teaching them that the present activity can be dropped at any moment and something else taken up in its place without commitment to continuity. What children want is guidance and direction enough to help them develop self-discipline. We can perhaps best meet their needs in this regard by helping them discover where they can take root for a while, totally absorbed in a task of ever-growing fascination. The choice of interests and directed attention is personal with each child and will unfold itself to the adult willing to pay close attention.

BE CONSISTENT WITH YOUR CHILDREN

It's a delicate matter to determine when it's important to let the child learn from experience, perhaps guided by the kind of wise questioning I've described above, and when we have to lay down the law simply and directly. You don't stand and gently reason with a child playing on the railroad tracks in front of an oncoming train: you grab the child and run. For better or worse, modern life requires us to be forceful and definitive some of the time without necessarily explaining why or allowing for the discovery process. So there are some areas in which we are driven by necessity to say, "You can do this and you can't do that, and that's all there is to it."

This is certainly better than bringing up children in an environment in which the limits of their actions aren't ever really defined, and what is acceptable at one time is not at another. Young people, of course, are always testing. The parents say, "If you do that again, just wait and see what I'm going to do to you!" but some of them seldom (if ever) follow through on the consequence. The child, who has been informed of the penalty, repeats the behavior, but fails to experience the promised result. This could make the child think the parent was really just joking, which can be confusing, and may provoke anxiety. The child, perhaps correctly, senses the adult is not willing to take the trouble to lay down guidelines for acceptable behavior.

By the same token, keeping promises to your children is also important. If you make plans to do something fun, like go to the zoo next Wednesday, it's permissible to change them, provided the child clearly understands there's a good reason for the change, and something equally delightful will be substituted.

Children, of course, need to test reality, and will sometimes do so by staging dramatic showdowns over issues of control. What they really want in these situations is to be told what the limits are. You can provide this information most effectively if you are not emotionally involved. The worst thing to do is react to the child's behavior according to how you are feeling at the moment. You want to develop a sense that meaningful and consistent limits can be counted on.

At other times children may be frustrated because they don't yet have the skills, the knowledge or the approach to do something important to them. At such times you can be helpful in providing assistance — not by telling them how to proceed, but by asking them questions which will help them structure the task for themselves. This is best done in a disinterested spirit: the child should know you are willing to help if help is wanted, but you have no investment in providing it if it isn't — you want to assist, in other words, but you don't want to meddle. It's important, though, throughout everything that happens, to take what the child is doing seriously.

QUESTIONS FOR THINKING ABOUT DOING

Questions can be useful to guide the thinking of someone trying to move ahead with a task. Here are some useful ones.

1. What are you trying to do?

This question allows the person to define the task at hand. Sometimes just deciding what you are trying to do makes it easier to get it done. The question elicits a sense, at least, of the direction to be taken. At the age of four I set out to dig to China. The task was clear, and so was the goal. All I had to do was apply a shovel to the ground enough times and I knew I would eventually see blue sky and the sun shining below my feet, together with the puzzled expressions of the people whose territory my shovel had invaded. In my mind's eye I could see these upside down people staring quizzically at me. So, had the question of my goal been raised at the time, we would have proceeded quite soon to the next question. Note that *why* I was trying to dig to China was no one's business. I did not want to hear (and still don't) the sneering remark, "What are you trying to do *that* for?" Our most cherished goals may be a mystery to others, and perhaps should remain so.

2. What do you think it will take to accomplish the task?

Here the person is asked to look at the task and to define it realistically in order to see what's needed to accomplish it. Perhaps we are beginning our task too soon, not having taken time to determine, at least to some extent, what it involves. For example, in digging to China I did not stop to consider how wide the hole would have to be if I were to get down inside it and continue to dig. Thus I began the task without any notion of how things would proceed after I'd been at it a while. I might at that time have enjoyed looking at the action I was taking in order to see what the next few steps might be. I wouldn't have wanted anyone to tell me I couldn't get all the way to China, which would have taken a lot of the romance out of life. But I might have enjoyed thinking the task through a little more than I did before I started. This would have helped me later in life think through many things I needed to get done and would be able to complete.

3. What resources do you have available to get the task done?

We often ignore the fact that there's a wealth of tools or people available to help us complete a task. We may spend hours stuck at something, when asking the right question could get us unstuck very quickly. It is not so much that we are unwilling to ask as that we don't think to do so. But if we believe asking is a sign of weakness, we may go to a great deal of useless trouble to be heroic. This happens a lot in classrooms. Children need to learn not to exercise such heroics, while at the same time being willing to take full responsibility for what they decide to do. (This is such an essential matter, I've devoted all of Chapter Nineteen to it.) My answer in the case of digging to China would have been simple enough: "a shovel." That answer was sufficient to get me to the task itself, and keep me going for quite a while. Fortunately, I was able to ask the question and answer it all by myself.

4. When you have completed the task you have set for yourself, what will you be most pleased about?

If I consider the rewards of the activity, I will find it easier to determine how much energy I want to invest. If the rewards are great enough, I will not give up at the first difficult juncture, but if they are meaningless, I may come to see that I am wasting a lot of energy on something I don't need to do. I remember, as a child, questioning my mother about why she ironed the underwear. "I have my standards," she said. I didn't feel this answered my question at all. Of course, the "why" question was none of my business, and thus we couldn't go on. I should have asked her, "What pleases you most about having the underwear all ironed?" If she had thought about that question enough, she might have decided she didn't need to iron it. On the other hand, she might have delivered a glowing little talk about how wonderful it is to feel you are the only person on the block who irons every last piece of the laundry. She might have basked for hours in the satisfaction of knowing there wasn't anywhere in the house a piece of clothing that was wrinkled. Had I been able to see and share in this satisfaction, I would have felt much happier about her ironing the underwear, particularly after hearing her talk about how she was the only slave Lincoln hadn't freed.

As for me, I found digging to China at the age of four an excellent preoccupation, for the reasons I have already mentioned. I also entertained the notion that I would then have a short cut to a foreign land. Whether these joys would have been enough to sustain me through a lifetime and several quadrillion dollars of investment is a moot point, because my enthusiasm for this impossible project would transfer later to other, more possible ones. At that time it was enough for me to delight in thinking about the projected rewards of the task I had chosen and honor myself for being wise enough (given the understanding I had at the time) to choose it.

5. *What do you like best about the way you are doing this now?*

We often lose track of how well we are really doing at something, and need to be able to remind ourselves of this. If success is not immediate, we may feel as if failure is overwhelming, when in fact the effort expended so far is quite admirable and likely to bring success in the long run. It is all too easy to feel, when you are involved in a creative task, that no one understands you, or believes in what you are trying to do. This question implies approval and support, rather than dissatisfaction with the fact that the task is not yet finished. Thinking back on my digging to China, I am proud of myself for having the idea and putting some actual sweat behind it. Even though I didn't get very far, I was willing to put my idea to some test, which meant I didn't just sit around daydreaming. I have always since been fascinated by digging and the romance of what you may get to as you dig deeper. Of course there are plenty of ways of digging that don't involve actual physical activity, and my digging for the underlying meanings of things today may be partly a result of my pleasure then at my own willingness to give it a try with an actual shovel.

6. *If you could add one thing to what you are now doing in order to make everything happen better, what would it be?*

It's much easier to look at what is missing if we see it in positive terms. If I evaluate my effort as good and then consider how to make it better, I will be more likely to proceed than if I see only that I am failing — that my efforts are inadequate. What's missing that, if present, would make the situation even more delightful? This question keeps my attention on the fact that the process of moving toward a goal has value in itself. I suppose in my digging operation I would have liked to involve the rest of the neighborhood. It's lonely digging to China all by yourself. Fortunately, I enlisted the girl across the street in my project — until we quarreled and I went home in a huff, leaving her parents to fill in the hole in their back yard. Since then I have been rather good about getting lots of people involved when I wanted to undertake a momentous task. At least if there are more than two, there's someone to referee when a dispute breaks out.

If you find your children involved in activities that are not working well for them, it may be that by asking these questions and similar ones, you can get them to think productively about the logic of their own activities so they will have a more realistic view of what it takes to get what they want out of life. Meanwhile, try using these questions to evaluate some of your own activities.

DON'T WORRY ABOUT RESISTANCE

You may meet some resistance when you try to use questions like these, particularly if you have not used them before. Often someone who is frustrated just wants to dramatize the frustration and doesn't really feel, for the moment, like finding a solution. If this is happening, point it out, try to determine what kind of emotional support is needed, give that as best you can, and then invite your child to ask for additional support when things become a little clearer.

DO IT YOURSELF, BUT NOT ALONE

Here's a saying that may be useful to keep in mind while thinking about your activities. "You must do it yourself, and you cannot do it alone." The first part of the statement means that if I am to do something I consider to have value, I must take full responsibility for it, while the second part assures me that no matter how I go about fulfilling that responsibility I will have the help and cooperation of others. Even if I appear to be working entirely on my own, I am using tools acquired from social contact with others, such as language and thinking skills.

DON'T TAKE AWAY THEIR STRUGGLES

One mistake we often make as parents is trying to help our children avoid all the suffering we went through. First of all, this is impossible, and second if it were possible, it would deprive them of some important learning opportunities. To be supportive, understanding and sympathetic should not mean depriving others of the opportunity to feel in charge of what they are doing and responsible for the achievement. Nor does it mean depriving them of the right to grow through suffering.

Lest you think I advocate suffering as a means to learning, I don't. However I do think it sometimes comes inescapably from experience; and when that happens learning and growth are possible. But it is wrong willingly to impose suffering on others with the object of getting them to learn something.

Meanwhile, as young people struggle with things that may not be working for them at the moment, we must be prepared to accept their failures without criticism. These are stepping stones to success — important learning experiences. For example, when a young person loses a friend, the experience could lead to the kind of sensitivity that makes friendships work better in the future. So failures should be appreciated and valued for what they have to offer. They must not be trivialized, explained away or over-dramatized. It is annoying to a child when a parent insists on trying to feel his feelings for him. He knows, or will discover, that failures are a necessary part of the life process, and should be given their appropriate place in it.

THEIR PURPOSES, NOT OURS

Our children do not belong to us, and were not born to fulfill our wishes. They were born with purposes of their own, which it is our job to help them fulfill without burdening them with our fears. Useful structures and rules can be discovered by testing reality. When we work them out for ourselves, we believe them and can use them better than if we are forced to learn them second hand.

THE MOON SHOT

Still, there's a point at which vision can be generalized, and needs to be shared. I remember one night in the early 1960s I happened to be out walking while President Kennedy was addressing the nation. In every house I passed, I could see the TV set tuned to the President and everyone gathered around to listen as he told us there would be someone walking on the moon before the end of the decade.

It struck me at the time that this was a rare moment in history. The entire nation was brought together around an exciting vision of the future. Over a hundred million people at that moment heard the same words and were moved by similar thoughts.

Over the years since then our nation has been torn by upheaval and fragmentation. We have experienced more dissension than vision. But vision comes not only from our political leaders — it must come from within, from ourselves.

Helping or encouraging our children to a vision of their own is a gift of the highest kind. For there can be no more powerful force to structure and order one's life.

9

MAKING YOUR LIFE THE WAY YOU WANT IT

*We learn and teach crucial attitudes without being aware
of it. By heeding and directing these subconscious
thoughts, we can use our minds more
purposefully and positively.*

Every single minute of your time contributes to making your life the
way it is — so you have at least sixty chances every hour to improve it. You
can do so most effectively by learning to control your paraconscious
thoughts. These are the thoughts just below the surface of awareness to
which you can easily direct your attention, but usually don't.

TAKE A LOOK AT WHAT YOU'RE THINKING

As you read the above sentence, you were conscious of what it said.
Meanwhile, at the paraconscious level, there were other thoughts you
didn't pay attention to. Go back, now, and read that sentence again. Then
write down everything that might have occurred to you slightly outside your
consciousness.

Here are some items one person's list contained:

I'm hungry.
It's like a pool you can submerge yourself in.
I'm glad nobody can read my mind.
This might lead somewhere.
The fan is blowing in this room.
What did she say to me last night?
I'll have to remember to open a new bank account soon.

My father used to cook eggs deliciously.
What's the next step here?

THERE'S GOLD IN THEM THAR THOUGHTS

Our paraconscious thoughts determine how life goes for us. If our life is satisfactory, our paraconscious thoughts are working for us. If it's not, they may be our enemies. They can affect whether we're rich or poor, whether we're loved or hated, whether we succeed or fail. They also influence what happens moment by moment in life.

Now let's look at where they come from.

Paraconscious thoughts stem from attitudes recorded in our minds as a result of the sum total of our experiences. Many of our childhood experiences laid the groundwork for them. Here's one example of how they work.

LEARNING TO BENEFIT THE ASPIRIN MAKERS

If you were often told to bundle up warmly so you wouldn't catch cold, then any time you go out in too little clothing you probably do start sniffling. Maybe you think that's got something to do with germs — that anyone who suffers a drop in temperature is required by the laws of medical science to catch a cold. It might even be disloyal (possibly illegal) not to catch one.

Then there's the social side of a cold. It gives you something to complain of, and to commiserate about with fellow invalids. Plus, you can discourse — both learnedly and experientially — about how a cold is something one has four of every year. The common cold has something else going for it as well, because it doesn't respond to medication. We all know the best treatment in the world will clear up a cold in a week, whereas left to itself it will take a full seven days. You have to admire germs that can hang in there like that. And besides, what would happen if everyone gave up having colds? Think of the impact on network television.

LIVING IT UP AFTER HOURS IN SIBERIA

But not every culture responds to the common cold the way we do. Some folks are said to be trained to sit out all night long in sub zero temperatures without a stitch on. As if that weren't enough, they have to soak a towel in water, wrap it around themselves, dry it out with their body heat, and then repeat the whole process three times the same night. They don't even get a runny nose.

The reason they don't catch cold and we do is that their paraconscious thoughts function differently. People who perform stunts of this type believe they are capable of generating enough body heat to withstand all that cold, so their minds instruct their bodies to act accordingly.

In somewhat warmer regions devotees of a different sort learn to walk across flaming coals without burning themselves. A friend of mine leads workshops in firewalking, recently demonstrating his skill on television. He says almost anyone can get it right the first time, leaving me to ruminate rather heavily on the meaning of that word "almost" — I haven't yet accepted his offer to give it a try myself. Others learn to be buried alive for three days and survive. Still others gobble up only one fourth the amount of oxygen physicians used to believe was necessary to maintain life. (One illustrious practitioner did that on B.B.C. Television.)

WHAT ARE YOU GOING TO DO WITH YOUR PARACONSCIOUS?

Now I personally don't see the point of learning any of these skills. I'm content to bundle up when the temperature drops, and if my feet are uncovered at night I might get a sniffle. Occasionally I taunt my health food munching friends with the fact that I once used Hostess Twinkies to nip a cold in the bud. But in general it hasn't (yet) struck me as worth my while to train my mind and body in these particular arcane arts. I suspect it would take more time than I would care to invest.

But I believe it is important to use my mind effectively, for my own sake and for others as well, because the problems of contemporary life cannot be solved without effective thinking. If you agree with me, I suggest you try using your paraconscious to help your mind do its job better.

REMARKS THAT CHANGED OUR LIVES

Let's think some more about those early experiences. If you're like most people, you probably heard a good deal when you were a child about your stupidity, ugliness, awkwardness and bad behavior. Even one offhand remark to this effect can be deeply and indelibly painful to a child. Friends, siblings, parents and teachers may have seemed in disheartening agreement about your supposed shortcomings. As one of my associates remarked, reflecting on how for all his success he often feels inadequate, "Life is a conspiracy to make you look stupid."

HOW TO RAISE CRUMMY CHILDREN

Young children are impressionable and tend to believe what they are told. If we convince them they're inadequate, they're likely to turn out that way. Remarks from parents, friends and siblings become the content of the subconscious recordings that later shape their lives.

No wonder that as a result of early influences you may often catch yourself having thoughts like, "I can't do that," or "He doesn't like me very much," or "I wish I were better looking," or "How could I have said such a stupid thing?" Such thoughts hold in place a standard of performance that may remain consistent throughout life. Psychologists call this performance I.Q., and some of them are under the impression it's fixed and may be inherited. Actually, I.Q.s fluctuate substantially and have sometimes been permanently changed by changing the content of the paraconscious. Improvement seems to happen so rarely because the necessary conditions are seldom encountered. But they are easy enough to create.

CLEANING UP OUR LANGUAGE

Fortunately everyday life provides endless opportunities to transform your paraconscious thoughts. One way to begin is by identifying and destroying the ones that are doing you in. For example, pay attention to the language you habitually use. Every negative word instructs your para-conscious to give you a hard time. Never mind if you're only joking. The paraconscious has no sense of humor — it doesn't distinguish between a joke and a serious intention.

Try to become aware of your habitual negative thoughts. Then practice thinking the reverse until it becomes a habit. For example, years ago, when asked how I was I would always say "terrible." I thought it was boring to hear everyone else parroting back "fine," and I guess I just wanted to stir up some more interesting discussion. If people really wanted to know how I was, they ought to probe a little deeper, I thought.

But it didn't work. People nodded and smiled anyway. I guess they weren't listening. But my paraconscious was, because pretty soon I noticed I was feeling terrible a lot more often. So I started saying things like "getting better all the time" instead. When I did that, my life got better. I also, by the way, got the attention I was looking for. People wanted to know why I was so ridiculously optimistic.

HOW I FOUND HAPPINESS IN BEING PRETTY

Then along came an even better opportunity to attract attention. It had to do with my discomfort about my personal appearance. I had been told I was ugly when I was little, and even though this was probably always a joke, it had left the ugly duckling in me exposed. The thought of bragging about my looks was unthinkable in those days. But I discovered if I jokingly said I was "pretty" I could trick myself into praising my looks without noticing that's what I was doing. Saying I was pretty made people laugh, so

I didn't take it seriously. After I had practiced calling myself pretty for a while, I noticed I was no longer uncomfortable telling people I am good looking. In fact, I became rather smug about my looks. Then I noticed others relating to me differently. It seemed that when I stopped thinking I was ugly I actually became more attractive.

THE HIGH PRICE OF MODESTY

We've been taught that bragging about our virtues is almost as bad as robbing a bank. Unfortunately, that means we're deprived of one of the most important tools we could have for improving our lives. False modesty has no value. It only helps transform our notions of personal inferiority into realities.

LITTLE GIRLS ADORING THEMSELVES

You may have noticed how most young children do not suffer from false modesty. It's delightful to watch a little girl admiring herself in a mirror. I've heard little girls say the most wonderful things about themselves — how squeezably delicious and ravishingly scrumptious they are. Unfortunately, little boys don't seem so easily smitten with their personal charms. Perhaps that's because they don't attract adoration of that sort from adults. At any rate I never did, though I can assure you my baby pictures are as lovely as Shirley Temple's.

GIVING UP MODESTY IS ALMOST AS HARD AS DIETING

When I discovered the effect of false modesty, I resolved to give it up immediately and do everything possible to communicate my virtues without looking and sounding as if I were describing a traffic accident. This was a mighty challenge, which I sometimes felt unequal to. How could an inferior person like me shamelessly practice false advertising? Would I be arrested for pretending to be something I wasn't?

Then I found a solution. I realized it was all right to proclaim my beauty if I also waxed eloquent on the charms of others. When I began doing so, I noticed everyone I met really was beautiful. Some had disguised their beauty rather imaginatively, but just below the surface a little smidgen of attractiveness would peek out anytime they weren't paying attention to how ugly they were.

I'm aware I'm in hot water here. Miss America contests would go out of business if what I'm saying were taken seriously, and the Hollywood ethic would disappear. But I've noticed that the current dominant standards of beauty are quite arbitrary and racist. In order to be beautiful, you have to have an ectomorphic body type and either be white or look as if you are a white person painted a different color. Mesomorphs and endomorphs are generally out of luck, as are Orientals, Africans, Latinos, Indians (of both kinds) and all sorts of other people who don't unconsciously bring to mind the absurd and presumably discredited prototype of the master race.

Yet in the Renaissance, standards of beauty were different, as they are today in some other cultures. A woman friend of mine, who can walk down any street in the U.S. without being whistled at, recently visited a different culture and found every man she met was asking her for a date. Having spent many years just getting by looks-wise, she suddenly found herself a beauty queen.

For any given group the standards of beauty are generally defined by individuals as being whatever reminds them of their closest relatives. I'm reminded of the incident in *Planet of the Apes* when an ape expresses affection for a human being, but also tells him she is repulsed by his terrible ugliness.

So I think generalized and media-promoted standards of beauty are one of the most significant ways in which society imposes unfair limitations on people. If we didn't have so many media images in our heads, we would probably have a far wider range of opinions about what you have to look like to be attractive. As it is, the Hollywood complex sentences both "beautiful" and "ugly" people to all sorts of unfairnesses in life.

A QUICK FIX ON UGLINESS

I once had a student who was noted for her beauty, but had the habit of pulling her lips unnaturally over her teeth. Her face was structured so she looked pretty if they showed, but if she tried to cover them up (as she nearly always did) she looked strained and uncomfortable. I asked her if there was a reason she did that. "Yes," she said. "One day when I was about nine I got on the bus with a friend and some boys started picking on her. I tried to defend her, but when I did one of the boys said, 'You keep your big ugly teeth out of this.' That remark hurt my feelings so much I could hardly stand it. So I started trying to cover up my teeth whenever I could, so people wouldn't see them."

Most of us could report similar experiences. As a result we may have come to believe that, at least in that particular respect, we're no good.

HOW YOU CAN MAKE YOUR CHILDREN FEEL GOOD

As a parent you can create an environment for your children that encourages them to feel beautiful, intelligent, lovable, talented, caring, and many other positive things as well, by pointing out the evidence whenever you see it. You will not usually improve a child's performance by being negative, but you'll see a pronounced improvement if you lay on the praise. Spread it on thick, then add an extra helping. You really can't overdo this, as long as you're sincere. Think about it: how many millions of words might be applied to describing something so magnificent as a human being — even a supposedly inferior one! Don't worry, the resulting improved self-image won't spoil your child. What does the spoiling is a bad self-image constantly clamoring for attention and getting it in all the wrong ways.

But I warn you, you can't get very good at this — you may not be able to do it satisfactorily at all — unless you do it first for yourself. For only when you have taken adequate pride in yourself can you be really good at offering your loved ones the praise they so richly and unquestionably deserve.

10

LEARNING TO DEAL WITH FEELINGS

*How we recognize and express feelings shapes the way we
deal with everything else. Negative emotions can suppress
thinking and block learning. Here are some guidelines to
help turn feelings from a negative to a positive force.*

Father's reverie as he quietly mops the kitchen floor is interrupted by
his young daughter, who storms tearfully in from a baseball game. "Betsy
stole my ball and took it home," Annie cries, stomping her muddy feet right
where he has just mopped.

What does the poor man do: tell Annie to get off his nice clean floor?
Say "There, there, your mother and I will buy you another one?" Grab
Annie's hand, go over to Betsy's and demand the return of the stolen ball?

None of these responses would be much help. If Father either ignores
Annie's problem or tries to solve it, he's not supporting her to work it
through for herself so she'll be better able to become an independent,
self-directed person.

There's probably a long story behind the drama on the ball field, only
a fraction of which has yet been told. At the moment Annie is in no
condition to give a fair report of the events. But later, after crying her way
through all the tears, stomping the anger out of her body, and thinking for a
while about what really happened, she'll be able to work out a reasonable
plan of action for herself. Most likely Father just needs to pay attention
while Annie talks, cries and laughs her way through a cycle of mental
processes that will lead to reasonable thoughts and actions appropriate to

her situation. Paying attention while they cry is one of the most valuable services we can offer our children.

QUIZ: WHAT WOULD YOU DO IN THESE CASES?

Billy has written a poem so good his teacher thinks he copied it. Just back from school, he slouches into the living room where Mother is reading and throws himself angrily on the sofa. When Mother asks, "How was school today, dear?" Billy mopes and says nothing. If you were Mother, what would you do?

Jeanette comes to see her math teacher to review some problems before a test. The trouble is, she can't concentrate on the problems at all. When the teacher asks what she is thinking about, she says, "My dog Josephine died this morning." If you were the teacher, what would you do?

Dramas like these are our daily fare. How often we come across someone in distress, wanting to express the hurt, but not knowing how.

MY EXPERIENCE AS A TEACHER DEALING WITH EMOTIONAL RELEASE

Every so often I encounter a student in need of a good cry. There might have been a death in the family, but more often some passing frustration is all that's wrong. Occasionally I've been frightened by threats of suicide mixed in with the tears. I do not take those feelings lightly — but later, after a lot of crying, I've met the student in the hall joking with friends as if nothing had ever been wrong. An amazingly effective recovery process has been at work.

It's inevitable that once in a while young people or adults need a little time to cry in order to take their next steps in life.

SUFFERING THROUGH GERMAN CLASS

Although the German class was actually great fun, Rosemary didn't think so. At the age of forty she had yet to have a good experience learning anything, though she was a competent and sensitive nurse. She cried through a whole hour of class. During a break I asked her to tell me about her experiences in school. The stories she told were sad ones, but having told them she felt much better, with the happy result that the German course became her first really successful learning experience in a classroom.

ON NOT DOING MUCH VERY EFFECTIVELY

In such an instance I don't have to do much. I just help the upset student realize I'm willing to listen. My sympathetic presence reminds the student that all is not lost, that life is not totally miserable. As the tears come, I receive them with a nod and sympathetic smile. This brings them forth all the more readily.

I think people may be uncomfortable when they see someone crying, because they mistakenly believe they have to cheer the sad person up or solve the problem somehow. Actually, there's no need to do anything. In healthy people, whenever enough negative emotions accumulate, the floodgates open and the healing starts. That's all crying is — recovering from a painful experience. It unburdens the mind so joy can return and make learning delightful again.

Therefore supporting the process of crying, shaking, or whatever other means the child (or adult) may be using to release hurtful feelings, is one of the surest ways to help genius blossom. In the words of Shelley, "If winter comes, can spring be far behind?" So when our inner discontent or others' is upon us, we must allow it room, feel the feelings until they are no longer troublesome, and then get on with life.

WE'RE ALL LOOKING FOR A SHOULDER TO CRY ON

Really, we're all quite eager to do this, and it's one of the most human things we can do. Simply talking, crying and laughing about what's been awful in your life can make you feel like a new person.

So one of the major activities most of us unconsciously engage in is seeking out opportunities to get someone to listen as we tell the story of our woes and sufferings. Perhaps you've noticed how popular this activity actually is. Once the border of shyness is crossed, conversations at dinner parties, for example, are mainly efforts to outdo each other telling snippets of our private dramas. Everyone wants the chance to be listened to while reliving the unresolved traumas of life.

BUT FOR DISTRESS, LEARNING WOULD NEVER STOP

When our attention is consumed by distress, there may not be much left for other things. Every moment provides new possibilities for learning. The more effectively we're listened to as we unburden ourselves, the more free attention we'll have later for the joyful things.

So if Father gives Annie the empathic attention she needs to talk through the events in her baseball game, she'll figure out for herself how to get her ball back — and perhaps her friend as well. And if Mother spends enough time persuading Billy to tell her what happened about the poem he wrote, Billy won't withdraw and decide never to write again. In fact, he'll figure out an excellent way to prove to the teacher his work was original. And if Jeanette gets enough chance to cry about Josephine's death, in no time she'll be solving those math problems without the teacher's help.

THE MARRIAGE BETWEEN FEELING AND LEARNING

Learning cannot happen well when feelings are unwelcome, for feelings and learning are as intimately connected as a married couple. People learn on many different levels, some of which are emotional. But like a married couple, feelings and learning may become so separated that neither is happy or effective.

When emotions are positive, the total intelligence is in gear, ready to move on to new experiences. Negative emotions interrupt this process, grinding thinking to a halt, causing repetitious replay of thoughts occasioned by the hurt. As these thoughts remain unlistened to by others, they clamor for attention with increasing insistence. Finally they may become so rooted in our thought process they grow to seem like part of us. Then telling them to others no longer does much good, because we state them as fact, instead of allowing them to be distresses that will pass.

THE MYSTERY OF LIMITED INTELLIGENCE

This provides a clue to a fundamental mystery about human intelligence. It happens there are billions of neurons in the brain, all capable of contacting each other through a maze of networks more complex than anything else we know. Only a tiny fraction of these are needed to transmit sensory input, and only a tiny fraction more to send messages out to the rest of the body. The remaining billions are left to converse among themselves. The number of possible interconnections that could be formed in this conversation is greater than the number of electrons in the universe. Now if there is so much potential in the brain, why isn't more of it used? Why should stupidity in any form ever exist in human beings?

The answer, I think, lies in the way the brain has been structured by its evolution. Since learning must be accompanied by a positive emotional state, as all information passing into the long-term memory is processed through the limbic system, negative emotions block the operation of the memory. Thus, when they are present, we simply cannot think well. I'm sure you can see this clearly if you remember a time you tried to take a test while suffering emotional upset. Usually when we're not feeling lucid, some type of emotional distress — be it worry, preoccupation, fear or anger — has gotten in our way.

EMOTIONAL UNBLOCKING IN THE CLASSROOM

A first grade teacher I once met always began the day with three questions for each child to answer. The first was, "What has happened in your life in the past twenty-four hours that's both good and new?"

The second was, "Have you any little upset you'd like to tell us?"

The third was, "Have you any big upset you'd like to share?"

Her students were a little shy, but they did warm to telling the good and new things. Occasionally a child would share a little upset. But day after day no one had a big one.

Then one day Eliza was late to school. Her big brother had been hit by a car the night before and she had been in the hospital with him for part of the morning. "I have a big upset," she said, interrupting the reading lesson in progress as she came in. Between sobs she told the story of her brother. The teacher let her take time enough to tell everything she needed to. When she was finished a little boy raised his hand. He wanted to tell how scary it had been visiting his grandmother in the hospital.

For the next hour the students shared stories of things that had frightened or saddened them. Then everyone seemed satisfied, and work resumed as normal.

But each morning after that the children found it easy to share their little upsets, and occasionally a big one. The teacher observed her students getting ever so much more involved in school and becoming gentler with each other at the same time. They seemed to be learning their lessons more happily and easily.

WHY STUPIDITY IS SO EASY TO LEARN

Failure to think clearly, then, is frequently the result of feelings partially blocking the functioning of the intellect. If feelings did not get in the way, we could think quite well about almost anything.

If we ignore our feelings, they do not go away. If I experience fear in a certain environment, for example, I am likely to re-experience it whenever I'm in another situation that reminds me of that environment. Thus if I was humiliated in a math classroom, I tend to re-experience feelings of humiliation and fear whenever I'm in a similar classroom — perhaps whenever I try to study math.

HOW TO UNLEARN STUPIDITY

Fortunately, stored feelings can be discharged. The humiliation suffered in a classroom will lose its grip as soon as it has been dealt with sufficiently. Dealing with such a feeling may involve crying if we are sad, laughing if we are embarrassed, yelling if we are angry, shaking if we are afraid. This process of catharsis is the means by which we clear from our systems and our memories those emotions that have blocked our thinking.

HOW WE'RE INFLUENCED BY POSTHYPNOTIC SUGGESTIONS

Often negative feelings stem from criticism suffered long ago. Our parents, other older people, our brothers and sisters, or our peers may have criticized us (perhaps unintentionally), and thus told us — directly or indirectly — that we were stupid, ugly or ineffective. It was hurtful to hear such things, and if we don't get a chance to release some of the fears and doubts these incidents caused, they'll remain stored and believed. It's as if we had been hypnotized to accept our nonexistent limitations. Thus, in a sense, all of us are under the influence of posthypnotic suggestion. The suggestion is held in place by the pain we felt when we first began to believe negative things about ourselves.

That's why it's important to learn to recognize and distinguish our positive and negative feelings. The positive ones should be enjoyed, the negative ones released and healed.

THE PHYSIOLOGICAL RELEASE OF EMOTIONAL STRESS

Discharging negative feelings is a physiological process that releases them from storage in the body. It is accomplished by talking, laughing and crying, by trembling and raging, by sweating and yawning. It is what our body wants to do in response to hurtful experiences, and what it will do unless someone interferes. If that happens, the results of storing the negative emotion begin to build up. It's as if you had decided to do away with trash collection and began keeping all that accumulated junk in your basement. Eventually it would take over the whole house. And that's what most of us do with our negative emotions, until we become rigid and inflexible in our areas of undischarged distress.

MOMENTS OF EMOTION IN CLASS

Thus it's wonderful to share those moments when negative emotions are not allowed to perform their usual function of clamping down on the intellect. Occasionally there's the unforgettable moment when a student is deeply touched and willing to share. I'm reminded of the time when I played a recording of a Beethoven overture for my class, and when it was over we all noticed one of the boys was weeping softly. We sat in silence a moment, waiting for what might happen. Then he spoke: "I wish I could thank Beethoven for writing that," he said.

Sometimes students have to do more than cry. I've been delighted with the improvement in attitude and study habits that can occur after someone has torn up a textbook while raging about all the frustration it has caused. Needless to say, this happens infrequently.

ON THE IMPORTANCE OF COMMON SENSE

But a word of caution: I don't mean to put the stamp of approval on raging in public. Control of the emotions is extremely important, and those who discharge them in inappropriate places are not demonstrating maturity or common sense. It's always possible to wait until there's someone around who can listen with understanding before you spill out all your feelings. And you can do it privately enough so you're not disturbing innocent bystanders.

ONE OF THE DEEPEST OF ALL THE EMOTIONAL HURTS

We're all susceptible to many different kinds of emotional hurt, a lot of which happen accidentally. One form of hurt which is truly pervasive, though, is the painful disrespect others have occasionally shown for our most deeply felt emotions. Perhaps when we first saw a suffering animal our tears were greeted with scorn. Early in life we find out that some people are considered better than others for reasons we do not understand. We see our loved ones being unkind to each other. We have cruelty inflicted on us. All these things are extremely disillusioning and produce a need to cry or shake with fear, but when we try to express how we feel, we may be told to be quiet and stop being silly.

IF YOU DON'T LIKE IT, PASS IT ON TO YOUR CHILDREN

The limitations we were told we had as children are stored in the memory and come, after a while, to seem natural. As parents we are too likely to reproduce and unconsciously relive this experience in our treatment of our own children, and perhaps others as well. It's pretty well known by now, for example, that most child abusers were themselves abused children.

Much of the distress we pass on has to do with our sense of limitation. We think we are average, so we teach our children they are too. We think our talents go only so far, so we believe we must protect our children from disappointment by convincing them that they, too, have limited abilities.

THERE IS A WAY OUT

To break the cycle of convincing each new generation of its limitations, we must heal our own distress that got started when we "discovered" or were told we had such limitations. We need, perhaps, to cry about how much it hurt to learn of these supposed inadequacies. To do so, we must realize that the hurt is still hidden inside, waiting to be uncovered.

If you are able to cry about the feelings of loss you experienced when your fourth grade teacher told you would never be a writer, (or even acknowledge where that belief came from,) you'll be better able to help your child discover talents and abilities still waiting to be nurtured. All have experienced the hurt and oppression of being told what they couldn't do. Too few have had the joyful news of what they could do announced with respect and delight, perhaps in the form of a celebration.

SOCIAL SANCTIONS AGAINST HEALING

Though the healing process is natural, our society has for many generations restricted it, both in children and adults, so we have learned to deny our feelings. This learned control is a problem in itself, causing many to be so afraid of their own feelings they avoid discussing them, while imposing their resulting irrational behavior on those around them. In fact, it is precisely this undischarged distress that leads to most of the unlikable behavior we endure from others. If stupidity is learned, then this is how.

If society valued the expression of emotions, perhaps we wouldn't need to disguise and redirect them so often. Emotional discharge is a healing process that frees the brain from the limitations imposed by pain, fear or grief. While we are influenced (even unconsciously) by these negative feelings and the shadows of memories that go with them, we cannot function with our full intelligence.

11

THE JOYS OF COOPERATION

*Working together as a cooperative group makes for a
better family, a better classroom, a better world
— and more successful individuals.*

In the past, competition was considered to be the key to survival and
the driving mechanism for all progress. Today this is no longer so. Despite
its current stint as a buzz word in corporate and government circles, there is
gathering evidence that, at least at the individual level, competition is less
productive than cooperation. And on the global scale there is growing
awareness that the benefits of cooperation far outweigh the dangers and
wastefulness of competition.

THE FUTURE OF COMPETITION

Competition may have a glorious past, but its future is not so bright.
Before 1900, when only one percent of the population lived above mere
subsistence level at the expense of the other ninety-nine, it was probably
needed for survival. But within the past few decades that situation has
changed dramatically.

The actual resources and the means for utilizing them which are
available now could support all the world's population at a decent standard
of living. Unfortunately they are being squandered, misallocated, and
misused on a global scale, with a proportional toll in human misery.

It is possible to envision a world with a political system that distributes
our common resources sensibly and equitably, where people are educated

to use them wisely. Some day a mere one percent of the population may do all the work that needs doing, while the other ninety-nine percent will be able to concentrate on human services, crafts, art, scientific investigation and other forms of spiritual nourishment.

How we will arrive at this brighter future is not my subject here. For those who want to pursue that question, I recommend *Critical Path* by Buckminster Fuller. For now it's enough to point out that within the next couple of decades if we're to survive we must learn that competition as known in the past will have to be replaced by cooperation, so we can make decent use of our time, energy and resources.

YOU DON'T HAVE TO CHANGE HUMAN NATURE

Many believe competition is fundamental to the human condition. Apparently, though, that's not true. Recent research on strategies for winning games has shown that in any human society in which people have ongoing relationships, cooperation is the best strategy. Robert Axelrod documents this conclusion in *The Evolution of Cooperation*, which convincingly argues that we all function best in situations that encourage us to work together. And in her book *Surviving: The Best Game on Earth* author Norie Huddle takes up this theme through interviews with many whose ideas explore the implications of a fully cooperative society.

We're so indoctrinated with the competitive mentality of corporate America, we've lost sight of the fact that even in corporations cooperation is a good deal more effective than competition. That makes it one of the most important skills to learn in school.

COOPERATION IS ALWAYS BETTER THAN COMPETITION IN SCHOOLS

Even if competition might be necessary for your survival in a famine, it is usually out of place in school. This is particularly true of highly competitive and selective private schools. It may be legitimate to make the entrance requirements tough to meet, but once the students have been accepted, pitting them against each other decreases their ability to function well.

Every study yet done demonstrates that cooperative settings for learning are more effective than competitive ones. This perhaps startling finding was made by David and Roger Johnson, and announced in a paper called "The Internal Dynamics of Cooperative Learning Groups," published in 1985 in *Learning to Cooperate, Cooperating to Learn* by R. Slavin and others.

The Johnson brothers did a number of experiments in classroom situations. They then reviewed the scientific literature on the subject and found their own observations confirmed. Cooperation was nearly always significantly more effective in learning situations than competition, though in a few cases the results were about the same. But *not one single study* revealed an instance in which competition produced better academic results than cooperation.

In their examination of what good classrooms should be, the Johnson brothers describe an educational system in line with the highest ideals of democracy. Such a system teaches democratic concepts and produces respect for others, a determination to help them do their best, and a sense of fairness.

The implications of this paper are so significant I would like to quote from its conclusion, which offers some principles that have practical application both to schools and learning environments in the home.

> From our research on the processes that mediate or moderate the relationship between cooperative learning experiences and (1) productivity and (2) interpersonal attraction among students, a number of conclusions may be drawn. Although the type of learning task may not matter a great deal, the processes that promote higher achievement and liking among students may include the promotion of high-quality reasoning strategies, the constructive management of conflict over ideas and conclusions, increased time on task, more elaborate information-processing, greater peer regulation and encouragement of efforts to achieve, more active mutual involvement in learning, beneficial interaction between students of different achievement levels, feelings of psychological support and acceptance, more positive attitudes toward subject areas, and greater perceptions of fairness of grading.

The Johnsons drew a number of implications from their work, which I've summarized as follows:

1. All academic tasks lend themselves to being taught cooperatively. But the more complex and intellectual the task, the more effectively it can be taught using cooperative teaching processes.

2. Cooperative groups should be so structured that it's easy for group members to air controversy. Respect for differing opinions should be encouraged, and any conflict of point of view handled constructively, so all members of the group can learn from the resolution.

3. Groups should be so led that, while the learning task is consistently adhered to, there's also plenty of chance to practice thinking with the concepts being studied, and thus to continue developing a better understanding of them.

4. Students should be encouraged to work supportively, always giving each other good feedback, keeping each other on task and ensuring that all group members participate fully.

5. Heterogeneous grouping is desirable. In general, students of different ability levels learn better from each other than if all are at about the same level.

6. The classroom atmosphere should be consistently positive, supporting positive relationships and feelings of acceptance among the students.

7. As students' good experiences encourage positive involvement with challenging subjects, they should be encouraged to take the next step, exploring each subject at higher and more difficult levels.

8. Working together to achieve a result is not cheating. This is something students need to have pointed out to them frequently.

THE EFFECTS OF COMPETITION ON CHILDREN

A highly stressed, competitive environment tends to make Jack a dull boy. He may be bright, but he tends to play to older people, and he's probably not much good at pleasing himself or making friends his own age. Because he doesn't enjoy what he's doing, he's susceptible to burnout. Or he may, in self-defense, turn his instinctive enjoyment of the leisurely growing-up process into a series of obnoxious conquests.

If we allow young people to mature at their own rate they'll generally do better than if we compare them to others. Obliging them to compete, we risk turning them into stressed, bored and irritating overachievers, or else into self-doubters burdened with too many unfavorable comparisons.

Interestingly enough, this observation has been borne out in what must be one of the most competitive environments in the world: the Olympics. Those young champion athletes who compete most successfully when they need to are not particularly oriented toward competition, except with their own previous performance. They are, by upbringing, people who can be clearly focused on doing their best in their own way, without necessarily agonizing over how someone else might do against them. Regardless of their national origin one thing they often — and unexpectedly — turn out to have in common is parents who tend to be supportive and flexible, not hard-driving and domineering.

FOSTERING CHILDHOOD BURNOUT

Today many parents, worried about whether or not their children will eventually get into prestigious universities, put them in competitive situations almost from birth. These environments are virtually guaranteed to decrease their ability to learn effectively.

Beginning with day care centers as selective, and therefore competitive, as possible, these parents push their children through private schools, drive them around to little league events in which there is often an overemphasis on pressure, and in general set them up for a life of unhappiness because of too little enjoyment of success, satisfaction, love, self-reliance, self-esteem, and power. It's their mistaken belief that if their children don't get a taste of the school of hard knocks early enough they may be forced to beg in the streets by the time they are adults. Pressure of this kind drives some children, never given enough chance to find out who they are or what they want to do with their lives, to prefer the very alternative their parents tried to protect them from.

Parents intent on preparing their children for the 'real world' could instead be allowing their offspring to experience life as it really is by attending the neighborhood school and getting to know many different types of people. Then, in the home, they can make up for any shortcomings of the school by building an intellectually interesting, stimulating and challenging environment. The exercises in Part Three should help make this possible.

LEARNING TO TRUST CHILDREN

Children, particularly when they are very young, often understand better than adults how to establish a cooperative, nurturing environment. If we observe them and allow them to instruct us, we can learn something about how the events in life can flow comfortably and naturally one into the other. Collaborating with children and providing resources for them is appropriate. Dictating their every action is not.

Some children, though, pick up competitive behavior at a very early age. It may be their early learning experiences have made them afraid they won't succeed or get what they need to survive. If there's evidence of too much pressure, discuss the matter with the child by pointing out the advantages of sharing and working cooperatively. Over time you should be able to teach more gentle behavior, provided you don't create tension or worry around this issue.

SOMETIMES IT'S TIME FOR TIME OUT

Doing what comes naturally involves periods of rapid growth and other periods of lassitude. I have known high school graduates to sit around for a year or two doing essentially nothing and then suddenly demonstrate the ability to get a large amount of skilled work done in a short time. The person who has a chance to drift for a while eventually feels the urge to become directed. This need to drift can occur at almost any time, and is often the result of having accumulated a great deal of information and/or experience and needing to allow time to put it all together.

WHAT THEY REALLY WANT

Allowing children to find their own way is not the same as abandoning them to their whims, though some children function well enough on their own. Rather, it means keeping open communication about what makes sense to the child and what makes sense only to the people who are trying to tell the child what to do.

I have spent a lot of time talking to young people, asking them what they really want from adults. The gist of what I've learned is they want to be treated like fully functioning human beings who can think for themselves and have some idea what is good for them. All the young people I've talked with were concerned that adults seldom treat them with respect.

One particular group made the following relevant points:

1. Adults should support us, but give us more freedom and trust us to use it responsibly.

2. They should stop trying to prevent us from seeing things the way they really are.

3. They should stop looking at the past and start looking at the future. (They feel adults too often make comments beginning with "When I was your age," rather than saying, "Perhaps things will be different in the future from the way they were when I grew up.")

4. We want to be treated like human beings, and we almost never feel as if we are being treated that way.

5. Why can't we just be friends?

6. Why can't the adults provide us with more structure and security in life? (By this they don't mean telling them what to do, they mean providing them with a social structure that makes sense and gives them a reasonable expectation of living out a normal life span. A great many of them — perhaps as many as fifty percent — expect their world will be destroyed by nuclear holocaust.)

As you can see, there's a lot of desire being expressed for a more cooperative relationship between age groups. These particular young people wanted life in the future to be exciting, stress-free, more enjoyable, with more rewards, fewer hazardous waste products, and less reason to be afraid of dying at an early age. It seems to me that these are reasonable requests. They certainly make sense in the light of Integrative Learning theory.

WHAT DO THE YOUNG FEEL WE SHOULD TEACH THEM?

I wanted to know, though, whether these young people felt it was wise to impose any restrictions or limitations on the young or give them any particular sort of guidance. What advice, I asked, would they give their children, assuming they maintained their present view of life once they became parents? Here again, once a solid sense of one's own being is established, cooperation and respect turn out to be important themes:

1. You should do what you feel is right and thus learn to trust your intuition.
2. You should listen more than you talk.
3. You should learn to think about what you hear and what you plan to do.
4. You should have confidence in yourself.
5. You should learn to relax.
6. You should learn to respect each other's abilities.
7. You should learn to find the wisdom in yourself — you don't have to be old to be wise.
8. You should learn to know how rough society really is.
9. You should temper your intuition with rational judgment.
10. You should learn mutual respect with all human beings.
11. You should go after what you want.
12. You should think positively.
13. You should learn to look at a situation from every point of view.

I can't guarantee these views are representative of what young people want, because they are the result of an interview with a small group of young people. Still, I had not met them before, and was not imposing my ideas on their thinking.

Perhaps you'd like to try interviewing some young people yourself, to see if you get different answers from these. Then read them these answers and see what they think of them. When you've got what you believe is a good list, you may find you are already doing everything on it. Check this out with the young people in your life and see what they think.

HOW WOULD YOU LIKE TO BE A YOUNG GOAT?

My fifth grade teacher always objected to the term "kids." She would screw up her face whenever it was used and say, "Do you mean young goats?"

Ever since, I've wondered about the dignity of that term; and whenever I get a chance I ask young people how they feel about being called "kids." Most say they don't like it, although usually they haven't thought about the matter much. Some feel it distances them from the person using the term.

By now I've become allergic to the expression. It's similar to my reaction when I hear a bank manager say, "I'll have a girl type out these papers and get them to you." I don't think an adult secretary is a "girl," and I don't think a young person is a "kid." Consistent use of such expressions not only belittles the people they refer to; it also reinforces that diminished image in our own minds.

ON THE ETHICS OF YOUNG PEOPLE I'VE KNOWN

Generally I find that young people tend to behave about as responsibly as they're expected to. In a milieu in which they are regarded as irresponsible, it's sometimes difficult to find evidence they aren't. But that's only a self-fulfilling prophecy at work. When they're consistently trusted and given responsibility, they often live up to it beautifully.

Although there's a widely accepted belief the ethical sense develops only in stages as we grow older, I've observed that little children can have a remarkably mature moral sense. I think a higher moral sense has something to do with caring about people you have never met and never could meet — people who may be starving on the other side of the globe, for example. I remember one of my daughters, when she could barely talk, offering the following comment about herself: "I love everybody in the whole world — even the people I don't know." Throughout her life she always behaved as if she had already achieved the highest level on the scale of ethical development. So I'm not convinced ethical stages develop sequentially, provided children have the opportunity to be around people who understand and respect their ability to think and act at a high level of responsibility.

What I think may be happening in some cases is that a child perceives something which appears morally wrong and tries to get the parents to acknowledge that it is indeed so. A cousin of mine, for example, happened upon some anti-vivisectionist literature at an early age. He was easily convinced it is a bad thing to perform needless scientific experiments on animals and thereby cause wanton suffering. When he tried to persuade his parents of this, they quickly reduced him to tears and sent him to bed without any dinner, proclaiming he was being obnoxious. Perhaps he was obnoxious on that occasion. But he was also trying to assert what he felt to be a moral truth, and people who are doing that often do it obnoxiously.

Thus, children may attempt to operate at a high moral level, only to be forced out of it by adults who, because they happen to disagree (or perhaps don't like to be instructed by children), make them feel powerless to assert any moral values whatsoever. Then, perhaps, in a state of emotional withdrawal, they make their peace with the world by retreating to the lowest level of ethical awareness and working gradually up from there.

So if we learn to treat children with respect and cooperation rather than demeaning them and imposing irrational authority upon them, perhaps we'll see higher levels of ethical and moral insight emerging earlier in life than might otherwise be the case.

RESPONDING TO EMERGENCY

A friend recently told me about a period in her life when she was so sick she had to remain in bed most of the time, despite the fact that she lived alone with a seven year old and could not afford to hire any help. "My son rose to the occasion unbelievably well. He made breakfast for me in the morning, got himself to school, kept the house clean, and did everything else I could not. He'd never shown any signs before that he could behave so responsibly, but when I really needed help he came through for me."

Such stories of young people behaving responsibly in emergencies are actually quite common in poor families. If there are no adults around, the oldest child assumes the role and takes care of the others.

It's pretty clear that if we don't see young people behaving responsibly it is often because we've set things up so they're almost never in a position to. Of course, if we do trust them, it's possible they'll still be irresponsible and make mistakes. But why not give them credit for the ability to correct these, and thus learn to do better in the future?

Cooperation and responsibility go together, since the basis of cooperation is responsibility to other members of the group. At the Thornton Friends School students learned to be so cooperative that when one student chose to demonstrate the competitiveness of most people with an in-class experiment, it failed because everyone cooperated, contrary to the expectations on which the experiment was based.

Not only did these students cooperate in school, they often took their cooperative behavior outside of school — to job situations or other schools. Many of them became quite skilled at subtly maneuvering a group toward more cooperative behavior.

WORKING TOGETHER IN AN ATMOSPHERE OF TRUST

When people of any age are gathered together to work on a project that has real meaning for them, they'll do it better if their thinking is trusted and relied upon. If they are not trusted, they will usually develop contempt for the task and do it sloppily.

Schools should be places where one can learn by working with others at something important. Families can function this way too. If you can't change your school, perhaps you can make your family one in which each person earns respect and self-esteem by doing what comes naturally.

I once knew a family of eight in which the father and mother were both highly respected professionals. They worked so well together they organized their own opera company, and everyone had a major role. (All were fine performers.) When I visited them for a week, I noticed that without any apparent planning, everything necessary happened right on schedule. Shopping, preparing the food and cleaning up went like clockwork, with no visible assignment of jobs or apparent planning who would do what, though I'm sure there must have been some kind of planning. The expectation in this family seemed to be that everyone would contribute a little extra.

A family that learns to cooperate to this degree has a lot of creative energy available to make their projects interesting and productive. The same is true of larger groups. Cooperation is one of the most enjoyable experiences we can have, provided it is perceived as voluntary and desirable. It assumes all members of the group respect each other and are bonded together to help serve each other's needs as well as their own. That is how things should go in the world at large.

PART THREE

FALLING IN LOVE WITH LEARNING

We come now to a collection of activities intended to inspire you to collaborate with your children or students in searching for the nuggets of everyday genius still hidden in your family or classroom treasure chest. Integrative Learning is much more than a way of feeling better about yourself: it's a chance to discover deep reserves of intelligence you might otherwise never use.

In describing these activities, I've put them in the context of learning situations I've experienced. This allows me to develop the theory a bit further.

These exercises are not meant to be done in a vacuum — they're supposed to help you gain increasing knowledge of the theory and philosophy of Integrative Learning by directly experiencing some of its processes.

They are not meant to be done in a particular order. (Many readers have enjoyed starting with "That's A Likely Story," in Chapter Twenty-three.) Nor are my directions to be slavishly followed. Think of better ones if you can.

If after trying a particular exercise you don't think it helpful, you have two choices — dismiss it as inappropriate for your educational needs and go on to something else, or decide that your difficulty may be caused by your inexperience with such an exercise and hang in there till you get something out of it.

For parents or teachers who wish to go beyond the activities given here, let me quickly sketch out a plan for designing Integrative Learning experiences. Chapter Twenty-four explains how to use mind-mapping, an innovative approach to organizing the material you want to teach or to learn. Mind-mapping will not only help you determine the core concepts that give the material its structure; it will also provide you with a new way of organizing information, so you can prepare to present it more clearly.

Once you've organized the material in this way, you want to do two basic things: (1) put it in a form that appeals to the imagination, and (2) file it away in the long-term memory. To accomplish these two goals, develop and explain the essential points in the material in the form of a story or dialogue which you can then read aloud with a background of concert music. Afterwards (at least a day later) develop activities around these central points, using exercises and questions like the ones in the following chapters.

When you construct your own exercises, look for suggestions for making them more enjoyable. In any learning experience, teacher and learner can collaborate in exploring new possibilities.

One test that should be applied to exercises is whether they can elicit a variety of interesting responses, all different. You want to get students away from trying to guess what the teacher or parent is thinking, so they're encouraged to do their own thinking. The best exercises will be simple and open-ended, equally interesting to beginners and more advanced students.

12

I NEVER HEARD A WORD YOU SAID

Most people never get listened to adequately. Those who
do, get better at thinking.

"My parents never listen to me," the teenage girl complained, in
words and tone I'd heard a thousand times before. Sometimes it seems as if
no one's parents know how to listen. Is this the fulfillment of the crusty old
saying that children should be seen and not heard?

"Alice never listens to us," her mother had said to me on the phone
earlier. Both mother and daughter needed to sound off about the constant
misunderstandings that resulted from their not listening to each other. Both
felt defeated and rather helpless. It seemed neither could sit still long
enough to find out what the other thought, because they were both starving
to be listened to themselves.

WE'RE ALL STARVED FOR ATTENTION

That's how it is with most people. We so seldom listen to each other
and are so starved for attention that it becomes progressively harder to listen
to anyone else. We are beaten up with inattention and strike back at
everyone else in the same way. Almost nobody gets listened to enough.
You can go through your whole life without ever being listened to for even
five straight minutes.

BREAKING THE CYCLE

Not being heard is one of the most frustrating experiences there is. But no one seems willing to break the cycle of mutual frustration by unilaterally offering an attentive ear. When is the last time you did? Have you noticed how thirty seconds into a conversation, right in the middle of a good story, you feel compelled to say, "Yes, that reminds me of the time I . . ."

Then there's the urgent compulsion to offer advice, or to blurt out such sympathetic nuggets as, "Boy, that's a fantastic idea! You ought to try it," or, "Gee, that's the worst thing I ever heard, I can't see how you put up with it." We seem to think our poor friends will wither and die without immediate feedback. It never occurs to us that these constant interruptions are a form of vandalism far more serious than smashing windows. Windows can be replaced. Original thoughts, once interrupted, may disappear forever.

AN EXERCISE FOR GETTING LISTENED TO

The remarkable thing is that getting listened to is so easy to arrange for yourself. All you need do is make a deal with someone: "I'll listen to you for x minutes if you listen to me back for another x minutes." It's the old barter system, and we can use it whenever we want.

We call this process a Think-and-Listen. The rules for conducting a Think-and-Listen are: The listener gives non-verbal support by looking into the eyes of the speaker. You can smile when the speaker is happy, look serious when the speaker is serious and nod responsively when you feel like it. Just DON'T TALK.

The speaker, on the other hand, doesn't have to look at the listener. When we're thinking, our eyes need to travel about. The speaker need not necessarily speak. Crying, laughing and other forms of emotional expression are to be encouraged, because they facilitate the thought process.

LIMITLESS OPPORTUNITIES FOR PRACTICE

The other day I went for a two hour walk with a friend. The weather was nice and the neighborhood lovely. I got to listen while she talked through a personal problem about which I really had no advice to offer. At the end she felt better, and seemed to know what to do. Then it was my turn, and I had the same experience. We'd both gotten about a hundred dollars worth of free therapy. I'm hoping the IRS doesn't find out.

With practice at Think-and-Listens you can begin to adapt them to specific situations. Sometimes you can be very informal and just listen while another person talks. Your friend won't even know a Think-and-Listen is happening. At other times you might want to have a specific topic.

"I'll listen to you think through your day if you listen to me think through mine," you might say.

Think-and-Listens can be particularly handy during a fight. Make sure each combatant gets so many minutes without interruption before the other person gets a turn. The fight will then work its way toward a solution more efficiently because the main thing that keeps people from resolving their differences is that neither really gets a chance to hear what the other is saying.

The amount of time you choose may vary. Beginners might have trouble with more than three minutes. Old hands like me and my friend often do an hour each way.

Once you've gotten good at not interrupting, you might want to take a more active role and offer reflecting ideas or ask clarifying questions once in a while. For example, if you've spent a long time telling me how you feel about your grandmother, it might eventually be appropriate to say, "Looking at it from the outside, it seems as if maybe your grandmother just needs a show of affection once in a while." Or I might ask, "Do you think there could be something your grandmother wants but is afraid to ask for?"

IT MIGHT TAKE A LITTLE GETTING USED TO

Introducing Think-and-Listens to the uninitiated is usually easy. Most people will agree that they haven't been listened to uninterruptedly for five minutes in their whole life. But they're also likely to say they find it difficult to keep still for such an enormously long time while another person talks — or to talk that long without any feedback. For some it's almost like being on a tight rope for five minutes. They're desperate. They want someone to say, "It's okay for you to say that. You're keeping me entertained. You're not really a fool at all, even though you may feel like one babbling on like that." Not getting reassuring comments in response, they're sure they're going to die of embarrassment.

Whenever I hear about the embarrassment people feel at not being interrupted, I say, "Yes, it is awfully hard the first time, isn't it? But a little practice can make a big difference. Do you think it might be worth the trouble to get the value of being listened to and finding out what you're really thinking?" Most people agree it's worth the effort.

Everyone needs a chance now and then to think uninterruptedly. Raw thinking is sensitive and easily sidetracked. It may come out jerkily or tumble forth like a waterfall. It may contain rotten ideas not yet hammered into good ones. Or seemingly good ideas that will later turn out to be misguided. That is why the listener should just listen and let the speaker work everything out independently. Given enough time, any of us can figure most things out for ourselves, provided we have the information we need.

YOU CAN GO INTO BUSINESS — JUST LIKE LUCY

Let me offer you a carrot along with the stick to get you to tough it out and actually listen to someone. The carrot is the chance to go into business for yourself. Remember Lucy's little sign, "The Doctor Is In — 5 cents"? Well, you can put up a similar sign of your own so people come to you and say, "I have a problem." Your reply is, "Sit down and tell me about it." They then describe their problem in detail while you do nothing more than listen. After a while they say, "Thank you very much, you've been a wonderful help. I know exactly what to do now." .

I can't tell you how many times I've done exactly that. I have a terrific reputation for giving good advice — but it's usually given with my ears. When, occasionally, I slip up and offer a person some actual advice, it's usually well received, but later I'm likely to find out how terrible it was. So if you can restrain yourself from that ego-satisfying tendency to want to feel superior by giving advice, you can be just as wise as I am whenever I can restrain myself, and you'll enjoy the same fine reputation for helping people with their problems. You might even make a nickel doing it.

A word of caution, though: it's extremely important that the subject of a Think-and-Listen be kept confidential, and that nothing said by either party be revealed or referred to again by the other, unless permission to do so has been explicit. The breaking of confidences uttered during Think-and-Listens can destroy friendships and cause discomfort to those who may have said difficult and perhaps painful things in the belief that their confidentiality would be respected.

USE THEM ON THE JOB AND IN THE MARRIAGE

Think-and-Listens are wonderful tools to use at home or on the job. When you get stuck on something, just look up a friend and say, "I need some time." You then set your watch for an agreed-on amount and talk until the time is up. More often than not, you'll find you've worked out your problem. The other person can take the same amount of time either then or later.

If there's no one to listen in the immediate vicinity, Ma Bell won't mind your using the phone. Every so often I get a very expensive long distance call from someone who just wants me to sit there and listen to them cry for five or ten minutes. A couple of friends of mine do this back and forth across the Atlantic Ocean to the tune of $600 a month. Still, it's cheaper than psychiatry.

Next time your spouse or your child has a problem, try saying, "Sit down and tell me about it. Let's take ten minutes each way." Then follow the rules of the Think-and-Listen. You'll soon discover quite a difference in the way people in your family communicate after you've tried this a few times.

And whenever there's a serious conflict between you and a family member, allot five minutes each way and keep taking turns until the problem has been resolved. It could be all day before you're finished, but it's the quickest and most efficient route to a solution I know.

THIS IS POWERFUL STUFF

The power of being listened to is almost unfathomable. Over and over I've seen it increase my students' effective intelligence. After all, how can we learn to think if we don't practice? And what better way to practice thinking than by having someone listen to us while we do so? Do you imagine you would have learned to walk if you'd had someone hanging onto your elbow all the time? Suppose when you first learned to talk every third word had been corrected or modified by an older person. So how can you learn to think if someone else is forever trying to improve on your first raw, unformulated expressions of ideas?

LET'S USE THIS TO INCREASE THE INTELLIGENCE OF OUR SPECIES

Our tendency to interrupt is another reason why stupidity seems so widespread in our incredibly intelligent species. Our specialty, after all, is thinking, but few of us are allowed to think in any responsible, independent way. How well do you think birds would do if they couldn't fly unless another bird were holding them up or otherwise correcting or interfering with their flying? Or suppose horses had to ask permission every time they wanted to gallop, only to find out that for the most part their galloping wasn't good enough. Would you want a dog defending your house that had to check in with all the other dogs in the neighborhood before barking? Why should every other species be so immensely more confident at exercising its specialty than we are?

HERE'S MY PERSONAL GUARANTEE

This, of course, would not be true if we had a social convention of listening to each other think through every idea. That social convention alone would turn most of us into geniuses. I challenge you. If you think I'm exaggerating, try doing Think-and-Listens on a regular basis for a year and see what happens to your thinking. I guarantee this will clear up a whole batch of your problems.

Take a moment now to think about your own experience. Were you listened to enough while you were growing up? Are you listened to enough now? How does it feel to really listen to others? Do you think you could grow to enjoy it more? Does it make you uncomfortable to think that really helping people might be all that easy?

THE BOY WHO FINALLY GOT LISTENED TO AND HOW HE GREW

My student Fred was almost unendurable. He never paid attention in class, never did his homework, seemed totally uncreative and was just plain obnoxious. Then one night we had a parents' meeting which his father attended. During the evening we had everyone do Think-and-Listens. Afterwards, the father said to me, "You know, all these years I've never listened to Fred without interrupting him. I'll have to do something about that."

The next week Fred told me he wanted to write a mystery story, and he wanted my help. This was a mystery in itself. I'd never seen him write more than a paragraph before, and never an interesting one. But that day he brought with him three pages he'd already written. So I listened to him while he developed the story further in his mind. A few days later it was complete. He'd written over twenty-five pages. I wish I had a copy of that story. I'd publish it in this book and dedicate it to all fathers who finally get around to listening to their sons for the first time.

13

I'M GLAD YOU WERE BORN, BECAUSE . . .

*When we hear good things about ourselves, we get
smarter. When we tell other people good things about
themselves, that also makes us smarter.*

Albert was one of the most self-defeating young men I'd ever met. He was enrolled in Thornton Friends School too late in the first term to receive a grade for that term, and was expelled before the end of the second term. So he never received a grade for anything, which was probably just as well, because he never did any work. The day after he was expelled, his father called and thanked me for expelling him. This didn't prevent my feeling guilty that the parents paid a year's tuition for only a few months of their son's inactivity and wasted time.

I don't feel guilty anymore, though. Four years later I received another call from the father: "I really wish you could come to my son's graduation from high school," he said. "He has turned out to be one of the best students in the history of his school. He's done outstanding work with literature and wants to go on to a career as an English professor."

Naturally I wondered what might have happened to contribute to this miraculous transformation.

"You told him he could do it," said the father. "The important thing is, he believed you. After you threw him out, he decided to get busy and apply himself. It worked. It really worked."

THE TRILLION DOLLAR RIP-OFF

But why should this obviously talented young man have had to wait until he was in ninth grade to hear any teacher say to him "You can do it"? And why should millions of others like him never hear that at all?

This story isn't unique. I frequently hear from parents that no one told their son or daughter they were any good until I came along. Sometimes I feel like an army of one to clean up the messes of hoards of insensitive teachers lined up in the backgrounds of my students.

But why are they so insensitive? Why isn't everyone doing this? Because we're trained not to believe in ourselves, or in each other either. Experience with the massive amounts of criticism we're likely to get while growing up trains us to believe the only way to make someone better is to criticize them. I sometimes wonder what that particular bit of cultural insanity is costing this nation every year in lost brain power and productivity. I'm sure it's at least in the trillions of dollars. Maybe it's time for a change.

HOW REBECCA WAS KIND TO HERSELF

At graduation the first year of our school a parent thanked me for helping to contribute to a turnaround in her daughter's attitude. "Things like this don't happen," she said. "But it happened." An important part of that turnaround had gone like this: One time I heard Rebecca saying something nasty about herself, and I jumped on her for it. "You can criticize me all you like, Rebecca," I said. "But don't ever let me hear you criticize yourself again. You're too good for that."

NO MORE ACTING FOR GILDA

On the other hand, I remember the time when Gilda, the daughter of a friend, attended one of my acting workshops. She came home bursting with excitement about the new possibilities she saw in acting. Her father and I were talking together at the time, so I saw everything that happened. Gilda made the mistake of sharing her enthusiasm with her father, who responded with a flood of criticism. Pretty soon she just left, her shoulders slumped and her chin hanging down — and that was it for acting so far as she was concerned.

SUCCESS IS SUCH A LITTLE THING TO ASK FOR

It's really not hard to tell someone they can do well. You have to mean it, of course — you have to believe in the person. But all of us were born with the ability to be outstanding successes, and the only thing it really takes is the right kind of encouragement. Stuff your children with praise for their successes and let life itself handle the criticism for the failures. We're so busy protecting our children from the school of hard knocks that we end up being the school of hard knocks ourselves, just to give them practice. That isn't fair. They're smart enough to work it out for themselves, even if we weren't. A friend who is a professional writer tells how he took a test designed to help him select a career, and the one thing he was advised not to do was become a writer. But he went ahead and did it anyway, and he's a great success at it. So let your children decide for themselves what their limitations are and don't invent limitations for them out of your own disappointments in life, which should have nothing to do with them.

EXERCISE — TURN IT AROUND

Next time you complain or hear anyone else complaining in your house, stop the complaint and make a deal. For every complaint it will be necessary to say something positive to counter it. Anyone who fails to do this will pay a fine — one cent, one dollar, a thousand dollars — whatever is appropriate. (You can put the money away towards a vacation.)

After that's been working for a while, go to the next step. Declare a No Complaints Day. Do this once a month. Anyone who complains at all during that day pays the fine. (It's always possible to convey the information contained in a complaint in some positive and supportive way.)

The No Complaints Day once a month can increase to twice a month after three or four successes. Gradually increase the No Complaints Days until there are only a few carefully chosen times during the month when complaining may occur at all.

Don't get me wrong. It's important to complain sometimes, or we'll become uncritical and put up with things we shouldn't tolerate. But complaining can't do anyone any good unless it is done responsibly. In our school we usually found it was necessary to set aside a day or two about the middle of the year when all the students could complain about the school all day long. After a few hours of getting the complaints off their chests, they would start to think more positively and initiate solutions to the problems they were complaining about. So finding a time and place for responsible complaining is a first step.

THE PUT-UP GAME

The art of putting each other down fuels our cartoon industry, our stand up comics, our political system and light hearted fun at teen-age gatherings and cocktail parties. Indeed, put-downs are sometimes seen as expressions of affection, and in some families they are a staple of conversation.

But no matter how much you may laugh when teased about your kinky hair, the bald spot in the middle of your nose, your tendency to set the fashion by wearing cast off clothing, etc., your own subconscious doesn't think it's funny. The subconscious, having no sense of humor, can't really tell the difference between a friendly jibe and an attack, and tends to record all put-downs as information to be acted on. So this habit of self-denigration ("I can't draw") tends to bring about the very qualities we're half-humorously describing.

The habit of putting down ourselves and others is so deeply ingrained socially, we need to learn how to reverse the process. Take it from me as an ex-put-down artist of the first water, the spring of jocularity will not run dry if you start being nice to people as a matter of course. There's plenty to laugh about without subtly trying to make your friends feel a little worse about themselves.

The Put-up Game is a happy way of breaking the habit. It is fun and easy to play, and especially useful in families with addictions to putting each other down. The game is played by means of little skits. For example, two people can pretend that one of them has knocked the other down accidentally. In the first version of the skit the two characters put each other down in the same creative way they are used to doing around the house. In the second version they say only nice things to each other.

As is the case with any addiction, you may experience withdrawal symptoms while learning not to put each other down. Parents may worry that if they don't remind their children continuously of their faults, the children will never be able to discover them themselves. Brothers and sisters may fear endless transgressions from each other. It may be hard while you're learning to be nice to each other. But if you all hang in there, the results will be worth the effort.

THE TRIUMPH OF THE BIRTHDAY CIRCLE

In our school we invented a wonderful way to make sure all the students got a chance to find out how good they are. The only thing that surprises me about this technique is that it wasn't invented centuries ago and hasn't become standard fare at children's parties. It's called a birthday circle.

What you do is sit the birthday person in the center of a circle of people, each of whom then tells the one in the center, "I'm glad you were born because . . ." and finishes the statement with their favorite thing about that person. No one is allowed to qualify the statement with comments like, "When I first met you I thought you were a freak, but now I realize you're really okay." Or by putting themselves down: "I wish I could paint Chinese dragons half as well as you can." Furthermore, the compliment must be sincere and believable to the person who hears it. It's not the time for meaningless flattery. And the birthday person has to drink it all in without saying anything.

TEENAGERS CAN BE PEOPLE TOO

If you could see a group of thirty or so teenagers go through this process, your belief in the future of the world would flourish. Far from the sarcasm and emotional defensiveness that often characterizes this age group, you would hear sincere and wise comments being shared by everyone. Affection, hugging and even crying are the rule in birthday circles. The fact is that teenagers are often silly, obnoxious and rebellious because our culture expects them to be that way, and teaches them how. Sometimes these expectations are really outrageous. Two of our students were almost killed in an automobile accident that was not their fault. Neither ever used drugs. As she was coming back to consciousness and having broken glass pulled rather carelessly out of her skin, one of the girls heard the nurse saying, "This ought to teach you to drive around under the influence."

So try it out next time you throw a birthday party. Make it the climax of the whole thing. Sit everyone down and give them a little lecture on how to do it. Tell them how much fun it's going to be.

HOW TO LIVEN UP SOMEONE ELSE'S PARTY

And don't stint your adult friends either. When I go to a party in honor of someone, I usually suggest a birthday circle, with excellent results. What if when Dagwood retires after umpteen years in the same office the boss, instead of giving him a gold watch (or in addition to it) has everyone in the office sit on the floor in a circle and tell Dagwood how they've loved his sandwiches over the years? If you think people won't go for it, you're wrong. Everyone is looking for an excuse to give and receive praise. It's a rare thing for me to stage a birthday circle and not see at least a couple of people crying as they say to each other what they've always wanted to but never felt safe enough to say before.

GIVE US HALF A CHANCE, AND WE'LL ALL LOVE EACH OTHER

Safety is the key here. Human beings naturally love each other when they aren't feeling something negative that is caused by unfortunate circumstances. We need to express that love, and this is an excellent way to begin the habit of doing it. The birthday circle is every bit as important to the person giving the praise as the one receiving it — we need to get off our chests how much we love, admire and respect other people.

ASSESS YOURSELF ON THE RECEIVING END OF PRAISE

Think about how it feels to you to get praise instead of criticism. Do you feel guilty? Do you believe there's something terrible about thinking well of yourself? Do you think the person praising you is only trying to manipulate you? Do you wish it would happen more often? Do you think if you got praise enough for what you do well you might get a whole lot better at it? Are you stoic and unaffected by such things? Is that the best way to be? Is that the way everyone is?

"GOD ISN'T HAPPY IF I'M HAPPY"

Some years ago a woman I knew was suffering from bouts of terror and wondered what was causing it. We talked for hours about the problem before we stumbled onto a major clue. It seemed that my friend was about to take on a new challenge in life and believed she was wrong to do this.

"My parents taught me that if I wanted to serve God I should go off to China and become a missionary," she said. "I never wanted to be a missionary. What I want to do is open a new study center in theoretical physics. I feel guilty about that, because it's something I enjoy doing."

"I really can't speak for God," I said, "but if I were God I'd arrange things so people really wanted to do what I wanted them to do. Do you believe that God doesn't want you to help people understand the secrets of the universe, and does want you to traipse to some other part of the world and do what you can't stand doing?"

Of course, my friend's parents had probably never even told her she ought to be a missionary. But somehow she had gotten the idea that if there was something she wanted to do — that made her feel good about herself, that gave her respect in the community, and particularly the respect of the people she worked with — then it was wrong. It was wrong simply because she enjoyed doing it.

Once my friend saw what she was doing to herself, she felt much better and began to make new plans based on what she really wanted to do and could do best. In the process, though, it was necessary for her to admit that she is a fine and indeed remarkable person. I think she had trouble doing this because she had had to grow up without hearing positive things about herself from anyone else. Obviously, her parents would have made a big difference in her life if they had said from time to time, "Louise, you're a wonderful girl, and we're really proud of you." As it was, if either of them ever said this, or the equivalent, she did not hear it. Birthday Circles once a year would have gone a long way to correct this situation and might have made a tremendous difference for the better in her life.

GRADUATION DAY — WITH A DIFFERENCE

Let me tell you about what graduations from the Thornton Friends School used to be like. I have to preface this by saying that our graduation classes were never larger than fifteen, so if in a large institution you were going to try something like what I'm about to describe, you'd have to break the class into smaller groups. Perhaps this activity could become part of the pre-graduation exercises.

We're in a room lit with hundreds of candles. The seniors enter in two straight lines and take their places in seats in the audience. Then each senior in turn comes to the front row of benches and sits facing the audience. For a timed period, anyone who wishes can speak. This is when parents, friends and even sometimes strangers stand and say things like, "George, your Mom and I are so proud of you, and we'd just like you to know that." Or "Gosh, Bill, remember all those late nights when we sat up and talked about our problems? I'll never forget the time you helped me figure out what to do about my snake collection. You've really helped me this year, Bill." Or humorous ones like, "Reckon you're going to have to go out and buy a new motorcycle now, Amy. The guys in college aren't going to want rides on that antique you've got now." When the ceremony is over there's hardly a dry eye. "What a wonderful school," people are saying as they leave. "These young people really know how to love each other."

Loving each other isn't the only thing in life, but what's the use of the rest of it if we don't do that?

14

THE ANNOTATED LITTLE MISS MUFFET

*The most wonderful buried treasure is in each individual
human mind. When we learn to make connections and see
beneath the surface, we can dig up that treasure.*

In the previous two chapters we explored (1) how being listened to
allows you to practice thinking and (2) how believing in yourself results at
least partly from hearing that others have confidence in you.

Now we come to the nitty-gritty of becoming an expert — learning to
deal imaginatively, creatively and independently with the materials and
opportunities life offers you. In this chapter we will deal with reading —
but not the kind that merely echoes words. It's the kind the mind does
constantly, whether or not words are involved. It's the kind we were born
able to do, but may have learned not to do.

LEARNING TO READ FROM A TODDLER REQUIRES YOUR BEST THINKING

You can enjoy guiding your young child toward this kind of reading.
In the course of the resulting conversations, you may find you're learning
to think better yourself. You won't get that benefit, though, unless you pay
close attention to the child's unique way of observing and thinking.
Learning to converse and play imagination games with children is more
challenging and important than designing rockets that penetrate outer
space, or redesigning traffic flow patterns in a city. This is an exploration of
inner space, an opportunity to redesign your own thought-traffic patterns.

So when it's time for the bedtime story, approach your child with the same spirit of inquiry, expectancy and destiny with which the ancient Greeks approached the Delphic Oracle. Like the Oracle, your child may seem to be speaking nonsense or indecipherable riddles, but if you listen closely, you may find some powerful new possibilities surfacing in your thinking.

THINGS ONLY CHILDREN SEE

As children we perceive many things in our environment that differ from what the adults around us see. When we report these experiences, we sometimes receive blows to our intellect and creativity. As an example, read the first few pages of *The Little Prince*, where the child draws a picture of a boa constrictor that has swallowed an elephant, and the adults see it only as a hat.

We give up our special perceptions while we're growing up, and thus give up ourselves. The loss is in the mind's ability to play with experience enough to find streamers of meaning radiating from it. On one level this takes the form of **symbolizing**, which is a way of responding to the abstract meanings of things. On another, it's deep structuring, or filling in details normally omitted from awareness because they seem too obvious. Let's see how these might operate in a simple sentence.

DIGGING FOR GOLD IN SENTENCES

For example, suppose I say to you, "Give me my hat." This ordinarily straightforward request, if it occurred in a dream, might symbolize my desire to cover and protect myself in your presence. If so, it could suggest the scene in Shakespeare's *Antony and Cleopatra* when the queen, about to kill herself, begins with the words, "Give me my robe, put on my crown." She is dressing for her final assertion of dignity, preferring death to the disgrace of captivity.

Another way to explore a sentence is to draw out its implications, in order to reveal its deep structure. "Give me my hat" implies that there are two of us, that I do not have my hat at the moment, while you are presumed to have access to it, that I feel in a position to request or command you to give it to me, that I do not need to be polite enough to say "Please," and so on. In other words, every time we listen or speak, we simultaneously understand many implications so obvious we're scarcely aware of them. But if these implications were not clear, we would become confused, and lose the thread of communication.

Perhaps these two processes of symbolizing and deep structuring are what make our thinking specifically human. At any rate, they can always be improved. For the most part, we do well enough to get by, but tend to be really clear only in areas of common ground. When we have trouble understanding, it's likely to be because we miss the symbolic meaning, or are unclear about the deep structure. When the symbols and deep structures are sufficiently confused, we are led to conflict, divorce, riots and warfare. As long as my backyard is your evil empire, it's difficult to persuade you to come over for a barbecue.

THE CASE OF THE COMPLIANT BLACK SHEEP

Many years ago a mother came to me in distress. "My son has been accepted into the University," she said, "but only on condition that he pass a summer course designed to improve his study skills. He's never been a good student, and we can't understand why. The rest of our family are academic whizzes."

Sometimes the black sheep of the family is psychologically locked into the role of scapegoat. It's hard for that person to be successful until this stops. Richard, however, seemed to want to learn. He was nice enough and willing to work. It was just that he didn't seem very intelligent. His mother asked me to tutor him and see what I could do.

Richard's glistening eyes and winsome smile signaled his eagerness to please. He always waited until I told him what to do. His cheerful comments were noteworthy only for their vacuity, and to have to converse with him at length could be depressing. I soon realized that he couldn't understand what lay beneath the surface of experience. I wanted to see if I could help him observe with more depth and penetration.

So I showed him a picture of a boat in the middle of a calm and beautiful lake. "What do you see in this painting?" I asked.

"It's a boat!" he said eagerly, pleased I had asked a question he could answer.

"Anything else?"

"No, just a boat."

"Well, what's the boat in?"

"It's in the picture," he said, his smile growing larger.

Richard apparently couldn't distinguish between talking about the picture as an object and mentally entering it and exploring what was in it, a process we might call suspension of disbelief. At the movies, you pretend to believe what you're watching is real — or rather you don't tell yourself, "Those are just images on a screen; it's not really happening." You let yourself get involved.

Richard couldn't get involved in the picture. I wondered, in fact, if he'd ever gotten involved in anything. Maybe he'd once been hurt playing a game, and decided never to play again. Whatever his background, he was certainly not playing my game. In fact, he seemed to have forgotten how to play.

"Is there any water in the picture?" I asked.

"Yes."

"Then why didn't you mention it?"

"Everyone knows if there's a boat there has to be water."

"Not necessarily," I said. "The boat could be in your garage, or on top of your car."

"That's true," said Richard. "We have a canoe in our garage. We keep it there when we're not on a canoe trip."

"Right," I said. "But this boat is in water. Why didn't you tell me it's in water?"

"It's obvious," he said.

"Okay, what other obvious things do you see?"

"I see a boat."

"You already said that."

"Well once I've said it, it's obvious."

"Okay, but you also said this boat is floating on water."

"No, you said that," he replied.

"Okay. Well if you were going to guess what else I might say about the picture, what would it be?"

"That it's a picture," Richard said. "That's obvious too."

Although I felt exasperated, it seemed as if I might be on the trail of something. Richard must be playing his own private game: he couldn't really be this stupid. He seemed to want to leave it up to others to do his thinking for him. Why couldn't he just report his reactions?

I thought about what his life might have been like. What kind of educational experiences could have produced such behavior? Suppose that early in life he had been quite sensitive and reported his observations, only to be told he was wrong. He might come to believe that nothing he saw, thought or felt made sense — that he must concentrate on telling others what they evidently wanted to hear. Since he never examined his own thoughts, he would then have no basis for developing insight into how others perceived things. I would need to draw his attention to his own perceptions.

"Do you see any sky in the picture?" I asked.

"Yes," said Richard.

"Describe it to me."

"It's just sky."

"Well, is the sky red, or is it blue?"

"It's not either exactly, it's got splotches of different colors in it."

"Describe the splotches."

"They're just splotches."

"Oh come on," I said, "can't you see how this one looks a little like an elephant?"

"Yes," he said, somewhat amazed. "Now you mention it, it *does* look like an elephant."

"Richard," I said, "didn't you ever lie in bed when you were a child and make shapes out of the funny marks on the ceiling?"

"No."

"Didn't you ever find shapes in clouds?"

"No."

"Well, do it now."

"All I see is splotches," said Richard.

"One of them looks like an elephant."

"That's what you said."

"Doesn't it look that way to you?"

"Yes."

"Find something else that looks like an animal or object."

He stared at the picture for a while, then looked blankly at me. "All I see is splotches," he said.

"Look" I said, "over here. This one looks a little like a giraffe. And that one looks sort of like a knife. Do you see?"

"Yes," he said, "yes, I see that."

"What else?"

He laughed. "That one there looks like my grandmother." As he looked at me this time, I saw something new in his expression. "There's more to this picture than meets the eye," he said.

From then on I found it easier to work with him. We made good progress, and as a result he was able to complete the course required for entrance to the University. Eventually he became a successful lawyer — a fine credit to his talented family.

THE MISSING LINK CAN BE QUITE SIMPLE

Richard had not learned how to look beneath the surface of his experiences. By exploring the deep structure of a painting, he opened his mind to other new possibilities, and thus became more responsive to implications.

Sometimes, though, the failure to look deeper can be very specific indeed. It's a matter of not being aware of what others assume about a given situation. For example, one of my students who had a lead in the school drama production had so little control over his lines I thought he had a defective memory. A year later, when he played an even more demanding role he was letter perfect in his part. When I asked him what had happened since his previous role he said, "Last year I didn't know we were supposed to take the book home and study the lines."

It was so obvious I hadn't bothered to mention it. In such a situation, a teacher might be tempted to feel exasperated or even scornful. But it hardly matters whether a student can figure something out or needs to have it pointed out, as long as the information is acquired and used. All of us from time to time fail to notice things that seem obvious to others.

Here's another example of helping a student shift from failure to success in a few minutes by showing him the importance of exploring the deep structure in written material. This student was able to generalize from a single instance — and thus came to understand what for years he had been overlooking.

AARON DISCOVERS COLUMBUS

When Aaron was befuddled about his American history course, it was difficult to see what the problem was. His textbook was, if anything, too simple. It started where most American histories start, with the voyages of discovery.

"I don't understand this book," he complained.

"What don't you understand about it?" I asked.

"It doesn't make any sense."

"Okay," I said, "read me the first sentence."

Aaron began to read: "'Before Columbus discovered America, the Indians had established a highly structured way of life of their own.'"

"Do you understand that sentence?" I asked.

"No," said Aaron.

"What don't you understand?"

"The whole thing."

"Okay, let's take it apart. First of all, who was Columbus?"

"I don't know," said Aaron.

Then I saw what the problem was. Aaron had been tuning out his education for so long he barely knew what America was. He had never heard of Columbus or the Indians. But the deep structure of that first sentence required a knowledge of these. So I filled him in. He seemed pleased: he could understand now.

"You see, Aaron," I said, "if you're going to get anything out of this book, you'll need to find out what it's referring to. If you don't understand the references in a particular sentence, ask your teacher — or look it up."

"I see." Aaron appeared satisfied.

"I guess we're going to have to work on this quite a bit," I said. "There's a lot of background you don't have. Come back after your next class, and we'll talk some more."

But Aaron never came back, and when I inquired I found he was making good progress in the course. It seemed it was only necessary for him to understand his problem in order to correct it. Once he got that insight he realized he wasn't stupid, just lacking some information which was easy enough to get. Then he began to deep structure his reading in the most literal sense. He filled in the background without which he could not understand what was being discussed in the text.

A FANTASY EXERCISE WITH NURSERY RHYMES

What Richard and Aaron had in common was a tendency to operate on one cylinder, because no one had ever turned on any of their other cylinders — or, perhaps, had actually turned them off. Whatever the cause of the problem, the solution was relatively simple. Learn to see symbolism and look past the literal, and you can figure out enough about the situation to function creatively.

You and your children can have fun exploring symbolism and deeper levels of meaning by creatively examining the implications of fairy tales and nursery rhymes. These simple stories have held their appeal over the centuries because of the powerful archetypal meanings lying beneath their surfaces. Their appeal is partly because of the way their significance impacts on the unconscious, causing one to explore the implications of what is stirred up deep in the mind. This provides the opportunity to verbalize and make safer some of those previously hidden thoughts. It also exercises the imagination, while teaching one to relate to stories not just by passively soaking them up like a sponge, but also by actively creating meanings and transforming them into new meanings — just what the mind is designed to do, and what Aaron and Richard had forgotten.

Relating creatively to stories at an early age may help prevent the child from later turning to the kinds of drug experiences that many young people are attracted to because they've lost the ability to stimulate their own imaginations.

So tell stories or recite nursery rhymes, asking questions as you go.

This will elicit responses on symbolic and deep structure levels. There's no need to analyze these responses.

"I COULD JUST KILL YOU" ISN'T NECESSARILY A MURDER THREAT

Children usually express what they need to at the moment. Though the thoughts they are verbalizing may seem distressed on the surface, the very act of telling them is usually a healing process for the child. So if the exercise elicits unsavory images, don't be shocked, but gently guide the discussion toward more benign ideas. If the child fantasizes blowing up the world or killing a baby brother or sister, listen and let these thoughts, through expression, clear themselves from consciousness. Then calmly point out that such actions must never occur, knowing the child will eventually accept this information. Have you noticed how often you, too, will say something outrageous when you're upset, only to find that later you'd rather forget all about it?

Your child may have even more need for such emotional clearing than you do. Children have to live in an unpredictable, sometimes frightening world, perhaps believing adults don't understand the intensity of their emotions. Fantasy exploration can provide an outlet for these troubled feelings, expressed symbolically because the child cannot handle them directly. Better the violent fantasy should exhaust itself through expression than bury itself in the subconscious. A negative reaction may only make the child uncomfortable for having unacceptable feelings. All feelings are acceptable; it is only the actions that may follow them that are not. So, remembering that art is an alternative to violence, and that story telling is an art, encourage your child to follow the thread of emotions as they unravel the labyrinth of fantasy.

But you need not accept this fantasy as your own. Instead, let yours model a more positive attitude. Just don't criticize or try to change the child's fantasies, because if you do, he or she may not trust you anymore.

WHAT'S A TUFFET?

Now for an example. Little Miss Muffet, you remember, sat on a tuffet. If you look up "tuffet," you may not find it in the dictionary, so I'll report my research on the matter. It seems that when, several centuries ago, Miss Muffet first sat down to dine on curds and whey, the meal occurred outdoors, and her tuffet was a tuft of grass. Eventually, though, someone moved her indoors (perhaps because indoor dining was more in vogue) and it thus became necessary to redefine tuffet. Someone appears to have assigned it the meaning "footstool," which is comfortably enshrined in the

Oxford English Dictionary, but apparently only for application in this particular context. The whole business seems to me to have been handled arbitrarily, so I think anyone who wants to has a right to assign the word a different meaning. After all, who but Miss Muffet herself ever really knew what it was she sat on?

Ask your child to decide what a tuffet is and draw a picture of one. What does it feel like to eat curds and whey sitting on one of those things? Why should anyone sit on one? Where was the tuffet? Was it in Little Miss Muffet's room? What else was in the room? A train set? An electric plum? Perhaps she also kept a circus or an octopus museum in her room.

Or maybe the tuffet was at Little Miss Muffet's school. Maybe it was what you had to sit on in the principal's office if you misbehaved. Then again, it might have been in the lunchroom, a likelier place for eating things. Or maybe the tuffet was in a special room that only Miss Muffet knew about, a room where you can hide and no one can find you and you can think Very Special Thoughts about Very Special Things. Maybe the tuffet was a magic tuffet that had secret compartments where Miss Muffet could keep her treasures, like her little toy roller coaster and her snow melting machine and her Godzilla doll. Maybe there's a manufacturing plant inside the tuffet where little men with long beards make stars to hang up at night. Maybe the tuffet is a magic carpet where you can close your eyes, make a wish, and be transported to any place you want to go.

THE GOURMET APPROACH TO MISS MUFFET'S DINNER

Anyway, there she was, eating her curds and whey. What are curds and whey? Can you get them at McDonald's? Do they grow in fields? Are they made in candy factories? Do they drop from the sky? Do you grow them in a little bottle in the basement? Are they manufactured inside the refrigerator? Do people get curds and whey on their birthdays or at Thanksgiving? Do you have to eat curds and whey if you're bad? Does eating curds and whey give you pleasant dreams? or heartburn? Does it make you secretly strong, so you can fly like a humming bird, or foam like a root beer float, or rise like a cat waking up and stretching, or fall like a dead leaf in a windstorm?

THE ONLY GOOD SPIDER IS A . . .

Enter the antagonist. What kind of spider is this? Perhaps a mommy spider with a lot of babies to feed, who wants some curds and whey for their empty stomachs. If only Miss Muffet would share a little of her meal, that's all the spider is asking. It might even have been Miss Muffet's pet spider, but sometimes a pet can make menacing faces at you — but it's really all right. The spider might have been an architect looking for places to construct a gigantic web complex, like a mall. Does Miss Muffet want a customized web in her room — a designer web? Maybe she could refer the spider to the principal's office at school where they need a few good webs to catch all the naughty children who talk when the teacher is talking.

Does the spider wear glasses and lecture like a professor? Does the spider, in fact, speak English, or some other language known only to those who live in dusty corners or under sofas or tune in from outer space?

What kind of spider is this? Is it time for a trip to the museum of natural history to find out whether there is a particular species that above all others prefers curds and whey?

EXPLORING MISS MUFFET'S SUPPORT SYSTEM

And, finally, what did Miss Muffet do after she was frightened away? Did she tell her Mommy that a naughty spider had interrupted her dinner and Mommy better step on it? Did she call the police or the fire department? Did she write a letter to the President, asking for a law against spiders in little girls' rooms? Did she ask someone on television to come take pictures of the spider so everyone could see it and not be afraid anymore?

KEEP THE OPTIONS OPEN

You'll probably find if you try this kind of dialogue with your child that there are times when the child wants to stick to the story as written, and others when it's fun to explore the side trails. Maybe you'll find yourself suggesting some of the ideas above and the child will giggle and say, "That's not how it is!" If you ask how it really is, you might get the answer "I don't know!" but keep at it. Even if the child says it's silly, new possibilities may be stirring in the mind — a more flexible picture of reality taking shape. This can have important consequences later in life.

Remember that children have to spend a lot of time getting things organized in their thinking, so it's good to play the fantasy game when they feel they want to; but don't force it on them.

IT'S GOOD FOR YOU TO HAVE A SILLY SIDE

Children also delight in seeing their parents being silly. It makes them feel more secure. "If Daddy can be silly like me, then I must be all right. And if when Daddy is silly I can order him around and tell him to stand in the corner with a napkin on his head, then there are times when I can be in charge."

Don't use this exploration process to impose your ideas on the child or indulge your fantasies. Just see what she will do with it, where it will go, and how her imagination develops as you let fresh ideas come into play. In the process, you help loosen boundaries so a wider variety of possibilities appears. Genius, after all, is partly the ability to imagine how things might be different. We all have that potential, but it has to be developed.

ADD MUSIC TO THE MIX

The bedtime story can become even more of an interesting challenge when created afresh with music as an inspiration. With the child sitting on your lap and classical music playing in the background, create a story and build it to a climax, making the rhythms fit the music. Then ask the child to continue it. After a bit, it's your turn again. Bring the story to another climax, and again let the child take over. See how long, complex and wonderful these stories become with nightly practice. See how much more responsive both of you become to the artistic possibilities of words spun out against a background of music.

HOW THIS IS GOING TO HELP IN SCHOOL

Later, in school, there will be plenty of times when it's important to explore implications. Those who have flexible imaginations find it easier to develop active mental interplay with ideas — keeping the options open and hunting for new possibilities. Flexible thinking will make it easier to decide wisely and well on important issues. Learning to see many implications in each situation — or rather, not learning *not* to see them — is one of the most important measures of intelligent behavior.

If, as is said, the battle of Waterloo was won on the playing fields of Eton, the great discoveries and new options of the twenty-first century may well be won in the nurseries of the twentieth.

WHAT ABOUT TEENAGERS?

Speculations like these on the thought processes of one of the world's best known little girls appeal not only to children, but also to Ph.D.s and corporate executives. I've seen groups of the latter embroiled for some time in discussions of Miss Muffet and her spider friend. Teenagers, however, may feel they are above such silliness. After all, the years between puberty and adulthood are when we dedicate ourselves to leaving childhood behind and deciding what's serious in life. Perhaps we're older then than at any time before or after.

So when we talk of weighty matters, the teenager and I, whether about Hemingway or The Grateful Dead, we'll probably end up assembling the meaning, structure and nature of the universe (or at least *a* universe, if only, perhaps, that of Sid Vicious). Little Miss Muffet may be passé in such company.

TEENAGERS AS FANATICS

I've discovered two types of teenagers — fanatics and non-fanatics. I was one of the fanatics, so I feel I understand that type a little better.

For the teenage fanatic, there is really only one important thing in life. Everything else has to be endured in order to buy time for the central passion. In my case it was Gilbert and Sullivan. I ate, drank, slept and preached the Golden Fourteen Operas, and the D'Oyly Carte Opera Company that spawned them. W.S. Gilbert, I believed, had dealt with all the profound questions, while Sir Arthur Sullivan had written all the music that needed writing. I believed that time not spent committing to memory or performing these Savoy Operas was time wasted. After school each day, in the privacy of my bedroom, I would join the D'Oyly Carte Opera Company (via His Master's Voice) in whatever I could wrap my vocal cords around. Now that I've discovered a little more about God and nuclear physics than I knew then, I've learned that this approach to the problems of the universe may have been provincial. But at the time any slight to the genius of the immortal masters of wit and melody was a personal attack on me.

OPPORTUNITIES MISSED

Parents, teachers and friends who downplay or recoil from the fanatical objects of teenagers' interests are missing a chance to harness that energy in the service of other pursuits. Most of us tend to react to the fanatic by running the other way. When we've talked to one for fifteen minutes, we've heard all we'll ever want to on the subject. Pity the parent who hates Heavy Metal, but for hours every day can't escape it. No wonder the subject is painful. But it's even worse that a rich warehouse of energy is never unlocked from too narrow commitments.

QUIZZING THE FANATIC

Teenage fanatics I've known personally have fixated on the Redskins, building organs (that play music), science fiction, *The Rocky Horror Picture Show*, Elton John, Hollywood films, automobiles (some racing them, some repairing them), skate boards, toy soldiers (by the thousands), the Grateful Dead, David Bowie, karate, Gustave Mahler (symphonies only), est, Civil War uniforms, composing atonal modern music, Walt Disney, horses, bench pressing, playing the guitar, the culture of Appalachia, Navajo culture, World War II fighter planes, the history of World Wars I and II, computer games, ham radio, stereo amplifiers, Christmas, photography, comic books, *Star Trek* and baseball.

All these subjects lend themselves to deep structuring in some way. One could talk for quite a while about the physics of skate boarding, for example, which could lead to an examination of the balancing process in the body, and might eventually develop into an in-depth study of anatomy.

Of course, you can't just impose this kind of study on the fanatic. Fanatics are super-sensitive to the difference between those who are interested, or might become interested, in their favorite subject, and those who are merely trying to manipulate. They live in a private world that must be entered with reverence, like a temple. Take off your shoes, cover your head, and don't talk louder than a whisper. Above all, listen your way through the sermon, put something in the collection plate, and wait for the versicles and responses. At that point you'll have to prove you've learned something. When the ritual is over and you're an initiate, start firing away with the questions. Like:

What appeals to you most about this subject? Describe how you fell in love with it. Who else is interested in it? How do you communicate with others who are? Do you wish you had more friends who were interested? What would you most like to be able to do about all this? How will it affect you ten or twenty years from now? How does it work? How could you train someone else? What are its most important aspects? What would you most like to study or do next about it? Whom do you wish you could meet that would share your interest? What important contributions do you hope to make to the understanding of this subject so the world can better share it with you? Does this subject have its own literature? What is most needed to contribute to and fill out that literature? What would you encourage someone to write about this subject that hasn't yet been written? Is there pictorial art associated with it? What remains to be contributed in that department? What sciences are most closely associated with this subject? Is there one you'd like to explore a little more deeply? What do you think the social impact or message of this subject is? What kind of legislation do you think ought to be passed in response to the importance of your subject? What kind of society would allow you to pursue this subject in an ideal way? What are some of your favorite trivia questions relating to this subject? Can you think of some questions even experts in your field might have trouble answering? Pretend you're going to form a team of researchers to enhance the understanding or effectiveness of your subject — what would you have them do?

Not all these questions will work with any given person. Skip the ones that get no response and settle on a few that start the ball rolling. Bear in mind you're probably the only one who will ever ask, and the poor, lonely fanatic has been waiting a long time for someone to show an interest. Be aware also that you're dealing with a phenomenon so intertwined with the teenager's experience it's almost part of his or her identity. You and I can say whatever we want to each other about a teenager's idol, but a show of irreverence will likely provoke cool and hostile defensiveness.

TEENAGERS WHO AREN'T FANATICS

Most teenagers, though, aren't fanatics. Some of them have a broad range of interests and come across a little like miniature adults. Some appear to have no interests at all. They may be apathetic, bored, interested only in hanging out with their friends, or downright furious with the world.

Beneath the surface, though, I've found there are certain things most teenagers think about and would like to discuss with someone they could trust. Chief among these are sex, music, dreams, and adultism.

If you don't already know how to talk about sex with a teenager, nothing I can say here will help much. However, in my experience, most teenagers don't so much want to discuss the mechanics of sex as the social and ethical questions, such as why there is so much teenage pregnancy, whether sexual issues should be dealt with in school, whether giving advice about birth control invites a person to go ahead and have sex, and what the effect of AIDS on sexual habits ought to be.

The other three questions, though, can be undertaken productively without too much previous experience, with one word of caution: If you build trust as a result of a conversation that explores intense feelings, remember that the shock of betrayal by a new friend is pretty powerful at this age, and if you violate (or appear to violate) this trust, it may be a long time before you're forgiven.

LET THEM GIVE YOU A MUSIC APPRECIATION COURSE

Music is central in the lives of many teenagers, and while preferences differ, most know a lot about what they like. You can learn about the standards by which such music is judged, who creates it, what the lives and values of the musicians are like, what they're trying to communicate and how it's affecting young people's thinking. Take some time to look over lyrics recommended by your young friend. What's the message, and how do you feel about it? Be honest about your feelings, but at the same time careful not to suggest that the teenager's feelings have no value if yours are different. Differences of opinion and agreements to disagree often resolve tensions that otherwise can grow stronger in an atmosphere of not knowing how people feel.

Should music that may have a seriously disturbing effect on young people be censored? Of course those you're talking with won't want the music they like censored, but they may feel there's a problem with other music and the effect it can have on its listeners. Discuss these problems openly with young people, ask them for information, and share with them what you know.

THE WONDERFUL WORLD OF DREAMS

Another favorite topic for discussion is dreams. We tend to sleep a third to a fourth of our lives, and to dream as often as six times every night. Some of us remember our dreams, and some don't. Dreams can occasionally play an important role in our lives, as is the case with my friend who writes novels based on his nightly imaginings.

We also live in a culture which, apart from the realm of psychiatry, has not yet recognized the importance of talking or thinking about dreams. But some dreams need to be talked through. This is particularly true with teenagers. "Last night," one girl told me, "I dreamed I was having babies all night long. Every time I turned around, out popped another one." Coincidentally, she'd just taken an important step forward in her creative awareness. As I listened to her talk about the dream, she discovered a connection in her thinking between having babies and personal growth. Talking about her dream had a very positive effect on her.

TRY LETTING DREAMS SPEAK FOR THEMSELVES

An excellent form of dream analysis is the Think-and-Listen. It's a good idea for people to tell their dreams repeatedly until they figure them out. A lot of important self-revelations can happen this way.

It's true that once in a while you can hand someone an insight about their dream they haven't noticed. Then there's a sharp intake of breath, a turning inward for a moment and a look of recognition on the face. Most often, though, your interpretation of someone else's dream fits you, not the other person, and is just extra baggage for them. But if you tell your own dream enough times you'll figure it out — at least to the extent you're prepared to deal with it at the time.

Most dreams symbolize experience and reflect hidden desires or fears. Psychiatrists may interpret them from a Freudian, Jungian or Adlerian point of view and find different meanings in them. But why not just let the symbols unfold their own meaning as you talk the dream through for yourself? Some things will quickly become obvious as you practice exploring your dreams; such as the fact that they often contain puns. For example, a person who was about to take a new form of training told me a dream about riding in a train and immediately saw the pun.

Though it's not usually a good idea to interpret someone else's dream, it's fine to ask questions that help reveal the deep structure of the dream. Here are some that may be useful:

SOME QUESTIONS ABOUT DREAMS

What's the most vivid dream you've ever had? What is your favorite dream? Do you think any of your dreams mean anything? Do you have your own theory or ideas about what dreams are and what they are supposed to do? Tell a dream. Tell it again. Do you have any questions about it? How would you answer your own questions? Do dreams remind you of anything — like song lyrics, poems, movies, television commercials, fairy tales, paintings, or fun houses? Do you ever dream of the future? Do you ever dream of something that happened exactly the way it happened? Who are the people you dream about the most? Do you think they dream about you? Do you wish anyone in particular would dream about you? Do you know of any literature, movies, songs, or anything else that deals with dreams?

Do you ever dream when you're not asleep? What relationship do you think exists between daydreams and dreams that occur in sleep? Do you think dreams are ever shared by more than one person? Have you ever turned a dream into a reality? Do you think you might ever do so in the future? What's the most valuable thing a dream might offer you? Did you ever dream you were writing a song or painting a picture and wake up wanting to actually do it? Are animals important in your dreams? How does that relate to their importance in your life? Would you ever use a dream as the basis for a story you might write or a picture you might paint? Do you dream in color? Do you hear vivid sounds in your dreams? Do you feel your body moving in your dreams? Do you ever dream of reading something? Do you ever dream of having an interesting discussion? Did you ever dream you were fighting with someone you would never fight with? Did you ever dream you were friends with someone you don't like? Have you ever done anything in real life as a result of having had a dream?

RAPPING ABOUT ADULTISM

Adultism, which is the systematic oppression of people because they are young, is probably the most rampant injustice in our society. No one has yet come forward as a spokesperson for the liberation of the young in a way that captures the public imagination and creates a movement like women's liberation or black liberation. Too many of us, once we grow up, choose to forget how we were oppressed and end up treating the next generation the way we were treated.

Being young is not a disease, an infirmity of mind or any other kind of incapacity. Young people often sense, though, that older people don't like them or don't respect them just because they are young. I have found most young people eager to talk about this subject if they are asked, and usually they haven't been asked before. I think if you create the safety to give honest answers, you may be surprised by what a group of young people will say in answer to the following questions:

SOME QUESTIONS ABOUT ADULTISM

Have you ever been mistreated purely because of your age? Is there anything you wish people older than you would never do to you? Is there anything you wish they would always do? Do you think age makes a person inferior in any way? Do you like being called a "kid?" If not, why not? Do you ever feel older people are deliberately distancing themselves from you? Do you feel there is something older people should learn from you? Do you treat people younger than yourself with complete respect? If you did, what would that be like? Is there an age when people become old enough to understand about life and another age when they need to be told what to do all the time?

What kind of a world are you inheriting from previous generations? What would you like to thank them for? What do you wish they had done better? Are there any messes you feel your generation is going to have to clean up? Do you plan to have any part in that? If you could design an ideal society, what would it be like? What kind of a parent do you think you'll be? Is there anything your parents did that you hope you'll do as well? Is there anything they did that you'll do your best to avoid doing? Is there any kind of support you wish you could get that never seems available to you? Is there any way in which you feel older people consistently lie to you? Is there any way you consistently lie to them? What is the best thing about being your age? What do you think is best about being thirty? What do you think is best about being sixty? How long do you expect to live? Do you think you have a right to bring children into the world you have to live in? Did your parents have a right to give birth to you? Do you feel you really wanted to be born?

What person your own age do you admire the most? What person older than you would you most want to model your life after? How would you feel about younger people modeling their lives after yours? What changes might you hope to bring about in the way young people are treated? What things should not change? What do older people most need to know about your age group? What can older people best do to support you effectively? What do they most frequently accuse you of that is not true? What do you most frequently accuse them of that might possibly not be true? When you get to be fifty do you think you'll be comfortable having a conversation like this with a teenager? What ideas that you have now do you feel fairly certain you'll change when you grow older? What ideas do you think your parents might have had when they were your age that they probably don't have any more? What do your parents have a right to expect from you? What don't they have a right to expect? What do you have a right to expect from them?

Recently I spent an evening asking a group of teenagers questions like these. I had a wonderful time, and so did they. They all wanted to come back for more. They all seemed to be doing original thinking, because no one had ever asked them any of those questions before. Let's hope that will change.

15

CORE CONCEPTS THAT STRUCTURE OUR THINKING

Such basic concepts as sequence and balance have powerful applications in wide ranges of thought. These core ideas and others can be experienced and understood through physical actions, even by young children.

We've considered ways to stimulate the imagination in everyday life, particularly in reaction to the spoken or written word. Yet there's not much value in imagination without structure.

The underlying structure of our everyday lives and thoughts depends largely on what I call **core concepts**. These might be likened to programs in a computer. We don't really see them when we use them, but they are the means by which we organize our thoughts and actions and maintain consistency in point of view, behavior and application of skills.

Core concepts are not necessarily clear to the person who has them — they are so much a part of the background of experience they may seem indistinguishable from one's basic personality. But the breadth and depth of these core concepts determine how, and how well, we think and respond to experience. They are formed from our earliest days, so it's important to think about their role in learning and in our lives.

THE IMPORTANCE OF UNCONSCIOUS LEARNING

Children need the chance to structure and develop their understanding. Much of this structuring takes place unconsciously, as the body organizes experience. The most powerful learning may happen while our attention is elsewhere. Though we aren't aware of learning, our perceptions are permanently altered. The same holds true for our deepest beliefs.

So this chapter will deal with how we move from the conscious process of absorbing and practicing something new to forming habits and automatic responses that operate outside conscious control. It will also explore how core concepts help build connections among our ideas and experiences. Let's begin by sampling a particular means of structuring experience, to see how extensive its effect on thinking may be.

WHAT'S MOST HUMAN ABOUT US?

Suppose you had to determine what sets the human mind apart from the minds of other animals — what would you say it was?

Common answers to this question include socializing and tool-making. But ants and bees are also social animals, while some monkeys have been known to use tools.

OUR SENSE OF FAIRNESS

One answer you might consider is that humans have a sense of fairness other animals lack. If we don't always recognize when we're being unfair to others, we usually know when they're not being fair to us.

The notion of fairness requires both counting and equalizing. If you and I are to divide a collection of bottle caps, we should either end up with the same number, or our collections should have the same value — that is, unless we agree that the values should be unequal.

Fairness is one of the most basic concepts we possess. It can be extended to every facet of life. It leads to the most complex philosophical and moral issues, to the most intricate mathematical operations, and to the world of subatomic physics. Yet fairness begins right in the home, when we divide things among family members.

GIVING BOB HIS DUE

Several years ago I was concerned about a student who seemed on the verge of becoming a juvenile delinquent. Bob came from a large family, and I think had gotten so little attention he was beginning to believe he would have to take it by force. Although I knew he was bright, he had not been doing his homework for several weeks when I asked him to come in for a conference.

As he walked into my office, I could see the anger in his macho posture. He was looking for a fight, and I knew it wasn't just with me — he was ready to take on the world. As he lowered himself stiffly into a chair, his head cocked to one side, he said, "I don't like the assignments you've been giving."

"I understand why," I said. "They're beneath you. You're too smart for that kind of stuff."

The macho drained from his body. He seemed to relax, then sat up straight and looked at me a bit doubtfully. "You think so?"

"I know so," I said. "You're one of the brightest students I've worked with. Let's make up some other assignments for you. What would you like to learn about?"

This seemed to be what Bob he had been looking for. If he'd missed his share of the attention too often, perhaps now he was getting more than his share. Together we worked out some assignments that were just right for him, and he did them brilliantly. After that things went better for him. Today he's a leader in the field of education.

THE CONSEQUENCES OF GETTING TOO MUCH

But giving children more than their share can also make them uncomfortable. They may say they want something, but when they get it, they sense an imbalance, and as a result their behavior deteriorates. They'll keep on testing, though, to see whether they can get more than they deserve. When they do, there's likely to be trouble.

In extreme cases, persons possessing great power or wealth who have never been held to any limits, may spend a lifetime in a protracted temper tantrum looking for them, while countless innocent people suffer the consequences.

How do we judge fairness in the first place? Perhaps we were already struggling with the notion when we got up on our hind legs and began to walk. We discovered how vulnerable we are to falling down. It was necessary to focus on balance, to keep equal weight on both feet, to treat both sides of the body equally. A four-legged animal can get along well enough with a missing leg. I had a three legged cat once, and you couldn't tell unless you looked closely. My cat would do everything a normal cat would do. But try walking on one leg yourself and see how noticeable it is. Yes, equality becomes a major issue in the life of a biped.

CRAWLING EXERCISES

To get up on two legs, we have to do a lot of other things first. The lengthy process of learning to crawl as a preparation for learning to walk provides a number of opportunities to bring into consciousness experiences that a four legged creature would merely take for granted. You can explore some of the experiences on which you've based your idea of fairness by getting down on all fours and crawling about the room, exploring your bodily sensations and new perspectives.

How does the world seem different when you crawl? Try taking three steps with your hands before you take any with your knees. Notice how your body wants to move in a natural sequence dictated by the momentum of forward motion. Notice, too, how important forward motion seems in crawling.

FORWARD MOTION

Now stop and think. How much of your life is conceived in terms of forward motion? Are you moving forward in time? Do you see human history as moving forward? Your body is constructed so you can move forward effectively, but what about moving backward? How and why does that feel different? How about your automobile? Notice the way you progress through a book, moving forward through its lines and pages. Notice the way you organize tasks. As Alice found out in Wonderland, it is important to start at the beginning and proceed through the middle until you come to the end.

Forward motion is itself a core concept. Nearly everything we do or think about is conceived in terms of forward motion. In this respect we are at one with the universe, because continuous motion in the same direction is the state in which everything exists. A body in motion will remain in motion until acted upon by an outside force. That means if you're floating free in space and something starts you moving, you'll keep going in that direction forever, or until something gets in your way. Even if you're at rest you're engaged in forward motion, since everything in the universe is moving.

And though it seems perhaps too obvious to discuss, one problem most of us have is to keep moving forward toward our goals.

SEQUENCING

Now look at the sequencing part of crawling. The steps must follow a certain order. We cannot do one thing until we have first done something else. Again, our lives are organized around this concept. Yet often we fail to find the sequence that will allow us to perform a given task most effectively. Any task can be analyzed into component parts so it becomes more manageable. In school your child will have to outline papers and establish a logical sequence of development among the ideas that make up the outline. Practice in crawling, and thinking about the process of crawling, will lay the foundation for this. Many tasks may occur later in life that cannot be done without proper sequencing. People who never add up their checkbooks, for example, are suffering from sequencing problems. Nearly everyone has trouble with sequencing something important, and the consequences of poor sequencing can be tragic.

Though sequencing must usually be rigidly maintained, there can be arbitrary components, variable according to preference. Strengthening your concept of sequencing may give you more freedom to work out sequences that fit your needs, as the best way to organize a task is not the same for everyone. From getting up in the morning to setting the alarm at night, you order events so often you may have long ago stopped noticing how you do it. Yet it is always possible that things will work out better if we rearrange the sequence in which we do them. One of the main things successful people learn is to organize their activities so the sequence of events will have the most desirable effect.

CONNECTING THE TWO

Let's connect these two concepts of forward motion and sequencing with the way the body operates. To do this, we shall relate them to balance. Thus we'll be teaching the mind to look for connections between physical experience and the structure of thinking — connections that may help develop a more conscious and well-reasoned style of thinking. We can experience these three notions by performing an exercise that introduces counting and relates it to all three.

PICK UP COINS

Place twenty coins of equal value in four rows on the floor so that when you crawl between two rows it will be easy to pick up a coin with each forward motion. You and your child will each crawl forward between two rows. The object is for each person to pick up all ten coins, one with each forward motion. At the end of the crawl, compare your collections of coins. How can you determine if you have the same number? You could put the coins in two piles and see if they are the same height. You could each lay down one at a time and see if you have the same number to lay down. This might be quicker if you lay them down two at a time, or even three at a time. Why not many more at a time?

You could weigh them. You could put them in a glass brim full of water and measure the amount of water displaced by the coins. Discuss with your child what seems like the best way to establish their equality.

Offer suggestions, but let your child lead you to the solution. (Piaget has shown that young children have concepts of equality based on incomplete interpretations of perception. Therefore, if your child gives what you consider an incomplete explanation, explore, but do not push, other possibilities. Learn at least as much as you teach — learn what your child is seeing and conceptualizing. Trust that this will change with time and maturity.)

TRADING COINS

Now start trading coins: "I'll give you one of mine if you give me one of yours." That makes the trade equal. Similarly, two of mine for two of yours will keep the trade equal. But unequal numbers will not keep it equal. Try unequal trades and see how it feels. Does your child like it best when you get all the coins, or the other way around? What's fair? Why should one of you have more than the other? Does your child care about this kind of fairness? (Maybe for the child there are enough coins so both of you can have all you want. Maybe the child momentarily wants to be sure to get them all.)

HAND TOUCH EXERCISE

Now sit facing your child and play Pease Porridge Hot, or another hand-clapping game, bringing the palms of your hands together. But each time your palms touch, you pick up one coin and your child picks up one. This involves some of the same motion as crawling, but now you are touching hands at the same time. So this shows how you can sequence together and collect coins at the same rate.

This exercise will help the child experiment with ideas of sequence, balance, forward motion, accumulation of wealth, fairness, sharing, equality, number and other things that may occur to either of you as you play. Many things are being explored simultaneously here, all at a basic level of bodily experience. The learning process is unconscious and will probably not be remembered, but later it will be easier for the child to understand many of these concepts when they're encountered directly in a more sophisticated form.

Once the child is comfortable with the exercise when equal coins are used, these activities may be expanded by introducing coins of differing values into the exercise. Now it will be necessary to establish why one coin may be equal in value to many others, as the reason for this is not immediately obvious. Begin with cakes of different sizes. Show that one piece of a large cake might be exchangeable for two of a smaller one.

WHEN IS ONE WORTH MORE THAN TWO?

Then move on to things whose different values are clear to the child. One piece of paper with a picture on it might be worth ten pieces with no picture. Or it might be the other way around — because you can still draw a picture on a blank piece of paper. Let the child make the value judgment. Different pictures, on the other hand, might be worth different numbers of pieces of blank paper. See if it is possible to set up a consistent value system. Does the child's evaluation of a picture change from time to time, so the exchange rate for blank paper rises or falls? This prepares us to understand fluctuating prices in the store.

Why should a quarter be worth twenty-five pennies? Well, perhaps a tricycle is worth twenty-five wooden blocks. If the child has to make choices among things while shopping, this ability to make one thing equivalent in value to several others may become clear as a basis for understanding how the monetary system works.

PLAYING WITH UNEQUAL COINS

When you've explored some of these ideas, try playing with coins of unequal value. The child may wonder why, though, the value of a quarter does not fluctuate in relation to pennies if the value of a jar of peanut butter fluctuates from day to day. This leads to the question of the importance of having universally agreed upon standards for certain measurements. Look for things in the child's life that always have to be a certain way. Is it okay to sleep under the bed instead of on top? Is it okay to wear pajamas to school? So we can wear different clothes from day to day, but there's a standard that says pajamas only at bedtime. Well, why not a standard that says a quarter always has to have twenty-five pennies? Both of these are arbitrary, because pajamas cover your body and keep you warm, so they could be worn to school. It's just that everyone agrees not to.

So some things are arbitrary, some things fluctuate and some things (like Mommy and Daddy) have value no matter what. I can trade pennies with you, but I can't trade my Mommy and Daddy for yours.

TRYING TO BE FAIR IN AN UNFAIR WORLD

Now we see that while it's important to be fair as much as possible, nothing really is fair. One family has a Mommy and Daddy, one family has only a Mommy, one has only a Daddy, one has a Mommy, Daddy, Grandma and Grandpa. That's not really fair, but everyone has a different situation, so while there are some things we can compare, there are others we cannot. We try to make things as fair as we can, and we accept that certain things will never be fair, or perhaps can't be compared at all.

But when are we going to try to make things fair and when aren't we? I'm not going to try to give you back your Daddy if you don't have one. But if you lost your lunch, I'll help you look for it, and if it can't be found, perhaps I'll share mine with you.

These are topics that should be discussed in the family. The child's thinking is important here, and should be explored carefully. The child may have insights you'll never see if you try to explain what you think is right. Perhaps the child can point to important inequalities or equalities you've never noticed. Perhaps the child can show you a new way of sequencing.

LOOKING FOR SEQUENCING

Next it's possible to relate this experience to activities as well as numbers. Look at objects. The table has four legs. Can it crawl? The dog has four legs. Can it crawl? The car has four wheels. Can it crawl? What things have forward motion, what things have sequencing, what things have balance?

Later in life, as a result of this exploration, your child will be better able to understand things like balance of trade in economics, a balanced diet in nutrition, a balanced personality in psychology, homeostasis in physiology, a balanced equation in mathematics, and so on. Meanwhile, you can start exploring such relationships right now. Can you think of any subject area in which balance is not a concept of central importance? How about forward motion and sequencing?

GETTING MATH AND SCIENCE INTO YOUR BODY

The exercises so far have dealt with basic and general core concepts, not those that relate to specific subjects only. Let's take a look, though, at what can be done with a couple of core concepts in math and science.

In mathematics the number line is one of the first and most important things to learn. Although all of us who can add up our checkbooks use it unconsciously all the time, I've found that many intelligent adults don't really understand the number line.

Mark out on the floor a number of spaces and label them. The central one is labeled zero, and to one side are positive numbers in order from zero — to the other side, negative ones. One player stands at zero. Someone calls out a sign, either plus or minus. The player turns in the direction indicated by the sign. Someone else calls out a number, such as "7." The player then takes seven steps in that direction, and calls out the number he or she is then standing on. For example, starting from zero, +7 would be +7, but then -8 would be -1. In this manner, by actually moving on the number line, the player gets the feel of how addition and subtraction work, and also realizes they are one process.

Now let's try working with a science concept this way. In physics we have the notions of velocity and acceleration. These are easy to understand in the abstract, but many beginning physics students have trouble with them, as well as the formulas that describe them. So get a small group into a circle and pass a ball around. At first make sure it is passed at a constant speed or velocity. Then accelerate the velocity. Then decelerate it. As you play the game, players may take turns calling out "constant velocity," "accelerate," and "decelerate." Simple as this exercise is, it should help lay the foundation for understanding the concept when it is encountered in physics.

In similar ways other core concepts in other subjects may be experienced through activities involving the body.

TRY IT OUT ON YOURSELF

Returning now to the more general notion of core concepts, see if you've gotten some advanced adult-level inspiration from this. Get a book on an unfamiliar subject. Look through it for ideas related to balance, sequencing, forward motion, and equality. How much of the book do you already understand as a result of what you have been doing? How many connections can you make between this unfamiliar subject and other subjects you already understand?

By exploring your body, building up your stock of core concepts and applying them in new and unexpected ways, you will be training your mind to provide guidelines for your child's education far more productive than the lock-step of traditional education. At the same time, you may open up some new possibilities in your own thinking.

16

IS IT REALLY YOU?

*You can waste your whole life carrying out other people's
programs. Why not carry out your own?*

The last chapter explored some of the underlying ideas and structures
of thought that make our experiences comprehensible, helping us to
penetrate beneath appearances and make sense of the underlying reality.
But no matter how well we understand the world around us, we can't feel
whole until we figure out who we are and how we relate personally to what
we observe or know.

The process of discovering the essential features of one's identity may
take a long time — for some, perhaps, almost the entire span of life. Yet the
first traces of the discovery seem present from the beginning. Once we've
cleared away mistaken impressions of who we ought to be, we're better
prepared to discover who we are. It's like wiping the mist from the
bathroom mirror in the morning. Yes, you could leave it there and imagine
the face behind the haze — an idealized view of yourself projected by the
imagination, but one that does you little good in knowing what you really
look like. Or you can simply wipe the mirror clean and deal with what you
see there.

Sometimes the notion of who we are is sharpened as we face a difficult
challenge. Or in the heat of emotional conflict, perhaps even despair, we
discover what we are made of, and what we will do under extreme
circumstances. Still, there was always something beneath, even before the
challenge that clarified our sense of purpose. So let's look at what that

might be, and how you might come to know it.

THE UNIQUE TREASURE THAT IS YOU

You were born with a treasure that is unique. It is the particular point of view and special character to which you alone give life. It is what your friends will miss most deeply when you're gone. Throughout history no one else has seen life quite the way you see it; no one has had your unique style of being, your special impact on what surrounds you. As surely as you leave traces of your presence with your fingerprints, so you also leave an imprint wherever you go, through your effect on the experience of others.

Notice the same phenomenon in your friends. Think of the loss when someone is gone forever. How would you replace that person? There are, after all, over four billion to choose from — can't you find another just as good? If not, what is the special quality lost forever when any one of us is gone? Try to sense this quality in each of your friends. Look for it, too, in famous people. Can anyone else sing as your favorite singer does, argue a case in court like your favorite lawyer, emote like your favorite movie star? Of course not. I once met a man who knew how to shine a doorknob as perhaps no one else ever has. Though I met him only once for just a few moments, he left an indelible impression on my nine year old memory.

But what exactly is this uniqueness that will be missed when you are gone? And what can you do to bring that special trademark of your being more clearly into focus?

Of course, each child also has qualities that in all of history will pay only one brief visit to earth, never to be seen again. But the oppressive forces that act upon children can distort their identity — indeed, are sometimes applied for just that purpose. However, if loss of uniqueness in the melting pot of life was what you wanted for the children and young people in your life, you wouldn't be reading this book. The most valuable gift you can offer them is to help them become aware of their opportunity to offer their uniqueness to the world.

HOW WE THROW AWAY OUR GREATEST TREASURE

Despite the fact that our uniqueness is our greatest treasure, we put much of our energy into activities and pursuits that tend to obliterate it. Forgetting that it deserves to be nourished with all our resources, we lightly brush it aside in favor of rewards that give us far inferior ways of feeling important. How much more magnificent than material wealth or hollow praise is a fully developed talent! Wouldn't you forgo a mansion in Hollywood or a position in the limelight for the genius of a Mozart, or a

Babe Ruth? Somewhere inside you is your own sort of genius — waiting and wondering when you'll care enough to call it forth.

So explore that talent. If you make a serious commitment to do so, this will help inspire your children to begin a similar exploration. Great talent sometimes runs in families, not necessarily for genetic reasons, but because of example and influence in the education of children. Why should all four of the sons of J.S. Bach who grew to maturity have become world-renowned masters of the art of composition, while none of his daughters took up their pens to compose? Surely we cannot expect the law of averages to arrange genes so conveniently as this — it must have been because women were not expected to be capable of composition. And so we lost, perhaps, half the great masterpieces of music, not to mention other works of genius, that we might have had prior to the twentieth century. Sexism exacts a high price.

STOP LOSING YOURSELF IN CONFORMITY

How much are you influenced by the widespread pressure to be just one of the folks — never to step out of line, never to rock the boat? How much, instead, do you look inside for the special gifts that only you can bring to light?

Think for a moment about the meaning of that word "gift." It is a blessing received, but it is also something that we are the instruments to provide for the world. If we fail to do so, it will remain ungiven, while we feel vaguely frustrated and oddly disappointed in ourselves.

HOW LOU FOUND HIMSELF

Many people discover themselves through writing. That is what happened to Lou, a student who came to our school in his junior year. He had been on his own for a couple of years, preferring work on a farm and pot smoking to attending school. When he first applied for admission, he was rejected. But the next year, at last deciding he wanted to make something of himself, he wrote an eloquent letter praising us for our "noble decision" in rejecting him the year before, and saying he was now ready to accept the challenges of a good education.

In my English composition class, Lou decided to push himself to the maximum he could achieve. His first few papers could have been written by a third grader: their sentence structure was awkward and over-simple, their ideas inane, and their vocabulary at best ill-used. But aware of his limitations, he was determined to work his way out of them. Each day he would ask for a special assignment. Soon he was creating his own assignments. He designed a set of writing exercises for himself that prepared him to think like a novelist.

Meanwhile, Lou had made friends with Sam, another student who was quite gifted as a writer, and who read James Joyce for pleasure. Lou found Sam a willing tutor, and pestered him for ideas about what to read and how to write. Sam gave him a remarkable tutorial in literary style and technique. It wasn't long before Lou's writing began to show the effects of his drive and Sam's influence.

What struck me most about Lou when I first met him was his ironic wit. As he matured in his writing and thinking, this came into sharper focus, and the ill-used vocabulary began to shape itself into a new perspective on language use. He learned the value of the unexpected word well placed for power and point. His writing captured your attention while ruffling you a little.

I don't know whether Lou will develop into a novelist or turn his talents in another direction, but he has delighted in discovering his own unique style and point of view. He was able to accomplish this at least partly because he was in an environment that appreciated it when it began to happen. No one tried to force him back into a pre-set academic mode — otherwise, he might have turned his back on formal schooling altogether.

THE ANCIENT PRACTICE OF HERALDRY

Lou's attempt to uncover and express his own individuality demonstrated the kind of thinking that is often inhibited in today's society by pressures to conform. Anyone, particularly a young person, who wants to engage in such creative self-discovery these days needs all the encouragement and examples he can get. One useful model can be borrowed from the ancient European art of heraldry, a means by which families expressed how they saw themselves, identifying qualities they valued.

Not a bad idea — it's a shame we don't think so clearly any more about family identities, preferring in many cases to keep them as superficial or indistinct as possible. How about your family or group? Have you ever tried to express a sense of common purpose and shared values? If you want to try developing these, you may find that symbolism can be helpful.

THE IMPORTANCE OF SYMBOLS

In the interest of-self clarification, it's worth while deciding how you see yourself and inventing symbols to share your personal vision with others. A symbol helps focus your thinking about yourself.

Symbols have great power and appeal for children. They often symbolize themselves in their drawings, for example when they "illustrate" a relationship between themselves and someone or something else. Such symbols may help a child develop a sense of personal power. This is naturally a concern for children, and a frequent theme of the stories which fascinate them. Stories in which the hero or heroine triumphs in a difficult situation encourage the child to overcome fear and helplessness by imagining what it's like to confront a threatening situation and survive.

AN EXERCISE IN SELF-DEFINITION

Begin in the manner of heraldry by making a shield with four sections. In the first, draw a picture that symbolizes something about you as you see yourself. If you love to cook, one of your symbols might be a pie. If you love to read, draw a book. If you love automobiles, draw a car. If you're a dreamer and always have your head in the clouds, draw a cloud. If you're an aggressive person always looking for a fight, draw a clenched fist.

HOW OTHERS SEE US

Once you've got your own set of symbols, find out from others how they see you. Ask your children to think through a series of symbols for you and draw them in the next section. After that they can draw some symbols representing themselves and/or their relationships to you. Then carry the exercise forward, expressing in the third section how you would like to see yourself, and in the fourth, how you would like the world to see you.

EXTENDING THIS EXERCISE

This process can be carried beyond your self-concept and used to symbolize goals, dreams and ambitions for the future, the types of people you like to associate with, your world view, your value system, your style of thought, and other aspects of your life. Make a series of shields, one for each of the concepts in the previous sentence. Make a scrapbook of them. Putting all these in symbolic form helps objectify them, and may lead to making clearer decisions about your life.

Try a weekly family activity devoted to symbol development. Have all the family members symbolize something they've been thinking about that week in relation to themselves. The exercise of putting stated ideas or objectives into a pre-verbal symbolic form helps connect them with something deep in the mind, making them clearer and easier to act on. Sometimes this can make quite a difference in one's life. And when you've had your weekly exercise in symbol-making, go back through your scrapbooks and remind each other of what your previous symbols were.

FORM THE HABIT OF PRE-VERBAL THINKING

As the whole family begins to form the habit of using pre-verbal thinking to solve problems creatively, there should be a gradual shift into a deeper form of communication among individuals. Members of a society that over-emphasizes the spoken language and downplays the role of symbols in its cultural life tend to be superficial with one another. So you'll enjoy the increasing depth of communication that comes from this and related exercises.

You might vary the weekly meetings by choosing themes: one week, dreams for the future; another, how our friends see us; or our value system; or how we see our friends. I don't want to be too specific about this, because the themes you pick should evolve from your thinking and communication among yourselves. In this way you will make more conscious the process of growing into mutual self-awareness. This self-awareness can have a powerful effect on what eventually happens in your lives.

SETTING THE STAGE FOR SUCCESS

Great and successful people probably all had childhood precognitions of their greatness. So have many who did not achieve greatness. The main difference is that the successful ones were encouraged in their dreams by someone they considered important, while the unsuccessful were made to feel their dreams were foolish and impractical.

Another well-established trait of successful people is the ability to define and articulate their goals. But the pre-verbal symbolizing of goals is even more powerful than writing them down, because it digs deeper into our mental processes.

We need to change our attitude toward our dreams for the future and realize that the most seemingly impractical ones can in fact become tomorrow's realities. These dreams instruct our paraconscious minds to bring them into being. By forming the habit of symbolizing our hopes and dreams, we set the stage for the successes of the future.

17

THE GARDEN OF MEMORY AND CREATIVITY

*Learning to trust in your creativity and freeing
the imagination to find its own way to
express ideas and solve problems.*

Creativity is a function of our whole personality and its interaction with the world, not something we turn on or off. The more we see ourselves as innovative and original thinkers, the more creative we tend to be. The exercises so far have been designed to enhance trust in our own thinking and stimulate our own creative impulses. But the mind itself contains deep resources to help us do this, which we can learn to tap directly.

The most obvious of these is memory. Tapping this resource is a fascinating, sometimes mysterious process. Understanding how we remember — how impressions enter memory and how they are recalled — gives us powerful insights for using and strengthening our creative powers.

For creativity is integrally related to memory. Our experiences and our reflections on them are uniquely our own, and they are the treasure on which all creativity is based — whether expressed in artistic, scientific, or any other form. So whatever else we may say about creativity, these three things are essential to it: we must value our uniqueness, we must trust the worth of our experience, and we must be able to draw freely and widely on the full range of that experience, which is the content of our memory.

THE LAND OF NO MEMORIES

Memory (or the absence of it) is the subject of a wonderful opera by

Bohuslav Martinu called *Julietta*. Based on a play by George Neveux, it tells the story of a visitor to a country where no memories are permanent. Since they do not last, there is a man who sells new ones to replace the old. The hero Michel, a visitor to this country, falls in love with Julietta, who sometimes remembers him and sometimes doesn't. Though he has seen her three years before, she says, "We meet for the first time tonight," and later, having bought a memory, she tells him of their trip together to Seville, where of course they've never been.

MEMORY IS INTEGRATED EXPERIENCE

Michel's nightmarish experience with people who have no memories, and who consequently shift their expectations and realities at every whim, says something about the function of memory and how we use it. For it is more than a collection of facts, it is all that we have integrated into our lives. We soon forget whatever we have no stimulus to remember, while things of great significance to us are remembered forever. How many times would you need to hear that you had just won a million dollars? We do not forget falling in love, the death of those close to us, or the accidents we have suffered (except when they're too traumatic to be remembered).

FINDING THE DUMBO IN ME

A few months ago I saw Walt Disney's *Dumbo* for the first time since childhood. Some parts of the movie were as familiar as if I had seen them yesterday: exact visual shapes had permanently etched themselves in memory. Others I might as well never have seen before.

So our memory selects what we feel strongly about, while rejecting what seems not to affect us. As we all know, however, that does not mean we can recall everything we want to. For what is important to us logically is not always what we remember. Because the seat of memory is in the limbic system, the emotional center of the brain, permanent memories are more likely to be related to emotional experiences than practical necessities. If we experience something with enough intensity of feeling, we cannot forget it. Otherwise, we probably will.

This peculiar construction of the memory was useful to our mammalian ancestors, who had to remember what evoked strong emotion in order to stay alive, find food and reproduce. Humans, with more complex social and business systems, have not had time to evolve memories that easily retain the details of balance sheets. So where such details are concerned, memory must be coaxed. The best way of coaxing it is to fall sufficiently in love with what you are doing, and then to assist this love with strategies for enhancing its claim on memory.

IF YOU REALLY LOVE IT, YOU'LL REMEMBER IT

Have you ever walked through the streets where you spent a happy time with someone you loved and recalled the conversation as you passed a certain place — perhaps many years ago? Can you imagine being so deeply in love with something that every tiniest detail of it would be a permanent part of your memory?

The great conductor Arturo Toscanini loved music so much he never forgot a piece once he had performed it. It happened that late in life he planned to perform a work by a composer named Raff, the score of which could not be found in time for the performance. It was a string quartet which Toscanini had played when he was nineteen. Fifty or so years later, when he could not locate the score, he was able to transcribe it from memory. Later, when the score was found, it was compared with what Toscanini had remembered. Every note was correct.

In fact, all of us have memories almost as good as this, except that we do not know how to tap them. This is repeatedly brought home by experiments with hypnosis. A hypnotized bricklayer can accurately describe the exact markings of a brick he placed in a wall years before.

People in concentration camps have been able to recall and write from memory works of music or literature they have once known. The positive emotional attachment such things have for them when life is otherwise totally bleak by contrast, intensifies so much that detailed memories may surface.

It is at least partly a lack of emotional commitment that keeps us from remembering many things we would otherwise have clearly in mind. If the subject matter is appealing and associated with positive experiences, we remember easily. As unpleasant associations are overcome or resolved, memories come back. Even experiences under anesthesia have been recalled to memory with sufficient counselling.

Therefore, to make a thing more memorable we must create an intense emotional context for it. We must come to see it as an essential part of our personality. A memory is not a mere scrap of information dropped in some remote corner of our brain; it is an integral part of our self. When something is experienced intensely, we may not only remember it, we may use it also as a powerful creative force.

WHO'S BEEN SLEEPING IN MY BED?

Now let's do another thought experiment. Imagine yourself standing in front of your bed wondering who slept in it last night. Was it you or someone else? Or were two of you together there? Pretend you have entered the country where Julietta lived, where memory shifts at random. The only way you can have a memory is if you buy one from the man who sells memories, and what he gives you will depend on what he has in stock. So you don't really know who slept in your bed last night.

Such a loss of memory would be a loss of yourself. If you have no connection with your previous self, it is almost like having no self at all. Add back a bit of memory, and you have a bit of self. Add more memory, and more self appears. But is this self the real one, or one created from false memories you've made up in defense against the real ones? And on what basis do you select the memories you choose to preserve? Why can't you recall your entire life, exactly as it happened?

USING THE SELECTIVITY OF MEMORY

The memories you have at any given point are the emotionally integrated ones. You have a special feeling about the place where you sleep, because it is there that you become most vulnerable. If some stranger slept there without your permission, you might feel violated. If someone else slept with you, you will probably feel that experience intensely.

But memories veer into fantasy: you do not remember everything accurately. In general, you remember what you want to remember, and forget what you want to forget. So if you want to remember something, infuse it with beauty — make it attractive to memory and imagination. This was just what Lozanov did when he used concert sessions to tap into the long-term memory by enhancing emotionally neutral material with appealing posters, an intense dramatic reading and beautiful music.

MUSIC AS AN AID TO MEMORY

You can also use music to encourage past memories to surface so you can play with them. Is there a memory that has a destructive effect on your life? Would you like to change it into a less virulent form? Let us say that as a child you were told you could never learn to write. Such a memory may have gained a compelling negative force in life because you loved and believed the person who told you this. Listening to music, you can bring that memory back in a less threatening form, because the music creates an atmosphere of pleasure, allowing you the safety to examine and reconsider it. Suppose you misheard the person, who instead actually said, "You will learn to write superlatively." Under the influence of the music, create a new memory that allows you to accomplish your desire.

But what if the relevant memories have become hidden, so you do not even know what makes you feel so negative? The music allows you to imagine positive experiences to counter the negativity. These positive experiences then take their place in your emotions, perhaps in the process bringing the negative memories to the surface so you can experience and transform their pain. Music, then, may be used to construct an environment in which it is possible to create a new direction for yourself.

THE USE OF GUIDED IMAGERY

What I've said of memory applies also to creativity. The creatures and images of our imagination can be manipulated as we choose until they find their way into the reality of physical expression. One excellent way to start this process is through guided imagery accompanied by music. The music allows the mind to play. The images may come from inside your own mind or from someone giving suggestions.

If you'd like to read a guided imagery to someone, you might try the following passage. This was written during one of my workshops by Linda Carlson, a certified school social worker in Chaska, Minnesota. I thought it a delightful way to talk to a young person who wants to get more out of school, so I asked permission to include it here:

> Hello. Let me introduce myself. I am your Magic Mind. Perhaps formal introduction is unnecessary, since I have been a part of your life and the depth of your being since you were born. This introduction is really intended to acquaint you more completely with the many ways I have been and will continue to be a resource to you.
>
> I use the word magic to describe myself because, as you know, a magician seems to make mysterious things happen with such ease. One moment we see only the shape of the black hat and the next moment we see a rabbit emerge, fluffy and white.
>
> I work in similar mysterious ways. Since you were born I have recorded all the sights, smells, touches, impressions and feelings you have seen and experienced. All the information you have gained about life events and facts has been stored in my memory banks. I love color and sounds and variety and change and seem to be as constantly hungry for action as a growing young person like you is for food.
>
> You can always count on me to learn for you everything you will need to know for a lifetime. As you get better acquainted with me, you will discover even more clearly the ways I work for you.
>
> When you read, the words you see are recorded. I want you to know I can handle words very quickly through my photographic mind's eye, so don't be reluctant about skimming quickly through the pages of books you are reading. I also record the words you hear and want you to know you can trust that I won't erase a thing. And,

of course, your experiences with life that allow you to feel, move, touch and taste are saved too.

You might be wondering how you can invite me to show you my tricks. Well, a tricky mind sometimes enjoys a tricky invitation. Of course, you can always say, "What was that fact on page 30 of my social studies book?" or, "What exactly is the name of my county?" and I may pull it right out of the magic hat. Or you may need to tell me what you need and then, after you ring my door bell, leave a note under my front door and climb a tree in the front or back yard and have fun while you wait for me to surprise you with the answer.

I'll be there . . . when you least expect me! Count on it!

This material works best with young people old enough to understand all the words. So I've made a new version of it for younger children as follows:

Hello. I'm your Magic Mind. I'm always with you to love you and help you whenever you need help. If you need help, just close your eyes and ask me to come, and I'll be there.

I'm magic because I come to you when you're not looking. If you look too closely, I may not be there, but if you close your eyes and just rest quietly, I'll come to you.

I'm always there to keep track of everything that happens: everything you see or hear or taste or smell or touch, or feel inside your body. You'll always be able to remember anything you want to, just by asking me. I love color and sounds and changes and seem to be as constantly hungry for action as a growing child like you is for food.

You can always count on me to learn for you everything you will need to know for a lifetime. As we get to know each other better, you'll find many new ways I can help you.

I'll teach you how to read, and enjoy reading. I'll help you use books to answer the questions you want answered and dream the dreams you want to dream. I'll help you love all books, but I'll also help you find the ones you love best. I'll help you remember all the things you need to whenever you read.

Maybe you're wondering how you can invite me to show you my tricks. Well, try anything you can think of to call me and I'll come. I might come while you're playing in the yard or taking a nap in your room or watching television or going to school. You'll think of ways to call me. You can give me a special name, if you want to.

I'll be there . . . when you least expect me! Won't I be a wonderful surprise?

Guided imagery of this type read to a gentle musical background like the Pachelbel *Canon* can provide a rich experience that lays the foundation for developing self-knowledge and new creative powers.

JASON DISCOVERS CAPTAIN CREATIVE

At this point I'd like to introduce you to nine-year old Jason Gebbia.

Jason's mother, Betty, told me that when he came home from school one day toward the end of first grade he was so distraught he ripped down all the curtains from the windows in his room. She told me it was always a struggle to deal with a learning disabled child who was continually frustrated because he could not do what was required in school.

Betty has been trained as a teacher of Integrative Learning. She decided to use the guided imagery techniques she had learned to help Jason one night when he was having trouble with his homework. The assignment was to write a composition using all the spelling words he had to learn that week. Betty felt the assignment was a good one, and that Jason should be able to enjoy doing it. They were having quite a struggle getting anything written.

"Jason," she said, "let's try something. I am going to ask you to lie down and pretend you are asleep, and I am going to play some music and help you pretend some things. Would you like that?"

Jason decided he would try it. Betty doesn't remember exactly what she did then, but it followed the general outlines of the guided imagery offered above. She also doesn't remember whether Captain Creative was her idea or Jason's. She rather thinks Jason invented him. At any rate, after the guided imagery Jason decided to use Captain Creative in a story about a ship voyage. Pretty soon Captain Creative was not just appearing in his stories, but helping to write them. After that, writing was no longer such a problem for Jason.

A few days later Jason came downstairs with a little toy man pinned in his button hole. "What's that for? " asked Betty.

"That's Bright Idea," said Jason. "He gives me bright ideas."

I interviewed Jason a few weeks later, and I'll let him speak for himself on the subject of Captain Creative, Bright Idea, and others.

"Did Captain Creative make writing easier for you?" I asked.

"Yes," said Jason, "a lot."

"What did he do?"

"He and his little fuzzy friend, Bright Idea, and the S. S. Pencil helped me write many very good stories and long stories, either with spelling homework or at school. Take for instance, my newest one, 'The Invasion of the MUSSCLES.'" (Jason was referring to "millions of unusual small strange creatures lurking everywhere.") "The last homework assignment I did was 'The Person who was Under the Dishes.'"

I asked Jason to read this latter, which he had written that evening. It went like this: "All across the land there were holes, half of them where things were in dishwashers, and some in garbage disposals. On Sunday, pictures were stolen. The pictures were of a bratty sister After who or what took the pictures, I don't know and can't write. If I knew and wrote out the whole thing, then I wouldn't have to walk again, the reward would be that great. The end."

"How do you think that Captain Creative helped you write that story?"

"Well, I took a little bit of it from a poster I saw on a movie store window that was about a movie called 'Creatures.' So I told Captain Creative about this, and his furry friend, Bright Idea, and so instead of using 'creatures,' we decided to use 'things.' I was thinking about doing another story at school that was called 'Things and It.' 'It and the Thing.'"

"Do Captain Creative and Bright Idea do about the same thing, or do they have different jobs?"

"They do mainly different jobs. Because Bright Idea, he's more for doing the really action stories. You can see him wearing a construction helmet with a little light bulb on top. So he's mainly doing action and like heavy stories, while Captain Creative does adventures and goes to distant parts of the earth and distant planets, since he's normally on a ship."

"So he's the adventurer."

"Yeah, he's mainly going out of this galaxy to three galaxies behind Pluto, or just around the world to Africa. Who knows where he's going to go — but he goes there and he comes back and tells you about it and me and him and Bright Idea try to put together and make like a title. And 'The Invasion of the MUSSCLES' was also started by one of the third grade aids that we have. I asked her if she could help me along, and then with my liking MUSSCLES so much, I had remembered an experiment I did in science with my first ten MUSSCLES. They grew in water. So I came up with that title."

"Before you met Captain Creative, what was it like for you to write a story?"

"It'd take me a whole writing period just to get half of it down. Now I can do one story and a half in a writing period. That's probably the highest I've done. Because I've done half of one story that I began and finished up that half. Then I go and I write a whole nother story and then right about when I'm ready to begin another story, it's time."

"What does the S.S. Pencil do for you?"

Jason's voice rose to quite an emotional pitch at this question. I could see it was a matter of great importance to him how Captain Creative got around. "If it wasn't for the S.S. Pencil, Captain Creative wouldn't be able to go anywhere. He could only go from where I'm standing now to maybe New York City before he turned into a piece of dust. And with the S.S.

Pencil, he can go from where I'm standing to Pluto or he can go around the world to Pluto, to another galaxy, and then back to where I'm standing with the S.S. Pencil."

I made a mental note that Captain Creative, like Jason, depends on something beyond himself for the powers that make him superior. He depends on the S.S. Pencil, much as Jason depends on him. This is the natural human tendency to go beyond ourselves, to reach out into the universe itself for inspiration.

"So you have Captain Creative and Bright Idea to help you with your writing. Do they ever help you with anything else?"

"When I need to have a thought that's really hard — like with Bright Idea, he's got a little light bulb for an idea. And he's got little suction cups on his feet so they stick to you, and with those he can feed the bright ideas into you and take out the old, bad, crumpled up ideas. The light bulb on top of his head starts working and it goes through his helmet, then on through his whole body, even though he's green, and out his feet into you, and then he reverses the whole process, only this time it's sucking in the bad ones, like the left foot is giving out, and the right foot is sucking in. It's kind of like if you're running water in the sink and then you put your hand under it, shaped like a claw, some of it would go off to the left, and some would go off on the right, and some would just go plain old down. Bright Idea sucks in bad, turns 'em into good and blows 'em out the other side. It's kind of like what a fan does — it sucks in air, and blows it out the other side."

Then Jason told me more about the S.S. Pencil. "It could take him to Pluto, or it could take him to 1951," he said.

Betty contrasted the first Captain Creative story about the ship with what Jason is doing now. "That one was a real trial," she said. "It was really difficult. This one he sat down — we kind of played with it. He said, 'I don't want to do this, Mom,' and I said, 'Well just do two sentences,' then, 'Well, since you've just done two sentences. . .' and pretty soon he had it finished. And he did that while I was making dinner. I wasn't sitting here coaxing or coaching or that kind of stuff, I was just kind of saying, 'A couple more sentences, a couple more facts. You're really going gangbusters, why stop now?' And I know it didn't take more than thirty minutes before it was done, and he used every single one of the spelling words in it, which is more restrictive than when he's writing on his own."

I asked Jason if when he did his math he had anyone to help him.

"Except for my math book."

"Do you think there could be somebody like Bright Idea that could help you with math?

"Umhm."

"Who could that be?"

"Probably the guy upstairs who's got a little diploma on his head." He went upstairs to get the cloth doll — College Graduate with Diploma.

"Do you think you'll ask him next time you have a problem how to do the problem?"

"Umhm. But you know, I have one more question. How am I going to use Plain Old Green Guy?"

"Could you use him in science?"

"I'm not sure."

"What do you have to do in science?"

Jason told me they were studying plant systems, and I suggested maybe Green Guy could explain the systems to Jason. Jason said no, they were explained in class, but he could use Green Guy to remind him to water his plants.

"I could have him sitting on a plant, and then I look over and there's Green Guy sitting on the plant, reminding me it needs water." This, by the way, is an excellent mnemonic device, widely used by memory experts. Jason appears to have worked it out on his own.

I asked Jason where else in school he might need help.

"Reading."

"What kind of help do you need in reading?"

"I hate it."

"Could there be somebody that could help you to love reading?"

Jason told me about a book he had loved reading called *Intergalactic Spy*. "One time I finished it in two days," he said.

"Suppose you had somebody to make you love each book that you read as much as *Intergalactic Spy*. Would that help?"

Jason nodded his head emphatically.

"Who could do that for you?"

"Green Guy."

"He sounds like he's very useful."

BUT WHAT'S THE USE OF ALL THIS FANTASY?

Later when I told a friend about this interview, she said, "Isn't he just learning to live in a fantasy world? Isn't he withdrawing from reality?" On the contrary: as Mardi J. Horowitz argues in *Image Formation and Cognition*, mental health is largely measurable in terms of one's ability to control one's own mental imagery. Jason clearly was able to summon and use imaginary characters to help him complete tasks he cared about. This kind of ritual is often used by creative people. It's a matter of setting the stage for the creative mental action you want — telling your mind what kind of results you're after.

Some of the imagery in this conversation with Jason reminds me a little of how Einstein described his delving into the relation between space and time that led to the theory of relativity. He imagined himself riding on a beam of light and noticed what happened as a result. Later he translated the resulting images into mathematical formulas. Thus the most creative part of his life work was done in a manner similar to the one Jason describes.

And if you read Jason's remarks closely, you may have noticed he is already developing a rather acute scientific imagination, because his ability to describe a particular kind of process using a model is characteristic of such breakthroughs in scientific thinking as the Bohr atom (loosely compared to the solar system) or the double helix.

Children like Jason who are diagnosed as learning disabled may actually have a style of learning and knowing that is not compatible with the way things are usually done in school. Thus they may have great difficulty with some of the academic demands made on them while they are children and later, as adults, make major contributions to knowledge. Recent breakthroughs in understanding learning styles can be helpful in rectifying this situation, and may be useful in preventing such children from suffering serious, if unwitting, harm from those trying to help them.

WE CAN USE HELP TAKING INVENTORY OF OUR RESOURCES

Another thing that is evident from my conversation with Jason, and from the results of his association with Captain Creative, is that the mind is capable of developing a variety of tools to help solve whatever problems it may face, but that often we do not fully appreciate the resources we have until someone else brings new possibilities to our attention. Jason's mother had opened up a new way for him to be successful in school. He had spontaneously developed this approach beyond the original form of the guided imagery. Nevertheless he needed the help of questioning to think of additional possibilities he hadn't considered before.

Whether or not Jason will make practical use of the ideas he thought of during our conversation remains to be seen. Perhaps Green Guy will stand at his side as he reads and remind him of Intergalactic Spy, thus helping him to become an avid reader. Perhaps not. Let me tell the story, though, of a student I once had who was able to clear up a serious reading problem after a brief conversation in which I directed his attention to thought processes he already knew how to use.

WARREN REBUILDS HIS VISUAL SYSTEM

Warren had serious trouble reading, so he avoided it whenever possible. He was a stereo nut who loved building and rebuilding amplifiers, but this was not paying off for him academically. His parents were nagging him to do better in school so he could get a college education.

I asked Warren to describe his reading problem. "I get half way through a sentence," he said, "and I lose track of it."

"Okay, let's suppose your visual system is like a stereo amplifier, and it's not working. What would you do to make it work?"

"Well, first I'd check out each channel to see if anything was wrong. Come to think of it, I don't think my eyes work together very well, I think I use one eye to read the first half of the sentence and the other to read the second half, and they don't match up. What I could do is buy an eye patch and try it with only one eye at a time until I get it right."

Warren followed his own advice and within weeks his reading improved significantly. Then his interests began to change, and he found he really wanted to go to college.

Warren's mechanistic approach to his own visual system is impressive in its results. Here's another story somewhat along the same lines that illustrates how powerful an image can be in making it possible for the mind to re-program the nervous system to deal with a severely injured body. This was told me by June Sasson, a colleague in Integrative Learning.

THE STORY OF BARBARA

"It was shortly after I had taken the Lozanov training," she began, "that I met Barbara. It happened a friend asked me to accompany her briefly to visit someone who had been seriously hurt in an automobile accident. When I entered Barbara's room I found she was being treated like a vegetable. Her head had been so severely damaged in the accident her face had been pushed over inches to the side of her skull. The major part of her brain had been destroyed, so the surgeon reported there was no possibility of her ever regaining any ability to communicate.

"So, as we stood in her room talking, I was surprised to notice her eye movements tracking what we were saying. I asked to be alone with her for a few moments.

"Then I told her an outrageous lie. 'I am a specialist from the West Coast,' I said. 'I have had great success with people like you, and have taught them to regain the power to speak. I would like to work with you and help you to learn how to communicate. I will come and visit you every other day for a while.'

"I'm not sure why I told her this. I guess I felt there could be no harm. If I did not help her, I would at least be giving her more positive attention than she was getting from anyone else.

"So I visited Barbara for two hours every other day. I told her that her brain was like a spider web of pathways and although some had been damaged, as she surely knew, we only use ten percent of our brain, so we could simply take another pathway that had never been used and groove it for speech. I asked her to make believe the path was overgrown with weeds and told her to spend some time that evening removing the weeds and rocks. The next day I began instructing her to *see* the words I was saying grooving a deep fissure in the path she had cleared. I repeated one syllable words with classical music playing in the background.

"Three weeks after I began this process I entered Barbara's room and greeted her. 'Hi,' she said to me. 'See, I told you you could speak,' I said. I felt scared to death, as if ice water were coming through my veins. The mixture of elation that she had actually spoken and terror at what I had tapped into was overwhelming. I went into the bathroom and leaned against the wall sweating and shaking. Finally I decided what was done was done and I couldn't wait to see how far beyond a simple 'Hi' she could advance. I came out of the bathroom and hugged her. 'Let's get going,' I said, putting on the classical music again. I was giggling madly inside.

"It took about two weeks for her to learn to say her first fifty words. It didn't take much longer for her to regain the ability to say almost anything.

"Before I left I told her she could use the same process to get her arms and legs to move. Once her family heard her first words they couldn't wait to help her. They became her willing therapists in helping her regain the use of her arms and legs, one finger at a time. When I saw her for the last time she was walking with the help of crutches, and the only indication she had a speech problem was a slight hesitation before certain sounds. She told me she intended to continue improving until she could move normally.

"When I revealed I had lied to her about being an expert, she said, 'I never thought I would be grateful to anyone for a lie, but I certainly am now.'

"Two things particularly struck me about Barbara's situation. One was the way her family used to argue about whose turn it was *not* to take care of her. Once she began to recover, though, everyone wanted to be with her as much as possible.

"The other was she told me how awful it was to be thirsty for water and have to wait until someone decided to give her a drink. Then she might be given fruit juice or something else she didn't want."

June told me this story several years after it happened. Except for the people in Barbara's family, she had never discussed it with anyone else.

"Clearly the doctor made a mistake," she said. "Her brain was not as damaged as he said it was."

"Didn't you know," I asked, "that it's now been established that brain functions lost through damage can be taken over by other parts of the brain, so it's possible to regain normal functioning even after a large part of the brain is destroyed?"

She hadn't known that, and was worried that someone would accuse her of practicing medicine without a license. "Nothing you did had anything to do with medicine," I said. "You were practicing education. Many people who suffer from brain damage must be re-educated, much in the way that you worked with Barbara."

THE LEARNER MAKES THE SUCCESS POSSIBLE

The key to June's success was her belief that Barbara could teach her brain new skills. She used metaphorical images to guide her in doing this. Such use of metaphor to guide the brain is precisely how some language works. Many words are metaphors used to describe subjective experiences we cannot comprehend by more direct means. "I'm fired up with anger" is an example of such a metaphor. This characteristic of language can sometimes cause or cure psychosomatic illness which, along with June's experience, demonstrates how powerfully our language use affects our bodies as well as our minds.

June provided the leadership and direction in this teaching success, but it was Barbara's determination to make it work that made success possible. The drive Barbara had as an adult to create new pathways in her brain is the same as the drive any child feels to find new ways of knowing, understanding and doing.

THE IMPORTANCE OF PRE-VERBAL THINKING

Thus, from earliest childhood, the way we use imagery in our thinking is important. Whether we discover our most useful images in fantasy or technology, they can help us think about the problems we face much more effectively than if we use logic alone. Because the mind naturally forms and recognizes patterns, it can access many more ideas when we think visually than when we use language alone. By invoking his pre-verbal learning experiences, Jason seems to have been able to overcome the conflict that apparently started when he confronted the excessively linguistic demands of school. Captain Creative helped him summon the images that could eventually be translated into words to help him succeed.

For several reasons this transition into visual imagery can be more easily accomplished with a background of relaxing classical music than it can be by guided imagery or questioning alone. For one thing, the transition from language into visual images is easier when language and music are played together. Another factor is that the pleasure associated with the music reduces tension and anxiety, and makes unraveling the problem easier.

PRECEDE YOUR DISCUSSION WITH MEDITATION

If you want to see how effective this combination of pre-verbal thinking and musical background can be, try it with other people. At the end of Chapter Sixteen I suggested some group exercises revolving around symbol-making. Now we'll add the element of music.

Get the family or group together and pose a problem for discussion. For starters, it is best that the problem be a hypothetical one, such as how to design an automobile that drives itself. This takes the pressure off, since no one resolution must be agreed on.

Select a piece of classical music like the Pachelbel *Canon* to share together. Suggest that everyone close their eyes and breathe deeply. Then start the music. When it is finished, the family members can discuss the ideas that came to them. Sometimes a person may have none at first but, as the discussion continues, will begin to think of some.

You can use the musical meditation exercise for problem solving, or for starting people to think about an idea everyone needs to discuss. Suppose, for example, you're trying to decide whether or not to buy a new house or move to another city. Let everyone take the problem to the music and then discuss it. The resulting discussion is likely to have greater depth.

In the next chapter we'll explore how to extend this idea further, to develop writing abilities. For now it is sufficient to let the music stimulate the flow of images — images which may pass in a moment, or become as central in one's life as Captain Creative has been for Jason, or that ride on a beam of light was for Einstein.

18

ON BECOMING A POET

Finding a well of inspiration with music and relaxation:
an exercise to increase writing ability and enjoyment.

It's time now to explore how to bring the inner uniqueness of the mind to the surface in order to become conscious of the special qualities you alone have to offer. Getting beyond the conscious worry that blocks original thought is a problem that has troubled even some of the most creative people in history. I would like to offer a comparatively easy way to solve that problem. Perhaps this exercise will help you, as it has me, to get past persistent stumbling blocks in your life.

AN END TO WRITER'S BLOCK

One of the most exciting experiences I've ever had occurred the day I broke through my writer's block and more than doubled my productivity as a result of a single forty-five minute exercise.

It came about in the following way: My friend Barry Morley and I together developed a new approach to teaching writing that we called "poetry and relaxation." It involved combining guided imagery with classical music as a prelude and inspiration for writing a poem. Barry used it with his students and I used it with mine. We found it to be extremely helpful in persuading reluctant writers to explore the creative impulses that lay dormant inside them.

MY WRITING BREAKTHROUGH

It happened that a couple of years after we developed this exercise (which by the way, I often led but never experienced myself) I was teaching a course in writing short stories. I decided to do my own assignments for this course. I had selected the theme for the story I planned to write, and decided to try using classical music to inspire me to flesh out the story.

For twenty minutes I allowed the music to stimulate my thinking and bring images to my consciousness. It went something like this: I listened to the music for a moment, and then an idea came for the story. I didn't like the idea, and so dismissed it from my mind and continued to listen to the music. Soon another idea came, and then another. Gradually I allowed the ideas bubbling up from inside me to intermingle and take different forms. I began to play with the shape of the entire story and as it went through many permutations, I felt it coming more firmly into existence. At the end of twenty minutes I had the story and was ready to write it out.

When I had finished I realized that the same story would have required several cycles of revision by my old method of writing. Listening to the music had enabled me to make these revisions in my imagination. The next day I used this method to write another story, and then another.

A PRIZE-WINNING PLAY IN A FEW HOURS

The climax came a few weeks later when a friend asked me to write a one act play for performance at a lunch time theater. As it happened I was reading a book that morning on cosmology, and when I decided to write the play and went through the process of listening to the music, I found ideas about cosmology were weaving their way into a delightful little domestic comedy. I finished writing the play in four hours, and sent it off to my friend, who didn't like it.

At about the same time, though, I read a notice of a national playwriting contest for one act radio plays. I entered my play in the contest and it won. A few months later I was able to hear a professionally acted radio broadcast version of my play.

PERMANENT FREEDOM FROM WRITER'S BLOCK

For a couple of years I used this technique of listening to music and allowing the ideas to work themselves out until I was ready to write. It was a phenomenal experience. Until then I had wrestled with myself as a writer, trying to force myself to face that inevitable blank piece of paper. But once I discovered the music could guarantee inspiration, I no longer feared the blank paper, and no longer postponed my writing tasks. Life ceased to be a matter of taking walks, eating peanut butter sandwiches, making phone calls and otherwise avoiding the task I had set for myself. Now I could just play the music and then write whatever had surfaced in my imagination.

After about two years of this, I no longer needed the music. I was now able to write whatever I wanted whenever I wanted. Often I would arise early in the morning and go to the typewriter. Only once in the ten years since then have I experienced writer's block.

FUN AND INSPIRATION IN WRITING CLASS

If writer's block was a problem for me, who had always loved to write, it was certainly a problem for many of my students, who hated to write — or feared writing and approached it with worry and defensiveness. The poetry and relaxation exercise helped many of them overcome their writing blocks, just as it had helped me. I found that by the time I used the exercise four times in a writing class even formerly reluctant writers were writing comfortably. In fact, for many of my students who had previously hated writing, putting pen to paper became one of their most meaningful and enjoyable activities. I'll never forget the boy who openly declared his disgust for poetry and subsequently became so excited by writing that not a class would go by when he didn't feel slighted if he couldn't read his latest adventure in introspection.

Apparently writing is a perfectly natural form of expression for all of us, just like speaking, but we get so many negative feelings about it as a result of too many red marks on too many papers, that we become inhibited. The poetry and relaxation exercise breaks down this inhibition and converts the student to a love of writing.

TRY IT YOURSELF

If you want to try the exercise yourself, you can use the guided imagery from the previous chapter (page 194) as a basis. Record that passage on tape and play it back to yourself while listening to classical music. Then just listen to the music for a while and consider what you want to write. When you're ready, start writing. It's as simple as that.

The only reason to use the guided imagery, incidentally, is to overcome some people's initial feeling that the music alone is not enough. It's an added stimulus, not at all necessary itself. Actually, the music alone may work better, because as you begin to think about words while listening to the music you will experience the delight of bringing the two hemispheres of your brain into synchrony. Thus the music will make a pleasure out of the search for ideas, which may previously have caused you frustration. You'll soon find you can train your mind to let the ideas flow whenever you want them. I trained mine so well that I can simply let the ideas flow as I sit at the word processor, without first having to go to the music, since my writing blocks have long since disappeared.

LEADING A GROUP

If you're going to use poetry and relaxation as a group exercise, tell the group to have a pencil and paper, so they can begin to write as soon as they feel ready to do so. They should avoid eye contact with anyone else in the room until their writing has been completed, because letting another person's consciousness interact with yours is distracting.

Tell the group to let their pencil do the writing, and not to feel that they have to have anything in mind when they begin to write. Their subconscious mind will write the poem while they are listening to the music. If they want to find out what it wrote, they can simply see what flows out of the pencil. It is surprising how many in the group will have just that experience.

If when the exercise is completed someone has chosen not to write a poem, tell the group that occasionally the exercise does not inspire someone the first time, but that by the fourth time it is tried, everyone will have had a good experience with it. I mention this only if I notice someone has had trouble, in order to reassure that person with what I know to be true. I do not mention it at the beginning, which might only suggest to some people that they should expect trouble.

When the poems are written I ask that they be handed in to me, and I then read them all anonymously. I do this because some people are uncomfortable at the thought of others knowing what they have written. New inspirations can seem a little strange and frightening, and it is only after trust and safety have developed among group members that they may want to acknowledge their poems.

TRY IT WITH YOUR FAMILY

Parents who have tried this at home with the family have had excellent results. It's a good exercise if your children are having friends over and a group activity seems appropriate. Don't force it. Just explain what you have in mind and ask if anyone wants to try it. If the atmosphere is right, a new family ritual may be established that can help everyone improve their writing while developing a wonderful sense of togetherness.

EXPAND-A-STORY

Another technique I've found remarkably helpful for developing writing skill is called "expand-a-story." I discovered it while teaching an adult who was trying to relearn to read after a serious brain injury. We were working with simple children's books that had a picture on every page, accompanied by a single line of text. Obviously, the text could not capture much of what was in the pictures, so I suggested he add to each page a line or two of his own. These additions we wrote on three-by-five cards and put into the book. The next time he read the book, he enjoyed reading a story he had helped create. The result was a decided improvement in the rate of his learning.

I then found this technique of expanding a sketchy story can be used to improve anyone's writing. I've used it with children just learning to write and with adults, some of whom are professional writers. At every level of ability this approach helps develop new skills and perceptions.

The reason it works so well is that usually when we make up stories we must create not only individual sentences, but an entire plot structure as well. Structure and details require different types of focus, and do not always combine well. Having enough structure in place helps writers focus on enriching their style and providing the detailed, cumulative effect good writing requires.

To create an expand-a-story for your child, write sentences on a sheet of paper with lots of space between them, in which additional sentences can be written. Here's a sample expand-a-story.

IT IS A BEAUTIFUL DAY IN THE COUNTRY.
THE SUN IS SHINING BRIGHTLY.
NEVERTHELESS, HAROLD IS SAD.
SOMEONE HAS STOLEN HIS COOKIE.
HE ASKS THE SNAKE, "DID YOU STEAL MY COOKIE?"
THE SNAKE REPLIES, "S-S-S-S-S".
HAROLD THINKS THAT MEANS "YES."
HE SCOLDS THE SNAKE.
NOW HE FEELS BETTER.
HE CAN APPRECIATE THE BEAUTIFUL DAY IN THE COUNTRY.

When you write an expand-a-story, you can work on any part of it at any time. Because you don't have to worry about chronological sequence, it's a little like working on a painting. You can fill in details in any order and keep hopping back and forth between parts of the story until you've got it the way you want it.

So try an expand-a-story with your child, and after he or she has filled in the spaces, suggest that the child create an expand-a-story for you to fill in. This sort of thing can go on for a long time, adding greatly to the enjoyment of the writing process.

19

ONLY THE HELPLESS NEVER ASK FOR HELP

*Really successful people are good at asking for help at the
right time. But some help is genuinely harmful, some is
disrespectful and some is a nuisance.*

Norie Huddle, the author of *Surviving: The Best Game on Earth* is one
of the most productively inquisitive people I know. Five minutes after
you've met her, she's dragged your whole philosophy out of you in an
interview which is one of the most incisive you'll ever experience.

Norie has a wonderful story that helps explain how she got that way.
She tells how as a little girl she expressed interest in a large, white house she
saw out the window while on a drive with her father. "Would you like to see
that house?" her father asked. When Norie said she would, he pulled the car
over to the side of the road, took her up to the front door, knocked, and
persuaded the woman who lived there to show the two of them around.

"Ever since," says Norie, "I've felt that if I wanted to know
something I could easily find out all about it. It was only many years later
that I realized there was a sign in front of that house that said 'For Sale.'"

Here's an example of how worthwhile it is to teach a child the value of
asking questions, while providing the experience that answers will come.
We all need to learn how useful it is to ask for help when we can benefit
from it.

There's a delicate balance, of course, between the inner awareness of
one's own unique answers and the need to receive help and guidance from
others. Unfortunately, much of the help many of us have received has been

so manipulative, controlling and disrespectful that we eventually come to distrust help in any form. In Norie's case the request was simple and clear, and the response was direct and unmanipulative. She learned that an inquisitive thought can lead directly to actions which provide prompt and thorough answers.

As I have previously argued, we are a cooperative species who have throughout history depended on each other's assistance. The role of parenting is itself based on this survival need for help and cooperation. The unusual length of human childhood provides the time necessary for a rich, complex growing and learning experience. During that time the quality of parental nurturing is of the greatest importance. Unfortunately, too often parents give more assistance than is asked for, stifling the child's desire to receive or even ask for it. But in the right atmosphere the child will learn to be comfortable asking for help from parents and then, later, from others.

COMING OUT OF LONELINESS

When George came to our school he was determined to do everything himself. The trouble was, he never completed anything. As soon as he hit a snag he would stop working and either declare that he couldn't do the work or that it wasn't worth doing. He was an isolated, unhappy boy.

Then one day as I was sitting next to George I noticed an original and remarkable style of drawing coming from his pen. I assumed he'd practiced drawing for several years, but I asked him, "Where did you learn to do that?"

"Eddie taught me," he said. "I just copied the type of thing he was doing."

I was surprised. Eddie was a student in our school whose art work had a distinctively different style. George had met Eddie only a few months before, so he hadn't been drawing for long. "But Eddie's drawing doesn't look like that," I said.

George seemed surprised. "You think it doesn't?"

"Sure. Eddie draws cars and airplanes. You draw geometrical abstractions. There's a little similarity in your styles, but not too much. George, your artwork is quite original."

George seemed pleased. Then, during the following weeks I noticed he was completing his work more often and seemed more willing now to take other people's advice. Evidently he had been so afraid of copying he had been unwilling to ask for help at all. But now he realized that getting help doesn't force you to do something another person's way. Soon George's work was blossoming.

NO MORE CHEATING

Traditional classrooms place students in rows facing the front of the room. It is assumed that all students should communicate directly with the teacher, not with each other. This will prevent cheating, it is argued, and keep the children from getting things wrong by learning mistakes from each other. Yet the old one room schoolhouse depended on the students to teach each other. The education it provided was often excellent.

With Integrative Learning there is no cheating, and it is assumed that students can learn effectively from each other. Since the class experience is designed to help all students learn to the fullest extent of their capacity, cheating becomes useless and irrelevant. No one can cheat when everyone is aware of how everyone else is doing and how much each one knows. The response to anyone's not knowing something is to supply the missing information with as little fanfare as possible.

REVERSING THE TEACHER-STUDENT RATIO

So the ideal classroom has students mingling with and learning from one another. This reverses the teacher-student ratio. In an Integrative Learning classroom, each student is surrounded by lots of potential teachers.

That works well if everyone knows how to ask for help effectively. But you can't ask until you know you're in need. In other words, you have to know where you are and where you're trying to go, and something about why you're having trouble getting there. In the lock-step procedure of many traditional classrooms that's never considered.

There's no virtue in pretending you don't need help if you do, and there's no point in asking if you don't need it. Learning how to ask for help intelligently will in the end make us independent, because it is the quickest way to get the background and practice we need to master the fundamentals of any field of knowledge.

OUR FEAR OF REVEALING WHAT WE DON'T KNOW

Most people in our society are afraid that they might be caught not knowing something. It's amazing how much this fear prevents information from circulating among us. If you're trying to keep someone from finding out how little you know, you'll do all sorts of non-productive things to hide your ignorance. But you certainly won't learn anything. So it is that crowds of fearful people, queasy about their lack of knowledge, engage in endless small talk — about the latest fashions, how the football team is doing, and where the bargains are. For some, this is simply escape from real communication. If the fear level is high enough, it seems necessary to blunt it with alcohol, which in the end (even in small quantities) damages the brain. And that's how a great deal of the social life in this country proceeds. As a marvelous teacher I once met was fond of saying, "Everything is based on fear."

A TENFOLD INCREASE IN INFORMATION FLOW

I think that one simple change in the way we relate to each other would increase the information flow in our society by at least ten times. As things stand now, if you ask me a question and I don't know the answer, I will (1) pretend I didn't hear (2) fake an answer, and hope I'm right (this is particularly easy with yes-no questions) (3) deftly change the subject (4) give a piece of non-information designed to look like an answer when it's not.

In the ideal society if you asked me a question and I didn't know the answer, I'd simply say (with great delight at the opportunity to learn something new), "I don't know, but when you tell me I will." That would give the other person the chance to provide information I didn't have, and would thereby increase my fund of knowledge. As a result I'd soon gather so much information that in most conversations I'd be familiar with anything that came up.

HOW TO GET EDUCATED FOR FREE

Let's carry this a step further. Suppose that every time you met someone who had any specialized knowledge you asked them about it. You'd probably get a personalized cram course on that subject for free. Your new friend would keep talking as long as time permitted, because it's always fun to share specialized knowledge. And you would have a presentation especially tailored to your particular interests.

I've found if I talk with a college professor for an hour I'll get almost as much information about a course as I would if I sat through several weeks in a classroom. What I get is a more condensed version with all the highlights, the stuff I'd be likely to remember after the rest of the course is forgotten. That leaves me a lot of extra hours to talk to a lot of other professors. And it's all free. What a great way to spend an evening!

PROOF THAT EVERYBODY LOVES TO HELP OUT

We all love to help any way we can. If you don't believe that, think about the times you've stopped to ask how to get somewhere. Usually it's as if you were doing a favor for the person who gets to help you out. Have you noticed how most people will drop everything to come over and talk? I've seen clerks and gas station attendants ignore a customer who is waiting cash in hand while they help me figure out the local geography. They'll let me look at their maps and reference books, and sometimes they'll personally accompany me where I want to go. Some people have gone miles out of their way to help me get where I was going. Once when I asked a man how to get somewhere, he went to such lengths to take me there I was sure he wanted a tip, so I offered him a couple of dollars, thereby embarrassing both of us — he'd only wanted to help out. Have you ever once asked someone how to get somewhere and been told, "Please don't bother me, I'm too busy right now"? It's obvious that better than ninety-nine percent of us love to share information whenever the opportunity arises.

FINDING OUT WHAT YOU DON'T KNOW

But it's hard sometimes to know what we don't know. We've been so badgered by teachers who make us feel guilty if we're not right all the time that we don't like to admit even to ourselves what we don't know. Therefore the following exercise should be as meaningful for you as it is for your children, because you'll find yourself sharpening your awareness of when you need help.

AN EXERCISE IN LEARNING TO ASK FOR HELP

Blindfold one member of the family. Everyone else will have the opportunity to help the blindfolded person find his or her way around — but only when the blindfolded one asks for help. When help is requested, it should always be given sensitively and thoroughly. Take turns being blindfolded while you go about your daily routines.

You can practice this exercise for any desirable length of time. It could be a couple of minutes, or it could go on for an entire day, depending on how people feel about it. What each will discover is how much fun it is to hone up the other senses by temporarily ceasing to depend on vision. Notice how you get better at performing ordinary tasks while blindfolded. Notice, too, how you become better able to be specific about the kind of help you need.

BLOCK PILING EXERCISE

Another chance to use the blindfold is the block piling exercise. Spread some blocks around on the floor. One person piles them up while someone else is there to give information when it's asked for. At first just concentrate on making the pile as high as possible. With more experience the blindfolded person can try more complicated structures.

FORMING A FAMILY COUNCIL

After you've all learned from the blindfold exercise how to be more specific about the kind of help you need, form a family council that meets regularly. All take turns talking about the kinds of help they need to accomplish their goals. The Think-and-Listen format I described in Chapter Ten may be used here. Agreements can be worked out so everyone gives and gets the needed help. Divide the time evenly so each person can get a fair share of attention.

TRY SOME SPECIAL PROJECTS

When everyone is comfortable giving and receiving help with ordinary daily tasks, you might consider undertaking special projects. If anyone in the family wishes to do this, the family council can consider it and decide what help might be needed and how it should be given. For example, when I was young I started a theater company. I could not drive a car at the time, and I often needed my parents' assistance to chauffeur actors around to rehearsals. Because there was no formal structure for doing this, I always felt guilty asking, and would wait until the last possible minute. Had we had a family council, it would have been much easier for me to ask, and there would have been less conflict between my parents and me. The family council is a wonderful way to teach responsibility.

HELPING WITH HOMEWORK

Helping with homework is a particularly thorny problem. This is because it is too easy to give the wrong kind of help. When you are working with your child, you shouldn't be the one to do the thinking, you should support your child's thinking. But withholding desired information for too long doesn't help either. That's likely to turn into a power play between parent and child.

One time, for example, my mother was helping one of my brothers write a composition. My other brother was listening to this process. For fun, he wrote down everything his brother said, but left out everything my mother said. What he wrote went like this: "Uh-huh. Yeah, that would be good. You think so? Okay, I'll write that. I don't know. Yeah. Yeah, that sounds good. Okay. How do you spell that?" and so on. He had about three pages of this sort of thing, with not one single idea coming from his brother.

This got the assignment done, but it didn't help my brother become an independent thinker. He had to learn that in other ways. (When my mother read the transcription my younger brother had made, she laughed and immediately changed her ways. She was fond of telling this story at social occasions.)

When it's time to work on homework, give your child a Think-and-Listen, during which the child can determine precisely what help is needed. You can then ask questions about anything you think might prevent the child from being sufficiently independent. For example, you could say, "Why do you think you will learn more if I look that up in the encyclopedia for you than if you look it up yourself?" This question is tricky. It can easily sound like criticism or a put-down. So ask it in such a way that a well reasoned answer that had you going to the encyclopedia would be acceptable to you, and the child knows that. Another question: "Have you asked your teacher to explain more fully how to do this type of problem?" Your goal in giving help should be to provide the kind of support that leads to independence. This means you should be patient and loving at all times.

Learning to give and receive help can make a big difference in our lives. We'll feel less isolated, better able to face the challenges life presents. In the process we'll grow closer together as a family, developing really meaningful and powerful connections quite different from the squabbling and running off in all directions that typifies too many families these days.

20

MEANING DEEP DOWN TO YOUR GUT

The importance of being truthful about feelings.
Practice at expressing emotions can be fun
— and can promote family harmony.

In the last chapter we explored how you can strengthen the link between a person and a group to encourage the full development of that person's individuality. But how is individuality to express itself? There will inevitably be lots of feeling behind any true personal expression. So we need some way to explore feelings in order to become more comfortable expressing them, and more skillful in using them.

The role of emotion is a recurrent theme in this book, as it must be in any discussion of learning and education. We have considered (in Chapter Five) the Triune Brain Theory as to how information entering the long-term memory must pass through the limbic system which controls the emotions; the interaction of thinking and feeling (in Chapter Ten); and connections between emotion, memory and creativity (in Chapter Seventeen).

Becoming sensitive to and expressing emotions is vital not only to our psychological and social well-being, it is essential to our capacity to function rationally and intellectually. This sensitivity and expressiveness is an ability we can cultivate easily and enjoyably.

HOW ROSALIND TAUGHT HERSELF TO HATE WHAT SHE WAS DOING

When I first met Rosalind, she was a bright sixth grader who happened not to like school. In fact, she didn't like anything much except her Dad and her horse. When I pressed her on the matter I found that indeed there were other things she cared about as well: air, water, food, light, and so on. In other words, Rosalind had arrived at a pretty basic level of emotional turnoff to school work (and most other things as well).

I once asked her to do an exercise that helped her to learn, and she did it very well. But while she was doing it, there was a heavy frown on her face and in her voice. I noticed that the inflection pattern at the end of every phrase was a downward fall — almost a thud. Rosalind was telling herself through her expression and the movements of her body that she hated what she was doing, even though she was doing it well and it was inherently interesting. Clearly, in the situation we were working with the hatred was irrelevant to what she was doing.

So I asked her to smile as she continued the exercise, and to change the inflection patterns of her speech so her voice smiled too. A little lift at the end of each phrase instead of the dying fall helped significantly. Rosalind was beginning to teach herself to have positive feelings about something connected with her school work.

Being able to control and shape our feelings instead of being ruled by them can have a profoundly positive effect on everything we do — if we use that power wisely. The purpose of the exercises in this chapter is to enhance and practice using this capacity in safe and enjoyable ways.

LEARNING TO HIDE OUR FEELINGS

One of the saddest experiences of childhood is realizing that sometimes people don't tell the truth about their feelings. During their first months of life, children have to interpret adults without the assistance of language. In fact, our most basic acts of communication don't involve language at all. We cry, laugh, and remain silent — and thereby express the most powerful emotions, inexpressible in words, even by the finest poets. Actors earn their living not by what they say, but by the way they say it.

When we express our feelings fully and "own" them, we experience harmony in ourselves and in relation to others. When we deny them, even to ourselves, we feel disoriented. For children, expressing and owning feelings is perfectly natural. It does not occur to them to hide their joys, sorrows, fears or frustrations. But adults who have learned to hide feelings may lose patience with children's spontaneous expressions of feeling, wanting to suppress them. As children take on adult attitudes toward feelings, they tend to feel disoriented, uncomfortable in their bodies, and separated from themselves and their daily life experience.

Disorientation occurs when we learn to suppress laughter and tears, as well as other natural means of expression. Rejecting our feelings in this way may lead us to think ourselves fundamentally unacceptable. And by separating verbal and non-verbal communication we lose track of many of the subtle nuances that enrich our interactions, thus becoming more superficial in our feelings and the way we communicate.

LANGUAGE AS CONCEALMENT

As the child begins to understand and manipulate language, it soon becomes clear that words are used to conceal as well as to reveal meanings. Before language, the child knew how Mommy was feeling. Words may make it unfortunately clear that how Mommy is feeling and how she says she is feeling can be different.

As we grow older we become so used to the concealment of feelings we lose track of how disruptive this is to our sense of well-being and personal power. A lot of our energy is used up in guessing and interpreting, because the truth about feelings is so often disguised.

MEANING AND BEING

Archibald MacLeish wrote that "a poem must not mean but be." Meaning and being do not begin as separate concepts for the child, but become separated as a result of using language. With the concealment of emotion comes the need for seeking layers of meaning beneath the surface of human communication. This is not bad — in fact, it challenges the intelligence — but it can lead to confusion and insecurity.

Experiencing disharmony between what we say and what we feel leads to a vague sense of anxiety and not being at home in the world — a sense that some philosophers assume is an inescapable part of the human condition. However, the origin of this anxiety is not in human nature, it is in our withholding or even becoming unaware of what we really feel — in failing to live our lives fully. Accepting emotions helps us get beneath the surface in order to discover the rich and wonderful process of being.

Thus when I say "I am fine," you'll have little idea from the words alone what precisely I mean. Whether I am in torment or ecstasy, I report that I am fine. But if I fully and responsibly own my emotions, you will know how I am feeling without having to be caught up in my feelings.

ANGER AND DENIAL

As children we learn of concealment when our parents "protect" us from feelings they believe we can't handle, not realizing it is easier to know that someone is angry, afraid or unhappy than to have to guess.

Children are usually comfortable with expressions of strong emotion. When someone is crying they will give warm and affectionate attention. They know all about crying — it is one of their main activities. Recently I conducted a forty hour workshop for adults which was also attended by a seven month old baby. From time to time during the workshop someone would cry or express intense anger. Whenever this happened, the baby would attend closely to the expression of emotion. She was fascinated, but not distressed or anxious, and there seemed to me to be a loving expression in her eyes. Once the emotion had died down, the baby's attention would wander. Babies respond directly not only to their own need to cry and rage, but to other people's as well.

GROWING UP WITH SUPPRESSED FEELINGS

Children raised in an atmosphere of honest expression of feeling continue to have no fear when others express themselves, provided there is no danger present. But those who grow up around people who do not express feelings easily are likely to be afraid when outbursts occur. They have learned that something is wrong with the expression of emotion, since their parents tried so hard to avoid it. This avoidance or suppression of one's own feelings may be the worst crime one can commit against oneself. And feelings suppressed too harshly or too long can eventually emerge in explosions of dangerous rage.

In our society, which is so fearful of anger and so prone to vent it in inappropriate and dangerous ways — anywhere from the streets to the arms race — it is doubly important to learn to redirect our own anger productively, responsibly and without inhibition. It matters little whether I am shouting "I can't stand you," or "Peter Piper Picked a Peck of Pickled Peppers." The feeling behind the words, if it is the same, accomplishes the same relief. Yet not knowing this, we sometimes irresponsibly use our anger as an excuse to attack others, who may carry the wounds after we are feeling better. This is particularly true of children, who sometimes get attacked for reasons that have nothing to do with their behavior, but rather with whatever is happening in the life of the attacking adult.

THE VALUE OF PRACTICE

So it's good to practice expressing emotions in ways that don't attack others. If we can express emotions when we're not overcome by them, we can do a better job of controlling them in provocative circumstances. If I have played the game of anger, real anger doesn't bother me so much, either in myself or in others. I know that it all works out in the end, with no one getting hurt. I learn to see anger as a temporary condition that may arise in anyone, not as a personal attack on me. Thus I recover from my fear of it and am less confused about the reasons for any anger I or another may feel. This makes it less likely I'll displace my anger onto remote philosophical issues, foreigners or those less fortunate than I.

NUMERICAL FEELINGS

So try the following skit and practice it frequently. The more you practice, the better you will be able to communicate on the emotional level. Divide the family into an acting group of two and an audience of everyone else. The actors then play the following scenario: A is at home and B comes to visit or returns home. They are delighted to see each other, and hug and express affection. After a little conversation, though, a conflict develops between them. Gradually it turns into a noisy fight. After the fight has continued for a while, it is resolved and the two are friends again, hugging and kissing as they heal their conflict.

The entire skit is performed by counting. No words are used, only numbers and sounds. The numbers must be in sequence, and must go from one to one hundred. This means that the actors always know what to say and can keep track of where they are in the skit. Since they know they have to reach resolution by one hundred, they know something of what to expect from each other.

PRACTICE IN LEARNING TO RESOLVE DIFFERENCES

This skit can be performed repeatedly. It comes out different every time. The more it is performed, the more diverse and abundant the possible routes to resolution become. Performing it provides practice in accepting feelings and resolving confrontations.

After you have used it a few times as an exercise, you will notice that family conflicts become easier to resolve. People are less afraid of their feelings and less self-conscious about having them. They also learn that if they can turn their feelings on in a skit, they can turn them off before they go out of control. And they learn to be comfortable with the expression of feeling, as it becomes easier for them to admit and own up to their emotions and accept those of others. Also, they learn to read each other's non-verbal communication more effectively. This learning to control and purge emotions is one of the most important functions of drama.

YOU DON'T ALWAYS HAVE TO EXPRESS IT

A friend told me about a time she was angry with her husband and was going to yell at him. Then she thought, "Here I am at number 50. What if I just skip over to 100?" She did so and found she wasn't angry anymore. You may find this sort of response becoming possible for you as soon as you realize you can control your feelings, that you can express them when appropriate and keep them to yourself when they are out of place in the situation. Sometimes, after all, feelings are evoked just because of how we're looking at things. If we change our point of view, we don't feel so bad anymore. We can learn not to let the actions of others make us feel abused or put upon by them.

EXPLORING A DISAGREEMENT THROUGH SKITS

Suppose a major disagreement has arisen between two people. Let each of them become the director of a skit. For this purpose words may be useful instead of numbers. Let us say that Johnny took Jimmy's ball and Jimmy hit Johnny. First Johnny gets to direct other members of the family in a skit that shows his version of what happened. Jimmy plays the role in this skit that Johnny tells him to play. Next, it is Jimmy's turn to direct a skit. Johnny must now play the role that Jimmy tells him to play. The whole family participates, though, in acting out each skit. When both skits are completed, the family can discuss the differences between them and what they mean. Johnny and Jimmy will have developed more perspective on their disagreement and will be better able to negotiate peace.

This same exercise could be used for exploring outside disputes in which the family has an interest. If the discussion centers on a conflict among nations, for example, it might be interesting to do several skits, each exploring the conflict from the point of view of one of the nations. This will help objectify the conflict and provide more experience as a basis for making judgments. Often when we play the role of someone we are critical of, we can begin to explore that person's point of view for the first time. This has a way of opening up our thinking on the subject.

DRAWING FEELINGS

Many of us think we are expressing more with our tone of voice than is actually communicated to the listener. The following exercise will help you become conscious of how well your voice communicates feeling. It works well with small groups of three to seven people. Each person takes a turn and reads a sentence in several different ways. After each reading the other participants draw a picture representing the emotion they feel was conveyed by the reading. With practice, each participant will get better at eliciting drawings from the group that are (a) similar to one another, and (b) expressive of what the reader had in mind.

COMMUNICATING WITHOUT WORDS

After you have practiced the numerical feelings exercise enough to become familiar with it, try conducting skits without words or numbers. Just make sounds, and see how much you can communicate that way.

Music can be a wonderful vehicle for learning to express feelings. Put on some recorded music and pretend you are conducting the orchestra. The entire family can conduct the music simultaneously. Watch each other as you go, and get ideas from each other. It's a delightful way to get over your inhibitions about letting yourself be physically expressive. Letting the feeling of the music into the body and giving it expression allows you to experience emotional release and to practice being more open yourself.

Don Campbell taught me to expand this exercise in the following way: Pretend you are the world's greatest conductor and have total control over the orchestra. Conduct with your hands alone. Then with one finger. Then with your wrists. Then with your elbows. Then with your knees. Then with the tip of your nose. Then one foot. Then the other. Then one hip and then the other. Then pretend that the orchestra is behind you, and conduct it using the rear parts of your body. Then pretend it is above you. Then below you. Then allow all of these different parts of your body to come alive simultaneously as you conduct. Thus, by isolating parts of the body and investing them with the full emotion evoked by the music, we can enrich our sense of kinesthetic communication, and also can allow the feelings of the music to enter us totally.

IMITATION GAMES

Imitation games can work well with even the most diverse groups. They allow us to playfully practice expressing our own feelings and also to experience — and thereby intuitively learn — the feelings and experiences of others.

One simple exercise is to stand in a circle and have a member of the group make random sounds. All the others have to copy these sounds. Take turns being leader and followers. See how many different types of sounds you can invent and imitate.

I used to practice this exercise with my infant daughters while changing their diapers. Whatever sound the baby made I would imitate. The baby loved this game, and so did I. It led to lots of wonderful laughter and gave the baby a rare chance to feel in control of the situation.

We can imitate each other's movements just as we imitate sounds. Try the imitation game with movement, passing it around the circle, as you did the sounds.

HUMAN SCULPTURES

Another way to relate emotionally through movement is to create a sculpture made from human bodies, each holding a pose that expresses something about that person's relationship with the family. Start with a sculpture in which each person takes a pose expressing his or her role in the family. Now do another in which each takes a pose expressing something different from that role. Then discuss and clarify the different feelings experienced in those two poses. Would it be appropriate to try changing our roles from time to time?

Use human sculptures to explore ideas. What is a way of expressing mathematical relationships with the sculpture? How would you express an historical situation? How would you express the central idea of a work of literature or philosophy?

Learning to express emotion freely and responsibly is one of the most important experiences a family can share together. Practice in expressiveness will help the young grow up to be fully responsive adults. It is also one of the most powerful ways parents can learn from, and about, their children.

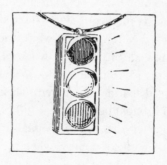

21

IT'S MY TURN NOW, BUT HOW AM I DOING?

*Each member of the family or group deserves a chance
to be heard. A respectful hearing communicates the
principle that everyone's opinion matters.
Here are some useful ground rules.*

It's great getting to know each other as members of the same family or group, as we've been doing with some of these exercises, but we'll grow together even more effectively if we have a few rituals to make sure there's equal time for all. It's good, also, to have an effective and non-threatening feedback structure.

MAYBE EVERYONE CAN TALK AT ONCE. . .

One of the cultural differences between middle class U.S. citizens and some Latin Americans is that at social gatherings the North Americans expect to take turns talking, whereas the Latin Americans may all talk at once, which doesn't seem to prevent them from knowing what was said. Partly because of this mixing of cultures there can be conflict between those who expect not to be interrupted and others who prefer to converse contrapuntally.

If you know that everyone understands everything you're saying even though they don't appear to be listening, it's not hard to develop confidence in yourself and learn to hold your own. But if you think you haven't been heard until someone has obviously listened, then it's important to set the scene so you can get what you need.

USUALLY THERE'S A NEED TO HAVE EVERYONE LISTEN IN TURN

Some families use dinner table conversation as a contest to see who gets the most attention. My mother used to tell the story of how one night at dinner she and my father were listening while I told what I had done in school that day. Meanwhile my brother Michael, who had just started kindergarten, wanted his share of attention. When asked what he had to say, he looked surprised that anyone cared. Then he said, "My teacher cried today, because I brought her a present full of needles."

Each person, however young, needs equal time, or at least an equal chance to be heard. It's hard, of course, when the youngest doesn't have much to say yet. So the family may need to cooperate to help the youngest feel equal. Otherwise, fifty years later we'll have an adult who's still crying because childhood was an experience of always being too young to participate. I have found this resentment widespread in my age group, proving it's never too late to cry because someone else was always spilling the milk.

MORE WORDS DON'T INDICATE MORE WISDOM

In a group discussion there is usually a tendency for the more verbal members to dominate. This doesn't mean others have nothing to say, it means they don't have the aggressiveness or inclination to speak up. Therefore, it's wise to adopt the following rule of discussion: no one speaks twice until everyone has spoken once, and no one speaks four times until everyone has spoken twice.

This will serve to include everyone in the discussion. No one can get out of participating, but there is always the option to say, "I have nothing to contribute right now." The practice of hearing from everyone is an important discipline, especially needed by those who have formed the habit of dominating. It will introduce them to the wisdom of those who are often silent, which their over-active mouths may have kept them from realizing.

I am reminded of my friend Thorny, an artist at silence. He used to spend a lot of time staring out the window. If you were with him you probably found yourself staring out the window too. Some of us got a chance to notice what was happening in the great outdoors for the first time in a long while.

But whenever Thorny did speak he could capture in a sentence what might have taken someone else a week to express. He was a member of our local writer's group. Most of his poems were only four lines long. Unfortunately for our time schedule, those four lines could monopolize the whole evening, for they stimulated many hours of thought and discussion.

THE GO-AROUND AND THE GOOD-AND-NEW

It is appropriate to use a variant of our discussion rule called the Go-Around whenever a group needs to react to some experience or take a turn at giving information. The simplest form of Go-Around is the Good-and-New, which should be used with any group that meets regularly. Start out the meeting giving each person a turn to say something good and new that has happened in their life during the past twenty-four hours. This focuses attention on positive experiences, and away from the habit of complaining.

Once in a while someone is unable to complete this assignment. In that case one of two things happens. The group "punishes" the person in the following way: three people each say something they like about the person. Or, if a painful experience has recently occurred, the group should give the person a chance to talk and, if necessary, cry about it.

The habit of thinking in terms of the Good-and-New increases the group's energy. It can quickly transform habitually negative attitudes. Soon individuals in the group will be opening conversations by saying, "What's your Good-and-New?"

The Good-and-New is an excellent Go-Around to begin the dinner table conversation. It brings the family together on a positive note, reviewing the most pleasant and meaningful events of the day.

SHARING MEANINGFUL EXPERIENCES

Go-Arounds can be adapted to different occasions. If the group has shared an enjoyable experience, such as a trip to the fireworks, a concert, a movie, or a wedding, a Go-Around is appropriate, perhaps in the car driving home. Each person is heard all the way through until he or she has no more to say. Each contribution is neither interrupted nor given much of a response later, though it may be referred to in building one's own thoughts. The habit of doing a Go-Around in response to important shared experiences develops a thoughtful attitude toward experience, as well as the impression that one's opinion is valued by others.

Go-Arounds have something in common with Think-and-Listens, in that they serve as a group Think-and-Listen, though usually on a focused subject.

The Go-Around can be used any time the people participate in one of the group activities suggested in this book. Then everyone should have a turn to evaluate and comment on what has happened.

Regular use of Go-Arounds (two or three every day) would build family rituals that bring out everyone's best thinking. Anyone who had the privilege of growing up in such a family atmosphere could be expected to become an articulate and powerful member of the community.

HOW AM I DOING?

An important part of learning something is getting feedback on how you're doing. If the feedback is mostly negative, you'll slow the process down or perhaps quit entirely. If it's mostly positive and you're having a reasonably good time, you'll keep going.

THE BOY IN THE BACK OF THE BUS

Recently while riding in someone's car behind a school bus I had a chance to perform an interesting experiment. Several children were looking out the back window making gestures. I waved and they all waved back. They gestured some more, and I selected one boy and imitated him. For a while all the children tried to get my attention, but I imitated only the gestures of the one boy. Within two minutes the others were just watching, while the boy I had selected continued with ever-growing enthusiasm to explore and expand his repertoire of gestures. For forty-five minutes this continued. Sometimes he made a gesture I was unwilling or unable to perform. When I did not imitate it, he went on immediately to something else. Later he might try it again, but he never tried anything I did not imitate more than three times.

So this boy, merely because I randomly selected him for positive feedback, continued the mimed conversation as long as our mutual journey would allow. Had I been his teacher giving him positive feedback on a task he had undertaken, the same thing would have happened. Had I ignored him, he probably would have quit within two minutes.

CONSTANT FEEDBACK ISN'T THE BEST

It's interesting, though, that the kind of feedback that will keep you at something the longest is intermittent. If positive feedback is constant, the behavior eliciting it will probably stop as soon as the feedback stops. But if it comes only now and then, the learner will assume it will eventually recur. This is because once we have started to try to achieve a goal, we're most likely to keep at it if we think there's hope of success even if there are some failures along the way. In fact, someone who receives intermittent positive feedback may try five or six times as hard or stay at the task five or six times as long as someone who does not. Meanwhile, the person who has been getting constant positive feedback may assume there is no more chance of success once the positive feedback is withdrawn.

Positive feedback can be a little dangerous because it is so powerful. A strong personality can lead a weaker one astray by holding out the hope of positive feedback from time to time. It's important, therefore, to internalize the feedback process as much as possible. In giving feedback, focus on communicating your reaction as being your reaction and nothing more. If you say "This is good," you seem to be articulating a universal standard. But if you say, "I like this," that's just your opinion.

THE IMPORTANCE OF KNOWING WHAT PEOPLE LIKE

Successful people are usually conscious of the likes and dislikes of others and know how to respond to them. Recently I heard a successful businessman say, "The two most important rules of business are to give people what they want and do business only with people you like. It took me a long time and a lot of painful experiences to learn them."

If this lesson can be learned in the home, it will prove useful in life for a long time to come. Being sensitive to what others want makes it possible for you to get the feedback you want, and also helps you keep in perspective the feedback you get. Also, if you take seriously only the feedback you get from people you like, you'll find it easier to believe that you and no one else should decide what's important in your life. Rejecting advice you don't like is just as important as accepting good advice.

We need to learn to evaluate the feedback we're getting for exactly what it is, and nothing more. For example, if a hundred publishers reject your manuscript, that only means a hundred individuals didn't like it enough to want to invest time and money in it. But there are millions of readers out there, so the hundred that have expressed a negative opinion represent only their personal lack of interest or their inability to see how your manuscript could be marketed successfully. Since many a best-seller has been initially rejected by many publishers, it may be wise to hang in there, particularly if you have evidence that a significant number of readers will like your work. I give this example, because rejection slips are legion and legendary in the writing business, and yet many would-be writers think a single rejection slip is sufficient cause to give up considering a writing career. Just so, a single rejection may lead one to abandon almost anything if one does not know that an individual opinion is not a universal judgment.

DON'T TRY TO SPEAK FOR THE WHOLE UNIVERSE

So teaching the child that your reaction, no matter how clearly expressed and definite, is nevertheless nothing more than your reaction, is important in leaving open the possibility for other reactions. This will relieve you of the burden of dictating your child's thoughts and beliefs.

A positive response can be just as misleading, or even devastating, as a negative one. For example, had my mother decided one of the best things I had ever done was attempt digging to China, I might have devoted my life to attempting to fulfill some promise she saw in that particular childhood project. After such misleading encouragement, many a life has been squandered on the meaningless, the trivial or the impossible.

Yet responses cannot be hidden, for they will be sensed even if unspoken. Therefore it's well to build feedback into a family ritual, making sure it comes from everyone as an individual opinion.

THE SELF-ESTIMATION

The Self-Estimation is the best tool I know for accomplishing this. It's quite simple. When it's your turn for a Self-Estimation, state what you are doing well in accomplishing the task being evaluated (whether it's living your life or painting the kitchen). Give all the information you think you have on the subject. When you've finished, others who have joined you in the Self-Estimation give their view of what you're doing well.

When you've exhausted the subject of what's going well, you have a chance to say what you feel is currently missing from your performance that might improve things if it were present. (Note the wording here. We're not focusing on what's bad, but instead on what good things are not yet present. This keeps the focus positive, even though you're exploring how to improve.) When you've said all you can, the others, as before, give their opinions. You may be surprised to learn that what you thought wasn't going well is actually humming right along, while other aspects of your performance aren't in quite as good shape as you thought.

Regular use of the Self-Estimation encourages people to think positively and creatively about all their activities. This perspective on performance fosters a sense of one's personal power to affect the world. It's a relief to realize how easy it may be to change your activities so you can spend most of your time doing the things you like best.

All these ways of sharing time so each person becomes important as an individual and establishes equal footing with the other members of the group will prepare them for taking a solid place in the world, sure of what they have to contribute, and of how it fits in with the contributions of others.

22

INTELLECTUAL SLEIGHT OF HAND

We all can be innovators. A game of invention can help us look at familiar things in new ways.

Up to this point everything I've offered you has focused on eliciting wisdom already present in the mind. The purpose has been to help you give this wisdom better shape, form and structure. Now let's consider some ways to develop your creativity more explicitly. Your unconscious can do a lot of the creative work for you, so you've probably already seen some surprising new ideas emerging as you worked on some of the preceding exercises. Beyond that, it's easy to teach your mind to increase its stock of creative techniques.

THE MIND AS PATTERN MAKER

Have you ever noticed how children at play love to discover new uses for familiar objects, new ways of rearranging the world around them? Young or old, when your mind perceives things freshly, it delights in making or discovering new patterns. It loves putting new wine in old bottles, or old wine in new bottles, perhaps discovering how to use a shoe to hammer in a nail or a soap box to stand on and give a lecture. All of our standard tools were invented in just such ways: by adapting something to a task not previously imagined for it. At the same time, the environment is now so filled with objects whose use seems to have been determined for all time, that we get relatively little inspiration or challenge to be inventive. This may create the impression that there is nothing left to invent.

WHEN PHYSICS WAS COMPLETE

I am reminded that at the end of the nineteenth century nearly every major physicist believed that all the essential discoveries in physics had already been made, give or take a few details. That was before quantum mechanics, the theory of relativity, and the general impression the universe is inexhaustibly unknowable.

Another example: eighteenth century writers mostly operated on the assumption that all good stories had been invented and needed only to be more elegantly retold. With this limitation in mind, Alexander Pope, one of the greatest English writers of the eighteenth century, set out to write "what oft was thought but ne'er so well expressed." That was before the romantic poets, the theater of Ibsen, and hundreds of other new breakthroughs in literary expression diversified literature and entertainment so much one can no longer claim to know what might be thought, or even what's required for good expression.

CREATIVITY GETS BLOCKED IN MANY LARGE AREAS

So there appear to be times when whole areas of creative possibility lie unexplored by anyone whose investigations are taken seriously, and once these areas are unlocked, huge new opportunities for genius reveal themselves. It's as if a veil has been lowered in front of our eyes to prevent us from seeing the gaps in our experience. But reflect that if everything useful had already been discovered or invented, then our lives would move forward flawlessly. Each difficulty you encounter, each moment of experience that is less than ideal, suggests an opportunity for some new development or invention — perhaps even the opening up of some new field of activity never before considered. What might some of these be?

POPULAR GROWTH INDUSTRIES THAT WERE ONCE UNKNOWN

Have you visited an olfactorium recently? That's a huge public gathering place where a sort of symphony of smells (called a symolfactory) can be experienced. It's highly popular, since, as everyone knows, smell is more likely to stimulate memory, imagination and emotions than any other sense. Symolfactories are composed by thousands of gifted smell artists, some of whom with banal imaginations grind out sterile combinations of perfumes, while others explore ranges of olfactory sensibility that move crowds to new horizons of emotional experience.

Or perhaps you're in the aquametropolitan business. Since six-sevenths of the earth's surface is under water, what could be more natural than to locate huge air bubbles about the ocean floor and build cities in them? Aquametropolitan real estate goes for such high prices (because of the rare opportunities these new communities provide for beautiful and healthful living in an ecologically controlled environment) that the boom in new developments in this field has jolted the economy to unheard of heights.

Not all new industries are so global in scope, though. The latest challenge to McDonald's as a neighborhood institution is the Shopper's Friendly Guide. Here is where you go with your weekly shopping list, and a friendly person at a computer routes your list through all the local stores, computing for you the most economical means of getting everything you want. Ten minutes at the corner SFG, and you've saved several hours, and anywhere from a few dollars to a few thousand in meeting your needs. (This popular new industry was developed by some people experienced in the travel agency business.) The SFGs have not only kept prices down, they've fostered the availability of unusual items, since local stores know that anyone who wants a stomach pump for a Raggedy Ann doll will be advised on just where to find it. This has eliminated much of the cost of advertising, particularly for specialty items. The SFGs have even developed psychological tests that help people identify needs and desires they didn't know they had, thus making life more interesting for the Shopper Who Already Has Everything.

Now that you've read these three ideas for future growth industries, how many of your own can you dream up? Is there anything on your list that might revolutionize some aspect of our living, helping to make existence more pleasant for everyone?

A WILD IMAGINATION IS AN IMPORTANT PROFESSIONAL TOOL

Science fiction writer and anthologist Frederick Pohl once pointed out to me that a higher proportion of scientists than general readers read science fiction. The practice this provides in imagining new possibilities helps many scientists think about their work more creatively.

Practice can help you be more flexible and creative and thus better able to discover useful and powerful new ideas.

THE NEW-USE-FOR-OBJECTS GAME

Have all members of the family or group write down their ideas about unconventional, humorous and even fanciful ways in which five randomly selected objects might be used. After a short time, read all the lists. Then repeat the exercise, allowing the participants to include whatever they liked from each other's lists. See how much longer each list gets the second time around. Notice how many ideas appear for the first time on this second round.

When you've finished the second round, use some newsprint or a blackboard and brainstorm additional uses for the five objects. To brainstorm, list every idea that occurs to anyone, no matter how bizarre or seemingly irrelevant it is. Criticism, or even discussion of the ideas is not allowed during the brainstorming session. When you brainstorm, you will probably find many more ideas are generated by the group thinking together than earlier when working separately.

By this process we stimulate the pattern-making function of the brain to give us new perspectives on what's already familiar in the environment. Thus the way is prepared for coping with the unfamiliar.

THE OBJECT-COMBINATION GAME

The next step is to think of possible useful relationships among objects. How could you use a stove and a firecracker together to accomplish something neither would be capable of separately? Using the stove to light the firecracker has some obvious drawbacks. Here's a better one. Some restaurants cook your food on a hot plate right at your table. What if, to enhance the display, tiny fireworks were set off while the food is cooking? I'm sure you can think of an even better idea for combining the stove and the firecracker.

By producing new interactions between objects that don't ordinarily go together, we can explore many wonderful new possibilities, some of which might prove immediately useful, but all of which will help convince you the world is full of infinite possibility. By making new combinations among things, you can do much that wasn't possible before.

INFINITE POSSIBILITY IS HERE TO STAY

Lest you think this exercise will only produce ideas already developed by others, let me point out something about the way number combinations work. There are twelve notes in the scale. Do you know how many tunes of the complexity of "Mary Had a Little Lamb" those twelve notes could make? Something on the order of an octillion. That's more tunes than could be sung by all the people on earth if all of them sang a different tune every minute for a hundred thousand years. Not all the possible tunes are good ones, of course, but there's an astronomically large number of good ones that won't ever get thought of, written or sung. (One night I was in the car with a composer friend, who suddenly had an inspiration for a new song. It was a wonderfully catchy little tune, reminiscent of the style of Gershwin or Cole Porter. I couldn't wait till it was fully developed and recorded. Then we stopped and went into a store to do some shopping, and when we came out, the song was gone forever. No one else will ever hear it.)

Now consider the fact that there are more than twelve different objects in your living room. When you consider combining many objects in original ways to create something new, you are thinking about an astronomically large number of possibilities, far more than could even be considered by all the inventors who will ever live.

It helps, of course, to have a depth of knowledge and experience in the area in which you're inventing. Ideas come more easily to the fertile soil of the prepared mind. So, think about the areas in which you work or have some knowledge, and consider how things might be improved in those areas. Then let the free play of your mind work with new combinations of objects to explore ideas that can be developed into a useful form.

Looked at from this point of view, it should be a relatively simple matter to create some technological concept no one else would ever think of. Let me state this more forcefully: if you don't think of it, no one will and the world will be forever deprived of your brilliant invention.

Whether it would sell, of course, is another matter. Even a super idea may have trouble getting marketed. Nevertheless, it's possible that by the fireside this very evening you could discover the answer to some problem that has troubled humanity for centuries, a solution which, statistically speaking, will never be thought of unless you think of it. Now that's power.

LUBRICATE YOUR IMAGINATION

You can't accomplish anything so grandiose, though, unless you lubricate your thinking skills by exploring improbable combinations of objects and push yourself beyond the obvious. The best combination of a door and a table is not just a door with a table in it, a table with a door on it, one made of the other, or anything as simple as that (though these combinations may indeed prove useful and not always as obvious as they might seem). You've got to get that table and door into an unexpected relationship, perhaps involving some other objects in the process. Also, you can deal with one of them literally, while the other plays a symbolic role. You might explore the possibility, for example, of a way of opening the door on new eating experiences. This idea could give rise to a box with a door on it. When you shake the box, some combination of foods is formed. You open the door to the box and discover what your dinner will be. This could make a lovely toy and might sell as a gift for the person who is tired of always eating the same old junk food. Users could keep shaking the box until they got a combination they liked. Even if they never got one from the box, it would stimulate new ideas for creative cookery.

ADD MUSIC TO THE MIX

At some point in this process (you be the judge of when) add a music listening experience to inspire you to go deeper in your creative process of inventing things. If you've used music for some of the other exercises in this book, you'll find it easy to adapt it to this one. Just play the music and tell yourself that it will inspire you to see new relationships among things and discover new uses for them. Then let your mind surprise you with some of the ideas it presents. Don't prejudge these ideas (which might seem outlandish at first) until you've explored them, perhaps in discussion with others. Some of the world's greatest new insights have seemed very strange when first encountered. Perhaps your off-the-wall fantasy could turn out to be tomorrow's new industry.

GET STARTED NOW

It doesn't take more than a few original good ideas to give one pride of invention and a sense of purpose in life. Anyone can learn to do it. The trouble is so few of us ever practice. So run, don't walk, to your living room. Select any two objects. Start imagining. Then ask others for their ideas on strange, original ways of combining the two. Have a contest for the best new invention. The prize? A liberated imagination.

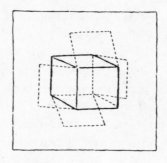

23

THERE'S MORE THAN ONE WAY TO BE RIGHT

The surprising number of right answers you can find
when you don't worry about givng wrong ones.

It's one thing to be able to put together new ideas, another to find new ways of arriving at old conclusions. Most of us have a few of our own approaches to problem-solving that may set us apart from those who would solve the same problem differently. A friend who seems to be a genius at repairing broken machinery says he asks himself, "If I were this machine, what would be wrong with me?" It leads him straight to the problem.

Unfortunately, too many school teachers don't accept this important fact about the diversity of human behavior and insist that everything be done according to strict formula. The student who may have a different approach or a different way of understanding is thus made to feel inadequate. More than that: unless the teacher takes the student's way of understanding (or misunderstanding) into account, it may be impossible for the student to understand what the teacher is driving at.

Sometimes the result of not paying attention to a particular student's unique approach to a problem can be disastrous, because there's nothing more devastating than finding out that your perception of the world is totally wrong. George Orwell explored the powerful implications of this disturbing feeling in *1984*, in which he showed the mental breakdown that occurs when a person is forced to accept as correct an answer he knows to be wrong.

HOW EDDIE AND MATH PARTED COMPANY

Unfortunately, many of us learn in school to mistrust our most basic perceptions. My student Eddie was an example of someone who did that. Eddie, who was quite verbal, impressed everyone with his fine intelligence, but he couldn't do any math at all. When it came to a math assignment, he would become passively resistant, eating his pencil, making paper airplanes out of pages in the textbook, or staring into space as if he had left his body and was cruising about in some alien universe.

Then one day he told the class why he did all this. "When I was in first grade," he said, "the teacher was teaching us to add. We had a board with squares on it like Monopoly, and we were supposed to move a little wooden figure along the squares. I had mine on the first square and the teacher came over and said, 'Move it two spaces,' so I did. Then the teacher said, 'Move it two more spaces.' I did that too. So far so good. But then things happened too fast for me. The teacher said, 'How many spaces was your marker on?' and I said five, because it really was on five of those little squares. I'm not lying to you, I've counted them over and over, I can even count them in my sleep. But the teacher said, 'No, four.' And I said, 'But, Ma'am, it's five spaces, I counted them,' and then the teacher hit me. Well, I knew after that nothing in math class could ever possibly make any sense."

Eddie was not happy about his failures in math. He had spent years eating away at himself about it. For the teacher, however, it was only a passing moment, long forgotten.

WHY DID THE TEACHER TREAT EDDIE THAT WAY?

We might ask why the teacher chose to inflict this deep scar on the boy's intelligence. He was doing the best he could. He had done nothing vicious or evil. I doubt there was even any insolence in his tone. He was simply reporting what he saw and understood, signaling his readiness to go on to the next step. But in the eyes of the teacher, he was wrong — permanently, irredeemably wrong. He had committed the most unpardonable sin. Everyone everywhere knows that two and two is four — how could this boy presume to waste her time with his insolence? And so she struck, as a snake might have struck an innocent victim and then slithered on with no notion of the life it had snuffed out.

This story of Eddie and the squares that added up to five, not four, is a particularly transparent case in which we can easily see what was happening. Teacher and student were operating on two different sets of assumptions. Both were correct, given the assumptions on which they were operating, but they came to a head over a situation in which there was supposed to be only one correct answer. The matter was not settled through reason or persuasion; it was settled by the superior physical force and authority of the teacher. But Eddie "won" in the long run. Passive resistance set in for the rest of his life so no teacher could ever bully him on that issue again.

IT HAPPENS TO ALL OF US

Such incidents, usually on a less obvious and less catastrophic level, occur thousands of times in the life of each child. Over and over we are told our way of reasoning, judging or perceiving things is incorrect. Someone bigger and stronger will assert another view than the one our senses report or our mind works out. Then we are left with no explanation of why we are wrong, only a feeling of anguish, perhaps having begun to suspect we are truly divorced from reality.

No doubt Eddie's teacher had received similar treatment any number of times when she was a child. She simply passed the abuse along to Eddie.

HOW TO AVOID INTELLECTUAL DISASTER

Incidents like this need never occur. You can avoid them by questioning the person who has given an answer you think might be wrong. Find out how that answer was arrived at. If you do not frighten your student, friend, child or lover, you should get a glimpse of the thinking that actually occurred, and then you'll discover the specific way in which it makes sense. Given the assumptions of the person who answered the question, the answer may well have been correct.

THE TEACHER WHO SWITCHED HIS STUDENTS

Several years ago I met a teacher who said he had once been assigned two classes, one a group of high achievers and the other a slow learning class. "I switched them in two weeks," he told me. "It was simple. With the high achievers, I punished them for wrong answers. With the slow learners, I rewarded them for *all* answers. If the answer was incorrect, I found some means to give the information needed to correct it, but I always gave credit for an answer, no matter what it was. In two weeks you'd have thought the slow learners were high achievers. And *vice versa*."

I guess he could see I was wondering about the outcome of this experiment, because he then said, "Don't worry, I put everything back."

"You made the slow learners slow learners again?" I asked.

"No, but you can bet I didn't keep the high achievers in the fix I'd put them in."

EXERCISE: HOW MANY RIGHT ANSWERS CAN YOU GIVE?

Let's try an exercise that might help us become more flexible in our thinking about right and wrong answers. I learned this in a workshop led by math expert Julian Weissglass. I usually do the exercise in a group in the following way: I hold up a picture of a cube and ask everyone present to tell how many sides it has. Most people say "six," but in a large group there are always a few who disagree — some because they don't know what "the" answer is, some because they have learned a different answer, and some because they are creative. So I write down all the answers, and then ask each person why their answer is right.

Here are eleven other answers and the reasons behind them:

Four: There are four sides, plus a top and a bottom. *Two*: Outside and inside. *Twelve*: Six outside and six inside. *One*: You can make a cube out of a flat piece of paper. When you're finished, only one side of the paper is visible. *Three*: Only three sides are visible from any point at one time. You have to assume the existence of the other three sides, and you could be mistaken. *Five*: Five sides and a bottom. (You don't usually put a picture in the sixth side of a picture cube, so for practical purposes it has five usable sides.) *Seven*: The side of the paper that remains visible after the cube has been made, plus the other six sides. *Eight*: Four sides, (excluding top and bottom), both inside and outside. *Ten*: You can see that many edges when you look at a cube without changing its position or yours. Who says an edge can't be called a side? Look at any two dimensional figure and you'll see what I mean.

Infinity: If you sliced up the cube you would keep on producing additional sides. Theoretically, you can keep doing this forever. You can get *multiples of all the above answers* (including infinity) by moving the cube through time. How can you do that? Take pictures of the cube. Each picture is of the same cube, but each one adds additional sides to the number you had before. This answer works or doesn't depending on how you define the identity of the cube. It gets very complicated and philosophical, and could occupy us for a thousand pages at least.

All of the above answers are correct, according to somebody's way of seeing things. So it looks as if a cube can have just about any number of sides you want. I haven't figured out how to get eleven out of it, though, and I'd be hard put to deal with the prime numbers after eleven, but perhaps a reader or two can help me out here.

WHY WE HAVE RIGHT AND WRONG ANSWERS

Of course we resist such latitude of response because it would create difficulties in communication. That's the problem. The reason we have right and wrong answers is so we can communicate with each other. There's no absolute reason to pick one set of correct answers instead of another, but there is reason to agree on something. It's only a matter of convenience, and should carry no stigma whatsoever.

This is particularly true in the matter of spelling. In Shakespeare's day the spelling of English words varied enormously. Then the printers got together and standardized spelling on the grounds that it would be easier to read if everyone spelled the same way. This was convenient for some of us, but made life more difficult for those who couldn't remember what the correct spelling was and were erroneously considered stupid because they couldn't. Whether you can spell or not has nothing to do with your intelligence, but try to convince your boss of that if you're a secretary.

YOU DON'T KNOW WHAT ISN'T RIGHT UNTIL YOU KNOW WHAT YOU'RE DOING

Anyway, there's no such thing as an error until you know what it is you're trying to do. Then anything that doesn't help get it done is erroneous. When you define error in someone else's terms, you can feel guilty. When you define error in your terms, you feel as if you are accomplishing something, like the pianist who played a concert to great acclaim from the audience, but felt he had played badly and therefore stayed at the concert hall to play the whole thing over again after the audience went home.

All you need do to help your child learn to deal better with mistakes is find out how the "wrong" answer was arrived at. The child doesn't want a nosey parent, but would probably appreciate a response of "Why do you think that?" rather than "That's wrong!" Once the child has explained why two and two is fifteen, then you can tell your version of what two and two is, and why you think that. Then give the child a choice of versions. Everyone likes to be able to make choices, and everyone likes to be able to communicate. Once the child is aware of your system, she'll probably enjoy using it now and again. Anyway, there's nothing at stake, it's all just fun and games. When there really is something at stake, we can agree on what's going to work and what isn't, and stick to that. Children don't usually have trouble with practical matters, they have trouble with rules and regulations that don't make sense because they are really power plays by adults who are too busy to bother with children.

DEFENDING YOUR POSITION

You can build your own confidence and your child's by playing the following game. Player one asks player two a question. Player two gives an answer. Player one says "No, that's wrong." Player two then gives an explanation of the answer. If the explanation makes sense to player one, player two is judged correct, whether or not the answer is actually right. Player one continues to ask questions until player two has given an answer player one finds acceptable. Then they reverse roles, and player two continues to question until player one has an acceptable answer.

The point of this game is to teach people to be persuasive in presenting their reasoning. Once you feel you can defend your point of view, you are less likely to feel defeated when someone says you are wrong.

THAT'S A LIKELY STORY!

This next game is great fun at the dinner table. Someone asks a why question, such as "Why are mountains high?" or "Why is the ocean wet?" The first person to begin gives an answer. This answer should be the most outrageous myth the player can concoct. For example, the story might go that mountains are high because the first people on earth needed to see where they were going before they set out on a journey, so they pushed up the mountains to climb up and get a good view of their intended journey. Or we might say the ocean is wet because long ago the moon was sad and cried for a long, long time. All the tears fell to earth and made the oceans. After that, the moon was happy again.

When the narrator has finished the tall tale just invented, everyone else greets it with the chorus: "That's a likely story!"

The purpose of this exercise is to relieve the tension around the possibility of giving wrong answers. Deliberately giving far-fetched answers to a question lightens up one's feelings about being questioned, thus making it easier to think under more serious circumstances.

Truth and accuracy are important and should be cultivated. They can best be cultivated in an atmosphere of freedom to think thoughtfully about what we have been asked to consider. If too much is at stake, we can't do that very well. But if we are relaxed, we are better able to see the truth, even when it is hidden from us by conventional wisdom.

24

INSTANT MEMORY THROUGH VISUAL THINKING

*Using mind-mapping to master large amounts of material
quickly and easily.*

If you approach problem solving from a variety of different angles, your thinking becomes more flexible. You can further add to its flexibility, however, by representing your ideas on paper in a way that reveals their inter-relationships. By thus gaining an overall picture of your developing networks of thought, you can more easily see how to improve their effectiveness. It's like any other form of revision — getting an overview of the current structure helps you develop one that's better and more efficiently organized.

Mind-mapping is the most effective mechanism I know for making this increased flexibility of thinking possible. Add to the verbal form of mind-mapping now widely in use the resources of seldom-used visual thinking, and you've got a tool that could save you months of time on a major project.

YOUR QUICK AND EASY GUIDE TO SUCCESS IN SCHOOL

Mind-mapping is, as I've suggested, a flexible way of organizing a subject that makes visible the relationships among its various components. This visual representation makes it possible to think about a subject more globally than if the outline were linear. And when you think globally, you increase your ability to understand both meaning and implications.

Visual thinking is a natural but subconscious facet of the human mind.

As an element of cognitive thought it was first explored by Rudolf Arnheim, whose book on the subject argues that for every idea, no matter how abstract, we have a corresponding visual image, which can be expressed in the form of a doodle. These doodles (or hieroglyphics), when used to represent ideas, can be many times more efficient than words in cross-referencing and storing information. That's because the mind is much better adapted to process visual images than words, since they more directly represent reality, exist in our minds prior to language, and are shared with some of our pre-human ancestors, which means the mind has been adapted to handling them for millions of years longer than we've had language. I believe that even apart from the other techniques we've considered in this book, the right combination of mind-mapping and visual thinking can effectively raise intelligence.

PROVING YOU'RE ALREADY AN EXPERT IN VISUAL THINKING

The following exercise will help you experience the universal reality of the ability to think in visual symbols which most people have never developed. Ask members of your family, or any other group, to number a piece of paper from one to ten. Then recite fairly rapidly a list of ten randomly selected words. Upon hearing each word, every participant is to make a doodle representing it, without also writing the word. Then, when you have finished reciting the words and all the doodles have been completed, the participants should go back and attempt to write in the words next to the doodles.

When I do this with groups, almost everyone gets a score of seven or better, with the majority getting perfect scores. However, I always say "If you got at least three of these right, you are already an expert at visual thinking." Here's what led me to that conclusion.

Stover was a participant in a course I was helping to teach that prepared people for the NASD level six exam, which requires the memorization of about 2,000 facts related to mutual funds and securities. Stover was at the time working for the subway and didn't think much of his ability to learn. When he took the little test mentioned above, he scored a three. Naturally, he was not impressed with his ability as a visual thinker.

In that course we were teaching people to mind-map the information they had to learn. When Stover took his turn at the board, I found he was translating every word into a corresponding picture. When I showed him how to represent concepts and not words, he understood better what we were doing, and began to mind-map successfully. That night he spent three and a half hours mind-mapping, having lost track of time because he was having so much fun. From then on Stover had no trouble mind-mapping, and was subsequently able to remember large amounts of technical information easily.

YOU HAVE IT — NOW USE IT

It's experiences like this that have made me practically certain that a large part of intelligence is the activation of the visual thinking process. All of us have this process operating at a subconscious level, but few of us make conscious use of it. It's as if, instead of using our legs to walk with, we continued crawling all through life — not a very efficient way for a human to behave. We all have this marvelous storehouse of visual imagery and a brain designed to think with it, but few of us ever make significant use of this powerful resource.

You may recall in an Chapter Seventeen I mentioned psychotherapist Mardi Horowitz's conclusion that the ability to control one's visual imagery is roughly correlated with mental health. Now I'd like to take this idea a step further. I believe we are mentally healthy to the extent that we have some purpose in life that is important to us. Purpose, however, is best represented and felt in visual terms, not merely stated in words. (We even use the word "vision" to express what we mean by this kind of purposefulness.) Those who can, in their mind's eye, clearly see where they are going in life seem much better able to produce results than those who just talk about what they plan to do — often without much show of action or results. Genius, then, is at least partly a matter of maintaining and developing productive and useful daydreams — reliable moving pictures that play and replay in the mind, pre-viewing the pattern of events eventually to become reality.

The secret of bringing your visual thinking usefully to life is to cultivate mind-mapping, representing each idea not just with a word, but also with a visual image. The practice this gives you could increase your intelligence, your sanity and your sense of purpose. On a more mundane level, since the mind can store pictures and retain them in memory many times better than words, it's relatively easy to memorize a mind-map made up of doodles, then reconstruct from these images the ideas they represent. Some of your initial doodles, of course, will not adequately capture your thoughts, so you'll need to revise your mind-map until you have it in a form that's easy to memorize.

EXPLORING THE INTEGRATIVE LEARNING MIND-MAP

Now let's look more closely at mind-mapping itself. You have probably noticed the mind-map of the material in *The Everyday Genius* at the beginning of this book. If I had used my own quick doodles, this map would not be clear to you. (Generally speaking, one can't use anyone else's visual mind-map, because successful visual images are unique and personal.) So we've used words and the drawings from the beginning of each chapter in this mind-map. Try making your own mind-map from it, replacing all the words and pictures with your own visual images. You'll find this much easier after you've tried the first exercise in this chapter.

Then see how long it takes you to memorize your new mind-map, so all the key points in this book are easily retained in your memory and available to be restructured to suit your own purposes in whatever new forms and combinations you choose to develop them.

PREPARE YOURSELF FOR A NEW COURSE IN A FEW HOURS

Mind-mapping makes it easy to approach a new textbook for the first time. If you mind-map the table of contents, you'll be surprised how much of the subject you already understand. Then, if the chapters have subheadings, mind-map all the chapters in the book, just using the subheadings. Then memorize your mind-maps. This process should take no more than a few hours.

After you've done that much, flip through the book at random and see how well you can guess the meaning and context of any sentence your eye happens to light on. My guess is you'll already know something about a fairly high percentage of the material in the course. The rest should be easier to learn after you've placed it in the context of what you already know.

Some people who have tried this have gotten excellent results, but still been a little queasy. "I'm so afraid I'll miss something," said one workshop participant. "That's why I like to read every word in sequence."

"Go down to the Library of Congress," I said, "if you want to get some idea of how much you're going to be missing no matter what you do. We can't possibly read everything, so why not read more books and get much of their information instead of a few and try futilely to get all of it?"

OVERCOMING THE TERROR OF THE BAR EXAM

This fetish for taking everything slowly and carefully really does some people in quite unnecessarily. I recall a young man who attended a weekend workshop I led on this subject. He was literally in a state of terror because he had to take the bar exam in a few months and couldn't see how he would ever learn all the material. As it happened, the material he had to learn was contained in two rather thick books he had brought with him.

After he learned mind-mapping, I went through part of one of these with him, and soon he was convinced it ought to be easy to learn the material in about two weeks. When he left the course he was excitedly looking forward to studying for the bar exam — certain for the first time that he would do well at it. Since then I've witnessed others change their attitudes toward difficult exams after learning visual mind-mapping.

THE ADVANTAGE CHILDREN HAVE

Children find it easier to think visually than adults do, so it should be easy to teach a young person how to use mind-mapping in school to cut down significantly on study time for homework. Young people, for some reason, don't always want to learn this way. After an English teacher in one school had taught the process to her students, they complained to the science teacher about what she'd made them do.

"Show me what she did," he said.

They then proceeded to lay out for him the complete lesson, just as she'd taught it.

"It seems to me that you've learned the material. It must have worked," said the science teacher to the chagrined eighth graders.

You'll probably find, also, that anyone who mind-maps a book this way ends up being able to read faster and more efficiently than before. The skill of actively reading to structure information in your own way, instead of just soaking up words, improves each time you practice mind-mapping.

FIGURE IT OUT YOURSELF

At this point I could give you detailed instructions in how to do mind-mapping, but I think that would only be confusing. Just study the mind-map I've included and figure out for yourself how it works. What you figure out will lead you to a better concept of mind-mapping than anything I could put into words.

I'll throw in a few hints, though, on what to look for in my mind-map so you can also put those characteristics in your own. Notice that it's a wheel with spokes radiating out from a hub. The hub contains the main idea of the map, while the spokes are main subheadings. Under each subheading you can add as many additional subheadings as you wish. At any level of the map you could draw a circle around a word and make it the center of a new map, developing in full a particular subheading, or sub-subheading from the original map. Thus you can take your subject to any level of complexity you wish.

The advantage of using the circular format is that whenever you wish, you can add additional ideas as subheadings. Any new idea can be squeezed in wherever it belongs. Since the relationship between ideas is fairly fluid in the map, you can then use it as a guide for making an outline in which you determine the final sequence you want to give your ideas, once you have explored them sufficiently. But since the map doesn't determine that sequence, it is easy to return to it and come up with a different outline. This means the material can remain flexible in your mind. You can give it new form and sequence any time you wish.

WHAT IT WILL DO FOR YOUR THINKING

What the map will do for your thinking is show you how you can access and deal with a wide range of detail in a short time, organizing it as you go, while still keeping it flexible for further possible organizing. Thus you never need feel you've locked the material into a final form, which means you can always expand and restructure your knowledge. In these days when new information is constantly becoming available in almost any field of knowledge, that's essential.

At the same time, your knowledge always remains in the context of the total picture. As soon as you've written a single word on the map, you've begun to envisage a structure. The next word you place on it has to find its relationship to the first, but the relationship can remain distant. Thus you can think about ideas in the sequence in which they occur to you, rather than having to edit your thoughts while searching for the next idea in the sequence.

ORGANIZING YOUR DAY

When you've learned to mind-map a subject as I've described here, you can then apply mind-mapping to other situations. For example, try mind-mapping how you spent your day today. Now look at the whole picture of the day and think about other configurations that might have been possible, and perhaps more satisfying. What useless actions might have been eliminated? What enjoyable activities might get a little more time? You'll soon appreciate how the mind-map gives you a global view of a time period, enabling you to make judgments that a linear outline would only obscure from your thinking.

One of the difficulties I have with scheduling my day in sequence is that it doesn't always allow me to do things in the order in which I desire to do them as I proceed through time. A mind-map, by not forcing me into a particular sequence, allows my activities to develop organically, yet I always know how what I'm doing fits in with the rest of what I plan to do.

RECORD A GROUP DISCUSSION

Mind-mapping can also be useful in keeping track of a group discussion. In fact, if you mind-map such a discussion, you'll later be able to repeat back every significant idea that was raised, though the order may be different, as you'll have had a chance to group ideas so they unfold more logically than they did in the original discussion.

This could be helpful if you want to write a book on the subject. Have some friends over, probe their thinking, mind-map everything they say, have some more parties and do the same thing, then organize all your mind-maps into one, go to the library and research the subject further, revising your map, then pinpoint any specific research you need to do to fill in missing information. After you've done that research, write your book.

Mind-mapping is also great for helping individuals or groups think through a problem. Use it in front of the group in a problem solving discussion, so everyone can keep track of what's been said, and how the whole picture vis-a-vis the problem is developing in the group discussion.

So use it as a tool for reading, writing, organizing your thoughts and your life, and communicating with others. The more you use it, the more you'll find new applications for it.

INTRODUCING MIND-MAPPING TO CHILDREN

And don't let anyone in your family go too long without realizing that mind-mapping can turn just about anyone into an A student. Teach your children about it not by lecturing them and forcing it on them (which is never the best way with children), but by doing some enjoyable family exercises with it. For example, you might plan a vacation together, developing a mind-map with each person's suggestions on it. Have soft music playing while you do this. The combination of planning the vacation, the soft music, and the general feeling of fun about what is happening should make the mind-map so appealing the child will start using it in school without any prompting from you.

Another way to use the mind-map is to have a discussion in the family about all the different ways to make learning a more enjoyable and successful experience. You'll probably have quite a lot to offer, but see what ideas your children can think of, and add them to the map too. Mind-mapping is a culminating activity in Integrative Learning. It ties things together conceptually and helps you get the most out of many of the other activities I've suggested.

THE CRACKERJACK PRIZE AT THE END OF THE BOOK

If you respond well to teasers (and read books from beginning to end), you may still be wondering when I'm going to make good on that promise in Chapter One that somewhere in this book is hidden the secret of teaching the planets so well that the whole class will want to become astronomers. Now that you've eaten almost all the Crackerjacks in the box, you're probably wondering where the prize is.

Well, the time has come to reveal that delightful secret, which is so good I wish I'd thought of it myself. I heard it from Car Foster, a fourth grade teacher in Kentucky. If you want to teach anyone in less than five minutes how to remember the names of the planets in order from the sun, just share with them this little nugget of guided imagery:

"Imagine yourself walking through the woods on a lovely summer day. You come to a clearing, where you notice the lush green grass. Strange to say, parked on the grass is a gaudy (or god-y, if you like) shiny red, spanking new Mercury automobile. Amazed to find such a vehicle parked here deep in the forest primeval, you climb a tree, better to observe it in this strange habitat.

"You don't have to wait long before the driver of the car presents herself. She proves to be a scantily clad woman with no arms, whom you instantly recognize as that lovely work of art, the Venus de Milo. Venus, primly rearranging her drapes, climbs into the front seat and prepares to drive the car, but before the motor starts, another woman comes out of the woods, whom you recognize as the popular hit singer, Eartha Kitt. Eartha is dragging behind her on a sled a giant five hundred pound Mars bar. She gets into the back seat of the Mercury, squeezes the Mars bar onto her lap, getting chocolate all over the ceiling of the car, and proceeds to cut a slice for Venus, who manages to eat it while simultaneously starting up the car.

"But wait! The car can't leave yet, because it has to wait for another passenger. Here he comes, bounding through the woods, flinging thunderbolts right and left! You immediately recognize him as Jupiter, King of the Gods. Too big to fit in this automobile, he leaps onto the roof. Then the car starts, and as it recedes down the path through the woods, you make out for the first time the license plate, on which you see the letters S — (Saturn) — U — (Uranus), and N — (Neptune). The curtain does not fall yet, though, for chasing along after the car, barking up a storm, is the little dog Pluto."

What I like about this guided imagery, which is kind of an auditory mind-map, is that it so beautifully clusters the information about a single visual unit. Furthermore, though there are nine planets, there are only seven units to be remembered, since three of them are combined in the single license plate.

If you wish to put something into a form that makes it memorable like this, create an organic unit among the parts, using colorful, bizarre images, full of action, (and — if it's intended for your own use only — perhaps some indecency), all in a dramatic format which is fun. Then offer the package to your child as a bedtime story. You'll find the story sticks. Try this planet story out tonight, if you don't believe me. Grandma will probably also get into the act and remember all the facts you're trying to teach the little one. And, of course, you'll remember all the planets too.

CLARITY BEGINS AT HOME

I've tried in this book to suggest that many of the problems we face in the larger world can be solved only as we change the conditions under which we bring up children in the home. Intelligence, like charity, begins there. It is less something we inherit than something we learn, and we learn it best from the people who model it for us early in life.

All members of the family can learn from each other. This fact is not unknown to the educational Establishment. Wayne Sanstead, Superintendent of Schools in North Dakota, has printed on his calling card this statement: "Every Adult Needs a Child to Teach; It's the Way Adults Learn." In North Dakota, by the way, they graduate 93% of their young people from high school, and 85% go on to college. No other state can better that record.

Children have as much to teach their parents as they have to learn from them. When we begin to act as a society on the profound truth of this phenomenon, we may be able to change the character of our whole civilization. For we will begin to understand that every human contact is a learning opportunity, and that the young have a freshness of perspective the old may have lost.

Any society that begins with the assumption that some groups of people are inherently better than others, whether because of age or any other attributes, dooms itself to being less than it could be. Adultism, racism, sexism, and other isms of that ilk, rob everyone — oppressors as well as oppressed — of the resources we might all be able to share if these social diseases did not exist. By limiting our view of what some can do, they discourage free and open communication among all people and slow down the progress of developing new ideas that might otherwise greatly increase the opportunities available to everyone.

There is no more certain source of wealth and new possibility than a well developed human mind, and no more certain block to these than a mind shackled with the diseases of prejudice and limited vision. Were it not for these maladies, we should by now be living in peace and plenty instead of suffering the ravages of crime, war, pollution and the spread of uncontrollable disease. For there is no problem, however great, that cannot be solved by creative and intelligent people using the full potential of their minds and then sharing what they have developed with a free and open-minded public.

Unfortunately much of the worst prejudice and lack of vision is spread by those who have the least excuse for such mental deprivation, since they have supposedly had access to the best opportunities in life. Fortunately, however, I have found that most such deprivations disappear rapidly when a person who has suffered from them is placed in a more supportive learning environment and allowed to hear directly from others how they experience life.

So let us incorporate into our national vision the awareness that whenever two or more are gathered together, they have a chance to learn from one another. Mutually exchanged learning, however, does not come easily to those who are not used to learning all the time and from everyone. For once we have forgotten the first fine careless rapture of infancy, learning itself becomes a learned skill.

Whenever you feel you are learning nothing from the person you are with, or the situation you are in, it is time to return again to whatever springs inspire in you the development of new learning skills, and drink as deeply as you can. Then you will be better able to discover that each person you meet has a fund of experience so rich that no matter what their differences in worldly accomplishments may be from yours, you can learn from them and they from you. Some of my own finest learning experiences have come from those who had lived long lives without the advantage of education or even literacy. Experience of any kind is always richly and uniquely instructive.

Once we have made our homes and schools places where the human mind can truly flourish, then it will be possible for us to do other things, such as build an economic system that benefits everyone, a technology that enhances the quality of all life on the planet, and a system of government that respects and draws the best from every culture on earth. Until we have accomplished these things, we are not entitled to feel that the teaching and learning we do is adequate to our needs.

APPENDIX ONE

HOPE FOR A BRAIN-DAMAGED CHILD

*A mother's experience in raising a brain-damaged child
and helping him to live a normal and productive life
offers lessons for all of us.*

Readers whose children have severe mental or physical difficulties may find it harder to accept many of my suggestions than those with normal children. I've noticed a tendency for such parents either to over-protect their children and focus family life around the misfortunes and limitations of the handicap or to deny reality by pretending the child is close to normal. Either approach can only make life more difficult for the child.

THE INNER BEAUTY OF THE LEARNING-DISABLED CHILD

The fine line between too little and too much protection challenges a parent to be sensitive in special ways. The resulting rewards can be profound. "Any children that have learning disabilities or handicaps of any kind have such inner beauty and so much to share with us and are so touching to our lives, that even if they are handicapped, it becomes quite irrelevant to what else they're giving us in return." That's how Mary Regnier describes those rewards, and she knows whereof she speaks, because she's raised a brain-damaged child. When I realized what a powerful message she has for parents like her, I interviewed her so she could share in her own words her experiences of treading the line between over-protection and denial.

WHO CREATED THIS?

First, though, let me comment on the ever more widely accepted belief that you create your own reality. This is easy enough to say to comfortable, middle class people whose current challenge in life may be deciding which brand of video recorder to buy, but harder to maintain in the presence of those who have survived, or perhaps still face, extreme, life-threatening challenges.

Mary Regnier believes absolutely that we each create our own reality, and she's willing to put her money where her mouth is. Mary didn't survive a concentration camp, but she did fall and drop her infant child down the stairs, permanently damaging his brain. I think it's easier to take unjust punishment yourself than to unintentionally inflict it on others, and I've often wondered what happens to people who after accidentally inflicting severe injury on children may find it difficult to get beyond unfathomable guilt feelings. If such a thing happens in an environment otherwise free of major conflict, the guilt may be all the more difficult to live with, because there is so little to distract one's attention from it. To such people, Mary has a lot to say that can bring new hope to their lives, and perhaps new power as well. To all of us, her story is one of triumphing over private despair in order to build an inspiring and productive life, not only for herself, but for her brain-injured son as well.

THE MIRACLE OF STEPHEN

She was willing to share with me her experience with her son Stephen, who at the time of writing has gotten himself admitted (against the advice of educators) to a highly demanding college and is earning an excellent grade point average there. That's a miracle, because the doctors told Mary after she fell with him he would never function normally in school, if indeed he lived at all.

"The most important thing I have to say," Mary told me, "is that you should praise the behavior that is working for a child and ignore everything else. After all, we live to be loved. I responded only positively to Stephen and I think that is the main reason that today he can do anything he wants."

MARY'S NIGHTMARE

I asked her what it was like in the beginning. "I spend very little time thinking about what Stephen looked like lying at my feet after I fell with him," she began, "because I would go crazy quite instantly. It's too damned scary. I had lost a child at birth before him. I remember that when he was unconscious at my feet, and I was aware it was an accident, I knew it was not my fault. That was an instantaneous decision. I picked him up and got him to the doctor. My first question was, 'Is he going to die?' and the answer was, 'Probably.'

"Then the terror that I had killed my own child took over. All I can remember doing is screaming, and screaming and screaming and screaming, and just being at the crib in which Stephen lay unconscious. I stayed there, knowing I could have killed my own child. When the neurosurgeon came in he looked me directly in the eyes and said, 'Mary, did you throw your child down the stairs?'

"I said, 'God no!'

"'Don't you *ever* forget that,' he replied.

"My commitment to Stephen after that was to nurture him as constantly as I could. He was only one month old when I fell with him. I was told at the hospital that I didn't need to be there, and that was *not* what I wanted to hear. I very much wanted to be there, nurturing, loving, caring for this child.

"That was a very important step I took right then, deciding not to pay attention to the fear, but to nurture the wholeness and spirit of that child. I believe those weeks I spent in the hospital, coming three times a day to be with Stephen, were a very significant part of his and my healing process.

"An important part of my commitment was accepting the fact that Stephen had a learning disability associated with his brain seizures. I had to live with the terror that goes with that."

THE BEGINNING OF STEPHEN'S ROAD TO INDEPENDENCE

"The surgeon told me if I took Stephen home and treated him as an invalid he would in fact be an invalid, so I could see I was carrying a lot of power. He was a teeny little baby with stitches all over his head, and I had to take him home and put him down on the floor to wrestle with his brothers and sister. I couldn't treat him as special, because if I did, he would pick that up and be affected by it the rest of his life in a very detrimental and neurotic way.

"I was also aware of the commitment I made to be there as support for Stephen on this walk we would take together throughout the time he would be with me. At each step of the way, I knew I had to do my part. At first, that included things like measuring his head every day to make sure there wasn't an increase in the swelling from spinal fluid coming up into his brain. I had to give him a medication I didn't even want him to have, because it was slowing him down, but I knew his life depended on it."

MARY'S ISOLATION

"I had to do most of the nurturing alone, because the people around me didn't want to deal with the emotions of caring for a handicapped child. I had to go to different doctors with him and hear things I certainly didn't want to hear. Yet listening to those things and knowing they were real was an important part of the process. And through it all I had to be with Stephen emotionally and help him accept it even when he was very young."

DEALING WITH GUILT FEELINGS

I asked Mary how she would have felt if she had been responsible for the accident. Suppose she had been drunk when it happened. How, in that case, would she have been able to deal with her son's injury?

"The only way out of something like that is forgiveness of yourself. I know — I am a recovering alcoholic, and I did do things with my children when I was drunk. It involves saying, 'I am a human being. I am capable of error. I am a sick person. I did this, and I now release myself for all eternity. I cannot stay in this hole and deal with so much suffering.'"

Guilt feelings, after all, don't accomplish anything, and if we are to solve the problem we have wittingly or unwittingly created, we must first banish them from our lives. We must accept responsibility for what we do and have done, but not in a way that exacerbates the very problem we want to solve. Unfortunately, feeling guilty is something of an American pastime. Our culture, by concentrating on the negative aspects of so many things, increases the probability most people will find something to feel guilty about, even if they happen to be innocent. Those who really are guilty obviously have a harder time.

Mary believes that had she felt guilty, self-forgiveness still would have made it possible for her to accomplish what she did with Stephen.

THE IMPORTANCE OF CHOOSING

"I had plenty of challenges around me to make sure I felt guilty. But there was a message in me that said, 'No, I am not — I know what took place, and it isn't my fault.' So I didn't let anyone convince me I was to blame. Perhaps if I had not gotten that clear, but instead had wallowed in the hell of guilt and feeling like a bad girl and a bad mother and that I had practically killed my child, then both Stephen and I would have been doomed. But anything's possible for a human being. It doesn't matter what the situation is, it doesn't matter how serious the crisis, a person has a choice: do I go forward, or do I stay in this hell? And it is absolutely your decision that determines the outcome. Both child and parent have to understand that, and if they don't — it's going to be a living hell.

"That's what you see in the learning-disability world — parents and children wallowing in a hole of darkness saying, 'This is all there is.' But the truth is, there *is* something else. They have to see other possibilities and choose them. Once they do, they can start walking toward them. There is only one out — forgiveness and moving on. Nothing else will work."

WALKING TOGETHER

"As I look back on seventeen years I see that Stephen and I have been on a journey hand in hand very quietly, and that lots of voices have come from other people — doctors, teachers and friends, and told me what Stephen could not do. I chose not to believe that, because although I knew Stephen had a handicap, I believed he could accept it and still be able to do anything he wanted to. I saw it as my responsibility to share that attitude toward his handicap with him until he could know it for himself.

"So when it was time for him to start school, I could accept the fact that even though he was five he was performing mentally as if he were two and a half. It was necessary to start by teaching him physical ways of caring for himself, as well as beginning educational concepts."

THE GIFT OF EXPERIENCE

Mary has a deep conviction that a child like Stephen is a gift, and that for her this gift included the terror and suffering she experienced. She believes she herself is a much stronger person because of that. The triumph of seeing how well Stephen has done gives her life greater focus and meaning. Now she wants to give to others as a result of the strength she has won from this experience. "There's no question," she says, "that every obstacle or crisis I've come through is my gift to humanity. It is my walking through it, experiencing all the pain, all the obstacles, all the terror, and getting to the other side that becomes my gift to parents whose children have handicaps of any kind."

FEAR KEEPS US FROM SEEING THE DISABLED

It's true our society tends to treat the disabled with condescension and pity. How often I have heard from a blind person or someone in a wheel chair, "Aside from my physical difference, I'm just like other people, and I wish I could be welcomed and treated with the same respect as a whole person. There's nothing wrong with my mind or my personality. Please don't show me pity or help me in ways I don't need. If you're in doubt about what I need — just ask me."

Yet the disabled are continually shunned because of the fear so many of us have of what it would be like to suffer such a limitation. Talking about this fear of handicapped children, Mary says, "We project it onto the children, but it has nothing to do with them, nothing to do with their learning disability. It is our particular terror about how that could be us, — how would we deal with it? — when in fact when children find themselves in a particular situation, they deal with it and do what they need to."

MARY BREAKS THROUGH HER FEARS

Mary herself wasn't always immune from this fear. She describes a time when as a parent she had to attend a fair given by handicapped children. When she first heard she had to go, she said, "It was physically disgusting to think about it. It was very gross, awful and terrifying. 'God, now I've got to go be with a bunch of children who have learning disabilities,' I thought. But this kind of experience can help you break through all kinds of delusion after the terror comes up. In the end, that day was unbelievable and we simply had to laugh at our fears. On the way home I talked with my children about the experience. We were touched. We will never forget that day as long as we live."

THE ISOLATION OF THE FAMILY OF THE MENTALLY DISABLED

Parents whose children are mentally disabled are even more isolated because society places such a heavy emphasis on what people can do with their minds. Knowing a child has mental limitations leads to premature judgments about what that child will be able to do. Schools and other institutions can be extremely condescending toward the parents.

I have heard many such parents complain bitterly about the hopelessness inflicted upon them by professionals who branded their children with limitations they felt might be overcome. To such parents Mary is a beacon of hope, because thanks to her belief and Stephen's strength of character, he managed to rise above his supposed mental limitations.

HOW THE SCHOOLS COOPERATED

Mary feels very positive, though, about her experience with schools. "I guess I never had a situation where people would not cooperate with me, so it's like what you believe comes to be, and if you expect the school people not to cooperate with you, of course they won't. But I always put it this way to myself: 'They will, because I'm going to ask them, and I'm a very friendly person, and I know they're going to fall in love with my son, and they're going to want to give him what he really needs.' For me it always worked. I always knew I could go and ask for what my child needed when he was still too young to do that for himself. I also asked for what I needed as a parent, and my expectation was I would get it. I never ran into a school system where that didn't happen. In fact, if anything, they gave me more than I asked.

"I know my experience was unusual, because I watched many other parents struggling. I can remember having picnics in my back yard and listening to what the parents were saying. Their experiences were very different.

"Parents should know it is their right as citizens to ask for anything they want for their child's education and legally it must be provided for them. I don't believe they need to get aggressive in dealing with the school.

"The secret is to be very, very clear about what it is your child needs, ask for it and make sure they provide it. I didn't get involved in any fights at all. I always received for Stephen the support he needed in every single school I went to. I took it upon myself to check out how those schools operated. It was my responsibility to get Stephen to school and to help him adapt to each of his different schools."

STEPHEN REJECTS HIS HEARING AID

Sometimes, however, Mary had to go a little beyond just asking for what Stephen needed. The story of his hearing aid is a case in point. It is the only story she told me that suggests a battle between her and any of his schools. "One of the biggest handicaps in the support system of schools for me was the labeling syndrome — stating categorically that a child cannot do a particular kind of thing because of his condition. I asked them to please stop doing that and not give Stephen that kind of message. I did not want him to have a crutch.

"In the particular case in point, because Stephen had lost the ability to hear high pitched tones, the school had asked for a hearing aid. As far as I could tell, Stephen always knew what he really needed. If I listened to him closely enough, I could always find out what we needed to ask for. He knew himself better than anyone else did. This was true from his earliest years."Stephen really did not want that hearing aid. It had been forced on him, because the school system said he had to have it. What I noticed was he had to fight to keep the support systems off. They continually badgered him about his hearing aid. This kind of thing creates a terrible challenge for a child. He can become so absorbed in fighting off the support system he has no energy left for learning. It's a struggle for control between the child and the authorities. Authorities tend not to ask children for information, but rather to assume they know what is good for them.

"So Stephen took off his hearing aid and it was driving the school crazy. So when I realized what was going on, I went to him and said, 'I'm aware you're not wearing your hearing aid.'

"He said, 'I don't need it.'

"I said, 'Do you hear what you need to hear?'

"'Yes.'

"'All right,' I said, 'we're going to straighten this out for you.'

"So we went to his ear doctor and I stood there while Stephen, by himself, told the doctor he knew he could hear everything he needed to. The doctor understood how he felt and wrote a letter to the school saying, 'Stephen Regnier will not be wearing his hearing aid anymore.' My support in this case consisted of listening to the child, believing in what he was saying, taking him to a powerful source that could do something with the school system, getting that information back to the school, and backing him up all the way. The school, of course, was absolutely appalled."

ENCOURAGING STEPHEN'S INDEPENDENCE

In this instance Mary's support of Stephen showed her belief in him and her unwillingness to let the school bully him "for his own good." This was an important part of her plan to help Stephen believe in himself fully enough so he could think well about his handicap and eventually overcome it. Mary knew he wanted as much independence as possible.

"He knew when he did not want any more support. He knew when he was strong enough to do something. I supported him totally in that, visualizing with him that he could compensate for any handicap he had, that his body would know how to do it differently, that he could count on his body, that he would just need to go inside and check that out, and he would soon know how to do whatever he wanted to for himself. He did this so well that by sophomore year of high school he knew he could get along without any more support. It was a bug in his ear, it was driving him crazy, and it was taking a lot of time. So I went to his school and said, 'I would like you to be available to my son, but only when he asks for it. From now on, I want Stephen to take responsibility for his life, and I want him to ask specifically for any support he needs. So you can have a check-in system if you want, but you cannot impose on him what you think he needs, because he now knows what that is.'"

A TURNING POINT FOR STEPHEN

Next, Mary told me about an important turning point in Stephen's life when he learned to become much more independent. As I listened, I was struck by the courage it had taken for her to respond to him as she did on that occasion.

"Stephen had just injured himself quite badly, and he knew he had allowed this injury to happen to him because people were forcing him to do something he didn't want to do. I simply asked him, 'Don't you think it's kind of ridiculous to let this happen to yourself when in fact you could have said no to all of this?' I could see he understood what I was driving at, so I continued, 'What I'm going to do with you today is hand you your life back. You're on your own and totally responsible for creating it the way you want it. You don't have to hurt yourself like this anymore. Just say no or yes, and tell us how it's going to be.'

"That's a pretty powerful thing for a parent to do for a child. The fact of the matter is it works because children know what they need and have the inner resources to carry out their own plans if we parents and teachers will only get out of their way. So from that point on I accepted myself as a cheering section, affirming Stephen's independence.

"But I told him that day — and it was a very critical day for him because he was in a lot of pain — that I would not be doing things for him anymore, that his mother was now out of the way so he had free range to create his life the way he wanted. All I was going to do was choose to love him and support him and cheer him on. Within two years, slowly but surely, he went from a D average to an A-."

HELPING STEPHEN AT HOME

In addition to running interference for Stephen when necessary, Mary taught him to use his mind independently. She never did the homework for him, but she sometimes showed him ways of learning it more effectively. "When he has a major test coming up," she said, "we will do some visual work and talk about how he knows he has all the answers within him and all he has to do is go inside and ask. It's his responsibility to prepare himself for the event, but I'm willing to be the cheering section."

In this way Mary provides Stephen with two kinds of support. First, she assures him he really can trust his inner conscious mind to provide him with answers. This is a powerful suggestion, because the information is stored just below the level of consciousness and will become conscious more easily if the student believes it is there and can relax and accept it. It's a matter of learning to hear the still, small voice within.

The second kind of support is the assurance that she is interested and excited by what he has to do. We are much more willing to perform for those we care about than just for ourselves. Parents provide their children with a great deal of motivation by assuring them they care about the results and are cheering them on. This is entirely different in its effect from putting the child under pressure by threatening to withdraw love if the results are not good. It is a positive way of saying, "I'll accept whatever happens, but I'm especially delighted by your successes."

THE IMPORTANCE OF LETTING GO

Mary is critical of parents who don't have the inner strength to give their children that kind of independence. It's not a matter of letting go prematurely and thus failing to provide essential kinds of guidance. Mary believes strongly in the value of guidance and structure.

"When they're young, of course you're guiding them and allowing them to know the parameters they can move in, because they don't have that themselves until they move into their teens. My children tended to have that quite early, though, because I gave them permission very, very early to make decisions for themselves. I can remember telling them in second grade, 'I would have no idea how to do your homework, you will have to learn how to do it for yourself. I don't know how to do that kind of math. You'll have to ask questions and figure it out for yourself. I will not be doing these kinds of things for you.' I gave my children plenty of opportunity to check out information for themselves because I did not want them dependent on me. I didn't like the way that felt. So as little children they were making very good decisions for themselves."

Thus, Mary is clearly committed to recognizing and valuing the independent being of the child — his or her right to follow a unique and individual path. "Most parents never do that," she says. "Their children could be forty years old and the parents still haven't gotten out of their way. They're still meddling and holding them up and making them believe the parent is the one that knows."

EMPOWERING THE YOUNG

Because of this failure on the part of so many parents, it is Mary's ambition to build a career empowering young people. "I want them to know I believe they can do what they want to exactly the way they desire. If their elders will get out of their way and just support them, they'll go and do it." Of course in many cases this doesn't happen because the child, reacting to excessive concern from parents, gets sidetracked struggling for independence and trying to manipulate the parents, which blurs the focus of the child's inner light.

Often we manipulate young people because of our unconscious (or perhaps all too conscious) need for them to make up for our failure to fulfill our dreams for ourselves. It may also be that our lack of belief in ourselves keeps us from believing in them. This can be particularly devastating in the case of disabled children, because it's always possible to find "evidence" that they cannot do what they want to. Parents manipulate their children by being over-protective or denying their handicap, either way trying to make them into something they are not. Mary is particularly concerned about this latter kind of manipulation.

WE MANIPULATE OUR CHILDREN BY DENYING THEIR HANDICAPS

"Denial is a big part of our culture," she says, "so it isn't hard to understand that parents would choose to deny. I think it's hard for them to accept the fact that their children have to wear braces or have allergies, let alone have a learning disability. I think that's extremely hard, because we'd like to believe we're perfect, and of course we're just human beings trying to do a great big important job. I feel it's disrespectful to the child to deny the reality of his existence. I think that's extraordinarily unfair. It's unfair to the child, and it's unfair to you, because you are making it much, much harder for the child.

"Sometimes it's very tempting to indulge in denial, but it never, ever works. You simply create more hell that way. Since the child knows inside what he can and can't do, for you to pretend he can is adding tremendous struggle to his path. Now he's got to make it right for you, and he's trying to make it right for himself too, and he's got a double burden. In situations like that, I'd like to be able to put parents aside, because they're such a trap for their children, they're such an obstacle, they're such a mountain that's in the way.

"Children can feel really powerless with parents and teachers, because they don't know how to get around these great big people who are trying to make them do something, and all they want to do is what they know they can do. If we would only allow them to do that in their own way, they'd do it. But parents and teachers don't seem to want to get out of the way, because we believe we know what we're doing, when of course we don't, most days."

TRUSTING BEYOND YOURSELF

What, then, should the parent do? "Acceptance and faith is the only thing possible. Just ask for whatever information you need. Don't pretend you know, when you're not sure. Ask. Because the problem is just too big for one person to walk around with. It's too big for the child, and it's too big for the parent. So you need to feel your powerlessness, in that you need to know you can't do it for the child."

Mary freely admits she is far from perfect at this herself. "As much as I yearn and pine to use my skills to do things for Stephen, it never works, and he tells me to get out of the way. He just laughs at me, because he thinks it's funny that I would try. So I force myself just to believe in him and send him off to school, saying, 'Of course you know I'll be with you, praying for you. I know you have everything you need to accomplish your desires.'

That's the only answer, so why deny it? The child won't deny it if you don't."

For all her optimism, Mary is quite aware of the difficulties parents of mentally and physically disabled children must face. She believes, however, the love of these special children is the only way out of the difficulties. "These parents must know the child is a very special love source for them. If they would go beyond the fear of what the child can't do and would accept what he or she can do and can be for them, then the fear would disappear."

DEALING WITH THE SOCIAL STIGMA

"But it's appalling socially to have such a child. People don't want to talk with you about your learning-disabled child. It's like talking about death. So you're very lonely, and you need a whole bunch of support. You need to be with other parents who have similar problems. Your child needs support because of feeling alienated, unique and different, and not being able to be the all-American boy or girl. The children face years of feeling alone, and the parents feel alone."

I'm reminded of one very successful friend of mine who triumphs over her physical handicap magnificently and is well loved by all her friends. She carries around the memory of her mother once saying to her when she was a defenseless child, "I wish that after I am gone someone would love you and take care of you the way I do. But I'm afraid that will never happen in your case."

Mary's message to parents and young people has been strengthened as a result of the struggles, the pain and the isolation she has faced. She glories in what Stephen has been able to do for himself and wants to carry the message of what is possible to all young people. "We need to love our children with all our power," she says, "because that's the clue to where our power is. And the most powerful way of loving them is letting go of them — letting them grow into their own unique power that is so different from ours."

I think that's one of the most important messages in this book. I've offered you many techniques in these chapters, but the dominant philosophy is to love others for their power, their strength and their uniqueness. "Whenever I think of Stephen," Mary says, "I come up not with tears of terror, but tears of joy." Those are the only tears our children should inspire.

APPENDIX TWO

THE PRINCIPLES OF INTEGRATIVE LEARNING

A summary of key concepts, mainly for teachers.

Several key concepts must be understood in order to clarify what Integrative Learning is and how it works. This section summarizes their use in a variety of instructional areas. Much of this material is presented elsewhere in the book, especially in Chapters Two, Three, Four and Five, but is summarized here for handy reference. It's mainly intended for teachers, and should not be read as a substitute or even as a summary of the book. Think of it rather as a rough glossary of key concepts in Integrative Learning.

THE THREE COMPONENTS OF LEARNING

The learning process has three components: **input, synthesis and output**. Learning has not occurred until all three components have been experienced. In traditional education, much emphasis is placed on **input**. It is possible, as the saying goes, for an idea to pass from a lecturer's notes to a student's notebook without passing through the mind of either. This parody of traditional education points to the fact that both teachers and students generally accept the concept that teachers should be primarily dispensers of information. It is then considered the student's job to absorb and learn the information once dispensed.

This leads to an exaggerated need on the part of teachers to have complete control over the information and always to have the correct answers, regardless of whether or not anything is learned. This tends to inhibit their ability to indulge in the free play of the learning process. It also prevents the teachers themselves actually learning something from their students during the progress of a class. At the university level, where right answers become increasingly less certain, the result is a general down-grading of teaching in favor of research.

Many teachers tend to see students first and foremost as lacking information they themselves have. It thus becomes their duty to transfer information from their minds to those of the students. Of course to do that the teacher must open the mind of the student, and this may be a somewhat violent process, perhaps involving threats and punishment. The tendency to see students as unwilling victims of their education fails to take into account the fact that learning is instinctive.

In Integrative Learning, though input is still important, we place equal emphasis on synthesis and output. In fact, because of the astonishing increase of information in modern times, most people have a greater need to learn how to process that information once they have accessed it.

Synthesis occurs when a student has compared the new input to previous experience, thereby establishing a working relationship between the two. As the new information is brought into contact with what has been previously learned, each transforms the other. This is why no two people observe the same event the same way. We interpret what we observe or experience in the light of our own individual experience. Thus, even when people seem to understand some new event or piece of information in the same way, they may actually be in deep, though unnoticed, disagreement.

OUTPUT

In most traditional education, **output** is part of a closed circuit. That is, a specific answer is expected, or a specific task must be performed. For example, if a student is asked to identify and discuss the causes of the War Between the States, assigning a probable value to each, he or she tends to assume there is a preferred probable value, or at least a preferred set of rules for arguing the question. Thus, expectation of a certain type of performance is established.

In Integrative Learning, expectation is replaced by expectancy. This is because specific expectations greatly limit the possible learning experience a student is supposed to have, while expectancy maintains openness to experience above and beyond that minimally expected, and validates all such experiences.

THE LEARNING CYCLE

These three components of learning interface with the learning cycle developed by Georgi Lozanov, whose research underlies the operational procedures of Integrative Learning. The learning cycle determines the instructional sequence. It also consists of three stages: **decoding, concert and activation**. These, however, are presented sequentially in the classroom, whereas the three components of learning interweave continually in the student's mind.

THE IMPORTANCE OF DECODING

In Integrative Learning **core concepts**, or key organizing ideas, provide the foundation on which the subject or skill to be learned is built. These are made clear to the learner during the **decoding**, so as to be synthesized into the entire thought process. Decoding prepares the way for the integration of new information into the long-term memory which the concerts provide.

The test of good decoding, however it is done, is the extent to which it has removed ambiguity by clearly presenting the core concepts to be studied. The amount of time spent decoding may vary from a few minutes to several months, depending on the degree of ambiguity inherent in the subject. This is because when there is little ambiguity about what is to be learned (as in a foreign language class) it is only necessary to expose the students to a new grammar and vocabulary. But when material is inherently difficult to understand, lengthier decoding is necessary for clarification.

Decoding may take many forms, such as a brief lecture or discussion, a charades type of presentation by the instructor, the use of participatory activities by the students (such as human sculptures), or actual research entrusted to the students. It may be either a direct or indirect presentation. Indirect presentations elicit the thinking of the students and allow them to structure their own sense of the core concepts.

THE USE OF CONCERT SESSIONS

Concert sessions may be used as part of the instructional process in Integrative Learning. New lessons may be presented in the form of a story or dialogue read with a background of concert music. The voice of the instructor is keyed to the emotional content of the music, not that of the material being read. By dramatizing the material with music, thus enhancing it with an emotional element, the instructor renders it in a form more easily acceptable to the long-term memory. We learn most effortlessly through stories with strong images and a musical background.

Whenever concerts are used, they should cover a larger body of material than that normally encompassed in a unit of study — as a rule, two to five times as much ground should be covered. Thus concerts are meant to be used sparingly, and as a means of challenging the learner to assimilate and integrate a large amount of material presented globally or holistically. Concerts of this sort should occupy no more than about five percent of the total instruction time.

In foreign language classes, two concerts are used, one active and one pseudo-passive. (The term pseudo-passive refers to the condition of the learner, who appears to be passive, but whose mind is in fact quite active.) The active concert, during which the students follow the text of the target language as it is being read, and can compare it with a translation, is used to put vocabulary and grammatical forms into the long-term memory. However, since the material is not read in the customary inflection patterns of the language, it must be read again, during the pseudo-passive concert, in a more normal tone of voice, so the students can assimilate the appropriate vocal patterns. During this second concert, the students do not follow the text, but usually put their heads back and close their eyes, allowing the mind just to soak up the experience.

In most other subjects, only a single concert is used. This single concert is read like an active concert, but experienced like a pseudo-passive concert. However, if two concerts are to be used, they should have different texts, the active concert being a story or dialogue, while the pseudo-passive concert is a guided imagery, in which the student is taken on a tour through the guts of the subject matter, such as a trip through the blood stream, or an eyewitness tour of events in history.

This form of presentation facilitates the mind's ability to synthesize new material. A single concert presentation is sufficient to establish it in the learner's long-term memory, provided activation follows after a night's sleep, and within a week. Concert music may also be used in the practice of developing skills, in the presentation of motivational or inspirational material, or in the exploration of new concepts, yet to be structured.

ACTIVATING THE MATERIAL

When concerts are used in Integrative Learning, material should be **activated**, usually a day or more after the concert has been presented. This allows the mind time, during a night of sleep, to assimilate the material from the concerts. Activations may include skits, games and discussions designed to help students bring the material above the threshold of consciousness and thus become aware of the extent to which they are already familiar with it. They are also then given the opportunity to structure it into the format they can deal with most effectively.

Generally speaking, activations are a delightful replacement for the boring drill and practice usually thought to be necessary in learning new information. Properly used, they can significantly reduce the amount of time required to achieve competence or mastery.

THE IMPORTANCE OF A POSITIVE ATMOSPHERE IN THE CLASSROOM

The classroom environment is so designed that experiences taking place there will seem positive to the students. All suggestions for activity and presentations of material are positive, and attention is never drawn to the student's failures, mistakes or other shortcomings without at the same time enhancing, or at least maintaining, the self-image of the student.

AMBIGUITY TOLERANCE

Though it seems unnecessary to say, we sometimes seem to forget that everyone learns best in an enjoyable environment. When students are comfortable, they are better able to consider and explore, as well as to avoid premature conclusions about the material. Anxiety provokes a need to achieve premature closure and take immediate action. The extreme example is panic. A state of panic may induce the worst possible response, merely for the sake of doing something. In the Integrative Learning classroom everything is dealt with in the most delightful way permitted by the structure of the subject. This gives enough latitude for ambiguities to be resolved naturally and comfortably, without premature closure.

RESPECTING THE STUDENT'S INDIVIDUALITY

Classes should be so arranged that no matter how clear and uncontroversial the subject may be, each student can still handle it differently. Therefore each class should be designed so students may examine and compare their personal styles of integrating new information. This is what it means to learn to think, and critical thinking should not only enable one to discover flaws in reasoning, but also to see the virtues of thinking in a style unlike one's own. For indeed, describing and appreciating the virtues of a new structure is as important a function of critical awareness as revealing the weaknesses of an inadequate structure or reasoning process.

Class discussions should do more than merely define some truth or other. Instead, students should clarify their personal relationship to the material, where possible clarifying the use they will eventually make of it. The Socratic method is too often used to lead students down a pre-ordained path of reasoning, too seldom used to lead them to the discovery and reordering of their own thought process.

When material is presented as absolute truth, students perceive less chance of developing their own relationship to it, and tend to become aware primarily of how little of it they actually understand. This diminishes their eagerness to learn. If it is clear that any person may, with enough thinking, arrive at a uniquely valuable point of view on the subject at hand, students are more likely to wish to achieve excellence.

With proper educational practices, all people may develop uniquely valuable points of view, provided material is presented to them in a way that stimulates the expression and development of their individual perceptions. These perceptions must then be brought into focus in relation to the subject, adequately modified through feedback, and effectively communicated.

PERSONAL STYLES OF LEARNING

By shifting the focus of the class from the transmission of material to the students' synthesis and output, the Integrative Learning teacher encourages students to discover and enhance their personal styles of learning. The teacher thus leads the student to develop his or her own approach to the material and take full intellectual responsibility for it.

Students also become aware of the unique learning styles of their classmates, because understanding the learning styles of others helps you better understand your own. Communication becomes more effective when these different styles are well understood. The purpose of understanding differences is not to reconcile them, but to be better able to interact creatively in terms of them.

Confusion about learning and teaching that occurs in traditionally taught classes may result from the fact that we not only perceive things from different points of view, but also learn most effectively in different styles. **Auditory, kinesthetic, visual, print-oriented and interactive learners** should be given equal opportunity to experience the learning process through their own strengths.

Auditory learners have the easiest time in traditional classrooms, where a great deal is meant to be learned through the ears. Print-oriented learners can often function pretty well on their own, given adequate text materials to study. Visual learners have a more difficult time, but their need for visual clues may be met by maps, diagrams and pictures. Good teachers often provide such clues during lectures by working diagrammatically at the board. Interactive learners can function well when there is an opportunity for them to be heard and test their own perceptions in discussion. Kinesthetic learners have the hardest time, since little is usually presented in their mode of learning. All these learning styles are widely distributed in all social, cultural and racial groups, so gearing classes to different learning styles for different groups is not valid.

Whenever possible in Integrative Learning we appeal to all five modes of learning simultaneously. Two excellent tools for accomplishing this are **drama and guided imagery**. A dramatic presentation of an idea in which the students become actors allows the idea to be presented in all five modes, if a script is used and there is discussion afterwards. Similarly, a guided imagery exercise can include suggestions in all five modes and the material can be in a dramatic format with interactive elements simulating discussion of the ideas.

THE SEVEN INTELLIGENCES

In a similar spirit, we make certain our classes engage all seven of the intelligences described by Howard Gardner in his book *Frames of Mind*: **logical-mathematical, linguistic, spatial, bodily-kinesthetic, musical, inter-personal and intra-personal**. The logical-mathematical is enhanced by having the students reason through the logical basis of the material being studied. The linguistic, by clarifying the vocabulary of the subject and giving students many opportunities to speak and write about the subject to a high standard of excellence. The spatial (visual) by using posters to lay out the fundamental structure of the subject, by teaching mind mapping, and by using human sculptures. The bodily-kinesthetic is developed primarily through dance, human sculptures and games or skits in which students perform with their whole bodies or at least manipulate objects symbolizing elements under study. The musical is educated through concerts, raps, mnemonic songs, musically guided imagery and dance music accompanying performance activities.

The inter-personal intelligence is developed through frequent class interaction and discussion, both with the whole group and in small groups, as well as through Think-and-Listens, which also develop the intra-personal. The intra-personal is further developed through opportunities to discover personal styles and relate the subject to the student's own priorities, as well as through guided imageries eliciting inner awareness.

HARMONIZATION

Because human beings are intellectual, emotional, physical and spiritual all in one, they must integrate everything they learn at different levels and in different ways. Paul MacLean's research on the Triune Brain reveals that the neo-cortex functions most effectively when it is in harmony with the limbic system. Meanwhile, the basic survival needs of the organism should never be threatened — so fear must be banished from the classroom and learning occur in a positive emotional context. Furthermore, since the two hemispheres of the brain have been shown to function differently, the degree of integration between the two hemispheres is important. **Harmonization** occurs as the student integrates different aspects of the personality in relation to the subject or concept being learned.

The teacher and the learning environment encourage harmonization by calling into play the emotional, physical and spiritual sides of the student, as well as the intellectual. The focus of activity should vary so that all these areas are touched on, and the student's understanding is consistent in all of them. The more effective harmonization is, the more powerful the integration that takes place, and the more power the new skill, concept or fact offers the student.

SOCIALIZATION IN LEARNING

Integrative Learning is also concerned with the relation between the student and his or her world. In traditional learning, **socialization** implies conforming to established social practices. In Integrative Learning it implies contemplating and effecting appropriate changes in social practices. The integrative learner is able to evaluate present realities objectively, envision superior alternatives, and seek the means to integrate the two.

Since social change is occurring so rapidly, this ability is now critical and essential. The integrative learner should receive encouragement to envision improvements and ideals for society, and opportunities to examine current social patterns in comparison with that ideal. If we know, for example, it is desirable to achieve equality among human beings, we may in some way relate all our learning experiences to that goal. This increases our general understanding of what we are doing and how it relates to the future we are striving for.

The effect of developing a world view in this manner is to help the learner progress more rapidly, since intermediate problems, such as completing a project or succeeding in a reorganization, seem relatively simple by comparison and are dealt with more efficiently and with expectations of success. Thus success in a literature course could be seen as the foundation for success in journalism, which in turn could become the foundation for raising consciousness about equality.

LEARNING IS A HOLISTIC PROCESS LIKE ART

The entire attention and potential of the student is most effectively engaged through the use of **holistic presentation**. Holistic presentation resembles the design of a feature film. The frequent shifting among the characters and situations, the revelation of the basic situation by implication, the tying together of the whole through an aesthetically sensed theme and sub-theme, the building to climax, the in-depth development of characters, symbolism, musical background, dialogue and other dramatic and cinematic techniques, are all used in holistic presentation. Thus in classrooms that use holistic presentation, course material is aesthetically arranged. Information is imparted in such manner that all parts of the course are relevant at all times.

INFANT LEARNING

As infants we learn in situations in which information is almost always available holistically. We do not learn our native language by getting it in small doses; we get it in its full complexity from the beginning. The mind is best adapted to dealing with subject matter in just this way, provided there is someone present who can help sort out the information and answer questions. So the teacher's job is to present the material and then help the students clarify and structure it in a way that is uniquely their own.

The learning process can be enhanced by simulating the infant learning experience (sometimes referred to as **infantilization**). Thus we use songs, stories, games, skits, myths, legends and other devices more commonly found in the nursery than the office. Use of these learning devices induces the rapid learning associated with the infant stage of development. The learner experiences this as fun, dramatic, bizarre, and as a pleasant reminder of childhood experiences. Resistance to infantilization is easily overcome in most learners if the rationale for it is clear, and if the students participate in it together.

THE IMPORTANCE OF DEEP STRUCTURING

One of the most important processes in infant learning is the **deep structuring** of learned concepts. The infant usually has a great deal of experience with something before even naming it. Most teachers, on the other hand, name things before the class has had a chance to experience them. This leads to superficial learning in the classroom. The Integrative Learning teacher allows the class to experience an idea in many different forms and allows each person to discover a personal relationship to that idea before it is named and accepted by the class as a basis for building other ideas. This may slow down the process of instruction initially, but in the long run it is significantly accelerated.

THE IMPORTANCE OF CORE IDEAS

All subjects have **core ideas** that can be simply stated, and to which everything in that subject relates. Understanding and articulating a core idea helps the student to feel grounded in that aspect of the subject and to judge each new piece of information in terms of its relationship to the idea.

Thus a framework is formed, so new information is easily remembered. Once familiarity with the subject has been established, skillful manipulation of the core idea makes it possible to reason out many things that are probably true within that subject area. The student who learns to explore and anticipate the implications of a core idea can more easily understand facts as they come to light, because the creative process has been elicited in seeking them.

GENERALIZING FROM CORE IDEAS

The integration of a few core ideas into a student's thinking sets the stage for exploring their application to other subjects. This in turn encourages the student to look for the core ideas in any newly encountered situation. Very often, these are easy to identify, and the student is then in a position to predict the unknown from the known with greater confidence and accuracy. Thus, students can learn to discuss unfamiliar subject areas with remarkable insight and to steer the conversation in channels that allow them to learn from others.

CHARACTERISTICS OF THE SUCCESSFUL LEARNER

Students who have mastered Integrative Learning should, first of all, enjoy learning. They should be able to think freshly and freely in all situations, should be adept at asking relevant questions when confronted by new situations, should be easily able to integrate the answers to those questions with information they already have, should have developed their own personal strategies for problem solving and creativity, should have internalized the learning process so that regardless of the situation it is always headed in a direction that serves the student's needs and interests, and should be dedicated to making a significant contribution to their world.